Chicken

Practical Cookery

Chicken

This is a Parragon Book
First published in 2000

Parragon
Queen Street House
4 Queen Street
Bath BA1 1HE, UK

Copyright © Parragon 2000

ISBN: 0-75254-099-8

Printed in Indonesia

NOTE

Cup measurements in this book are for American cups.
Tablespoons are assumed to be 15ml. Unless otherwise stated,
milk is assumed to be full fat, eggs are medium
and pepper is freshly ground black pepper.

Recipes using uncooked eggs should be
avoided by infants, the elderly, pregnant women and anyone
suffering from an illness

Contents

Introduction   8

Soups & Starters

Chicken Consommé 20
Hot and Sour Soup 21
Chicken and Asparagus Soup 22
Chicken and Leek Soup 23
Chicken and Pasta Broth 24
Dickensian Chicken Broth 25
Cock-a-Leekie Soup 26
Chicken and Bean Soup 27
Vegetable and Chickpea Soup 28
Lemon and Chicken Soup 29
Chicken and Sweetcorn Soup 30
Chicken Noodle Soup 31
Chicken Wonton Soup 32
Chicken, Noodle and Corn Soup 33
Spicy Chicken Noodle Soup 34

Clear Chicken and Egg Soup 35
Curried Chicken and Corn Soup 36
Chicken Soup with Almonds 37

Appetizers

Cranberry Turkey Burgers 40
Turkey and Vegetable Loaf 41
Parsley, Chicken and Ham Pâté 42
Sweet and Sour Drumsticks 43
Oat-Crusted Chicken Pieces 44
Sticky Chicken Drummers 45
Spicy Chicken Tortillas 46
Chicken and Almond Rissoles 47
Chicken and Cheese Jackets 48
Crostini all Fiorentina 49
Spring Rolls 50
Chicken Spring Rolls 51

Pot Sticker Dumplings 52
Chinese Omelette 53
Honeyed Chicken Wings 54
Bang-Bang Chicken 55
Steamed Duck Buns 56
Chicken or Beef Satay 57
Chicken Wontons 58
Sesame Ginger Chicken 59

Low-Fat Main Meals

Chicken with a Yoghurt Crust 62
Sticky Chicken Wings 63
Steamed Chicken Parcels 64
Thai Red Chicken 65
Teppanyaki 66
Spiced Apricot Chicken 67
Sweet and Sour Chicken 68
Ginger Chicken and Corn 69
Poussin with Dried Fruits 70
Harlequin Chicken 71
Chicken Tikka Kebabs 72
Chicken in Spciy Yogurt 73
Thai-Style Chicken Skewers 74
Chicken and Ginger Stir-Fry 75
Chicken with Two Sauces 76
Pot-Roast Orange Chicken 77
Two-in-One-Chicken 78

Karahi Chicken .79
Lime Chicken Kebabs 80
Filipino Chicken 81
Jerk Chicken 82
Chicken and Potato Bake 83
Mexican Chicken 84
Barbecued Chicken 85
Festive Apple Chicken 86
Crispy Stuffed Chicken 87
Chicken with Whisky Sauce 88
Honeyed Citrus Chicken 89
Springtime Roast Chicken 90
Baked Chicken and Chips 91
Lime Fricassée of Chicken 92
Spicy Tomato Chicken 93
Chicken and Plum Casserole 94
Chicken Tikka .95

Low Fat Main Meals (continued)

Mediterranean Chicken 96
Whisky Roast Chicken 97
Chicken with Vermouth 98
Chicken Tikka Masala 99
Chicken and Lemon Skewers 100
Cheesy Baked Chicken 101
Spanish Chicken Casserole 102
Spicy Sesame Chicken 103
Marmalade Chicken 104
Springtime Chicken Cobbler 105
Chilli Chicken Meatballs 106
Minty Lime Chicken 107
Chicken Fajitas 108

Citrus Duckling Skewers 109
Golden Glazed Chicken 110
Chicken with Lime Stuffing 111
Rustic Chicken and Orange Pot 112
Marinated Chicken Kebabs 113
Chicken with Bramble Sauce 114
Chicken Jalfrezi 115
Jamaican Hot Pot 116
Tasmanian Duck 117
Spicy Chicken Drumsticks 118
Duck with Berry Sauce 119
Turkey with Redcurrant 120
Roast Duck with Apple 121

Italian Dishes

Garlicky Chicken Cushions 124
Italian Chicken Spirals 125
Chicken Marengo 126
Mustard-Baked Chicken 127
Pan-Cooked Chicken 128
Boned Chicken and Parmesan 129
Chicken Cacciatora 130
Chicken Lasagne 131
Barbecued Chicken 132
Grilled Chicken 133
Chicken with Green Olives 134
Chicken and Balsamic Vinegar 135
Chicken Scallops 136
Chicken and Lobster on Penne 137
Skewered Chicken Spirals 138
Chicken with Orange Sauce 139
Chicken Pepperonata 140

Roman Chicken 141
Pasta with Chicken Sauce 142
Italian Chicken Parcels 143
Pasta and Chicken Medley 144
Parma-Wrapped Chicken 145
Chicken Tortellini 146
Rich Chicken Casserole 147
Chicken with Vegetables 148
Chicken and Seafood Parcels 149
Chicken Pasta Bake 150
Chicken and Tomato Lasagne 151
Tagliatelle and Chicken Sauce 152
Chicken and Spinach Lasagne 153
Garlic and Herb Chicken 154
Italian-Style Sunday Roast 155
Slices of Duckling with Pasta 156
Pesto-Baked Partridge 157

Chinese Dishes

Chicken Chop Suey 160
Cashew Chicken 161
Lemon Chicken 162
Celery and Cashew Chicken 163
Stir-Fried Ginger Chicken 164
Barbecued Chicken Legs 165
Braised Chicken 166
Yellow Bean Chicken 167
Kung Po Chicken 168
Green Chicken Stir-Fry 169
Chicken with Bean Sprouts 170
Chilli Coconut Chicken 171
Chicken with Black Bean Sauce 172
Garlic and Lime Chicken 173
Oramge Chicken Stir-Fry 174
Sweet Mango Chicken 175
Szechuan Chilli Chicken 176
Chicken with Mushrooms 177
Chicken with Vegetables 178
Cumin-Spiced Chicken 179
Spicy Peanut Chicken 180
Peppered Chicken 181

Chicken and Corn Sauté 182
Chicken with Peppers 183
Honey and Soy Chicken 184
Roast Baby Chickens 185
Chicken and Vegetables 186
Peanut Sesame Chicken 187
Chicken Fu-Yong 188
Coconut Chicken Curry 189
Crispy Chicken 190
Red Chicken with Tomatoes 191
Chilli Chicken 192
Lemon and Sesame Chicken 193
Chicken with Peanut Sauce 194
Chicken with Chilli and Basil 195
Honey-Glazed Duck 196
Duck with Pineapple 197
Duck with Mangoes 198
Duck with Broccoli and Peppers 199
Duck with Leek and Cabbage 200
Duck with Lime and Kiwi Fruit 201
Duck in Spicy Sauce 202
Turkey with Cranberry Glaze 203

Peking Duck 204
Red Chicken Curry 205
Barbecued Duckling 206
Indian Charred Chicken 207

Fruity Duck Stir Fry 208
Aromatic and Crispy Duck 209
Duck with Ginger and Lime 210
Noodles in Soup 211

Pulses, Grains & Noodles

Sage Chicken and Rice 214
Garlic Chicken Cassoulet 215
Orange Turkey with Rice 216
Chicken and Beans 217
Fragrant Spiced Chicken 218
Chicken with Rice and Peas 219
Cajun Chicken Gumbo 220
Chicken and Chilli Bean Pot 221
Golden Chicken Risotto 222
Chicken Risotto Milanese 223
Rice with Five-Spice Chicken 224
Hot and Spicy Chicken 225
Chinese Chicken Rice 226
Chicken and Rice Casserole 227

Chicken and Noodle One-Pot 228
Quick Chicken Chow Mein 229
Chicken Chow Mein 230
Chicken Noodles 231
Speedy Peanut Pan-Fry 232
Yellow Bean Noodles 233
Quick Chicken Noodles 234
Chicken on Crispy Noodles 235
Sticky Chicken Drummers 236
Chicken and Peanut Pizza 237

Salads

Duckling and Radish Salad 240
Layered Chicken Salad 241
Chicken and Spinach Salad 242
Chicken and Grape Salad 243
Chargrilled Chicken Salad 244
Spicy Chicken Salad 245
Waldorf Chicken Salad 246
Coronation Salad 247
Chicken and Paw-Paw Salad 248
Chicken and Noodle Salad 249
Potato and Chicken Salad 250

Oriental Chicken Salad 251
Chinese Chicken Salad 252
Hot and Sour Duck Salad 253

Index   254

Introduction

One of the easiest and least disruptive ways to reduce your fat intake is to change the way you cook. Trying new recipes, even with familiar ingredients, is fun and will result in the pleasure of eating delicious meals that are also healthier.

Chicken has become justly popular around the world and plays an important part in the modern diet, being reasonably priced and nutritionally sound. A versatile meat, it lends itself to an enormous range of cooking methods and cuisines. Its unassertive flavour means that it is equally suited to cooking with both sweet and savoury flavours. Because it has a low fat content, especially without the skin, it is an ideal meat for low cholesterol and calorie-controlled diets. As well as being an excellent source of protein, chicken contains valuable minerals, such as potassium and phosphorus, and some of the B vitamins.

COOKING METHODS:

Roasting

Remove any fat from the body cavity. Rinse the bird inside and out with water, then pat dry with paper towels. Season the cavity generously with salt and pepper and add stuffing, herbs or lemon if wished. Spread the breast of the chicken with softened butter or oil. Set on a rack in a roasting tin (pan) or shallow baking dish. Roast the bird, basting two or three times with the pan juices during roasting. If the chicken is browning too quickly, cover it with foil. Test for doneness by using a meat thermometer or insert a skewer into the thickest part of the thigh. If the chicken is cooked, the juices will run clear with no trace of pink. Put the bird on a carving board and leave to rest for 15 minutes before serving. Make a sauce or otherwise a gravy from the juices left in the roasting tin (pan).

Grilling (Broiling)

The intense heat of the grill (broiler) quickly seals the succulent flesh beneath a crisp, golden exterior. Place the chicken 10–15 cm/4–6 inches away from a moderate heat source. If the chicken seems to be browning too quickly, reduce the heat slightly. If the chicken is grilled (broiled) at too high a temperature too near to the heat, the outside will burn before the inside is cooked. If it is cooked for too long under a low heat, it will dry out. Divide the chicken into joints to

Introduction

ensure even cooking. Breast meat, if cooked in one piece, can be rather dry, so it is best to cut it into chunks for kebabs (kabobs). Wings are best for speedy grilling (broiling).

Frying is suitable for small thighs, drumsticks and joints. Dry the chicken pieces with paper towels so that they brown properly and to prevent spitting during cooking. The chicken can be coated in seasoned flour, egg and breadcrumbs or a batter. Heat oil or a mixture of oil and butter in a heavy frying pan (skillet). When the oil is very hot, add the chicken pieces, skin-side down. Fry until deep golden brown all over, turning the pieces frequently during cooking. Drain well on paper towels before serving.

Sautéeing is ideal for small pieces or small birds such as baby chickens. Heat a little oil or a mixture

of oil and butter in a heavy frying pan (skillet). Add the chicken and fry over a moderate heat until golden brown, turning frequently. Add stock or other liquid, bring to the boil, then cover and reduce the heat. Cook gently until the chicken is cooked through.

Stir-Frying is good when skinless, boneless chicken is cut into small pieces of equal size to ensure that the meat cooks evenly and stays succulent. Preheat a wok or saucepan before adding a small amount of oil. When the oil starts to smoke, add the chicken and stir-fry with your chosen flavourings for 3–4 minutes until cooked through. Other ingredients can be cooked at the same time, or the chicken can be cooked by itself, then removed from the pan while you stir-fry the remaining ingredients. Return the chicken to the pan once the other ingredients are cooked.

Casseroling is a good method for cooking joints from larger, more mature chickens, although smaller chickens can be cooked whole. The slow cooking produces tender meat with a good flavour. Brown the chicken in butter or oil or a mixture of both. Add some stock, wine or a mixture of both with seasonings and herbs, cover and cook on top of the stove or in the oven until the chicken is tender. Add a selection of lightly sautéed vegetables about halfway through the cooking time.

Braising is a method which does not require liquid. The chicken pieces or a small whole chicken and vegetables are cooked together slowly

in a low oven. Heat some oil in an ovenproof, flameproof casserole and gently fry the chicken until golden. Remove the chicken and fry a selection of vegetables until they are almost tender. Replace the chicken, cover tightly and cook very gently on the top of the stove or in a low oven until the chicken and vegetables are tender.

Poaching is a gentle cooking method that produces tender chicken and a stock that can be used to make a sauce to serve with the chicken. Put a whole chicken, a bouquet garni, a leek, a carrot and an onion in a large flameproof casserole. Cover with water, season and bring to the boil. Simmer for 1½–2 hours until the chicken is tender. Lift the chicken out, discard the bouquet garni and use the stock to make a sauce. Blend the vegetables to thicken the stock and serve with the chicken.

FOOD SAFETY & TIPS

Chicken is liable to be contaminated by salmonella bacteria, which can cause severe food poisoning. When storing, handling and preparing poultry, certain precautions must be observed to prevent the possibility of food poisoning.

• Check the sell-by date and best before date. After buying, take the chicken home quickly, preferably in a freezer bag or cool box.

• Return frozen birds immediately to the freezer.

• If storing in the refrigerator, remove the wrappings and store any giblets separately. Place the chicken in a shallow dish to catch drips. Cover loosely with foil and store on the bottom shelf of the refrigerator for no more than two or three days, depending on the best before date. Avoid any contact between raw chicken and cooked food during storage and preparation. Wash your hands

thoroughly after handling raw chicken.

• Prepare raw chicken on a chopping board that can be easily cleaned and bleached, such as a non-porous, plastic board.

• Frozen birds should be defrosted before cooking. If time permits, defrost for about 36 hours in the refrigerator, or thaw for about 12 hours in a cool place. Bacteria breed in warm food at room temperature and when chicken is thawing. Cooking at high temperatures kills bacteria. There should be no ice crystals and the flesh should feel soft and flexible. Cook the chicken as soon as possible after thawing.

• Make sure that chicken is cooked. Test for doneness using a meat thermometer – the thigh should reach at least 79°C/175°F when cooked – or pierce the thickest part of a thigh with a skewer, the juices should run clear, not pink or red. Never partially cook chicken with the intention of completing cooking later.

Basic Recipes

Chinese Stock

This basic stock is used in Chinese cooking not only as the basis for soup-making, but also whenever liquid is required instead of plain water.

MAKES 2.5L/4½ PINTS/10 CUPS

750 g/1 lb 10 oz chicken pieces

750 g/1 lb 10 oz pork spare ribs

3.75 litres/6½ pints/15 cups cold water

3-4 pieces ginger root, crushed

3-4 spring onions (scallions), each tied into a knot

3-4 tbsp Chinese rice wine or dry sherry

1 Trim off any excess fat from the chicken and spare ribs; chop them into large pieces.

2 Place the chicken and pork in a large pan with the water; add the ginger and spring onion (scallion) knots.

3 Bring to the boil, and skim off the scum. Reduce the heat and simmer uncovered for at least 2-3 hours.

4 Strain the stock, discarding the chicken, pork, ginger and spring onions (scallions); add the wine and return to the boil, simmer for 2-3 minutes.

5 Refrigerate the stock when cool; it will keep for up to 4-5 days. Alternatively, it can be frozen in small containers and be defrosted as required.

Fresh Chicken Stock

MAKES 1.75 LITRES/3 PINTS/7½ CUPS

1 kg/2 lb 4 oz chicken, skinned

2 celery sticks

1 onion

2 carrots

1 garlic clove

few sprigs of fresh parsley

2 litres/3½ pints/9 cups water

salt and pepper

1 Put all the ingredients together into a large saucepan.

2 Bring to the boil. Skim away surface scum using a large flat spoon. Reduce the heat to a gentle simmer, partially cover, and cook for 2 hours. Allow to cool.

3 Line a sieve (strainer) with clean muslin (cheesecloth) and place over a large jug or bowl. Pour the stock through the sieve (strainer). The cooked chicken can be used in another recipe. Discard the other solids. Cover the stock and chill.

4 Skim away any fat that forms before using. Store in the refrigerator for up to 3-4 days, until required, or freeze in small batches.

Fresh Vegetable Stock

This can be kept chilled for up to three days or frozen for up to three months. Salt is not added when cooking the stock: it is better to season it according to the dish in which it its to be used.

MAKES 1.5 LITRES/2¾ PINTS/6¼ CUPS

250 g/9 oz shallots

1 large carrot, diced

1 celery stalk, chopped

½ fennel bulb

1 garlic clove

1 bay leaf

a few fresh parsley and tarragon sprigs

2 litres/ 3½ pints/8¾ cups water

pepper

1 Put all the ingredients in a large saucepan and bring to the boil.

2 Skim off the surface scum with a flat spoon and reduce to a gentle simmer. Partially cover and cook for 45 minutes. Leave to cool.

3 Line a sieve (strainer) with clean muslin (cheesecloth) and put over a large jug or bowl. Pour the stock through the sieve (strainer) and then discard the herbs and vegetables.

4 Cover and store in small quantities in the refrigerator for up to three days.

Fresh Lamb Stock

MAKES 1.75 LITRES/3 PINTS/7½ CUPS

about 1 kg/2 lb 4 oz bones from a cooked
  joint or raw chopped lamb bones

2 onions, studded with 6 cloves, or sliced or
chopped coarsely

2 carrots, sliced

1 leek, sliced

1-2 celery sticks, sliced

1 Bouquet Garni

about 2.25 litres/4 pints/2 quarts water

1 Chop or break up the bones and place in a large saucepan together with the other ingredients.

2 Bring to the boil and remove any scum from the surface with a perforated spoon. Cover and simmer gently for 3-4 hours. Strain the stock and leave to cool.

3 Remove any fat from the surface and chill. If stored for more than 24 hours the stock must be boiled every day, cooled quickly and chilled again. The stock may be frozen for up to 2 months; place in a large plastic bag and seal, leaving at least 2.5 cm/1 inch of headspace to allow for some expansion.

Fresh Fish Stock

MAKES 1.75 LITRES/3 PINTS/7½ CUPS

1 head of a cod or salmon, etc, plus the
  trimmings, skin and bones or just the
  trimmings, skin and bones

1-2 onions, sliced

1 carrot, sliced

1-2 celery sticks, sliced

good squeeze of lemon juice

1 Bouquet Garni or 2 fresh or dried bay
  leaves

1 Wash the fish head and trimmings and place in a saucepan. Cover with water and bring to the boil.

2 Remove any scum with a perforated spoon, then add the remaining ingredients. Cover and simmer for about 30 minutes.

3 Strain and cool. Store in ther refrigerator and use within 2 days.

Cornflour (cornstarch) Paste

Cornflour (cornstarch) paste is made by mixing 1 part cornflour (cornstarch) with about 1½ parts of cold water. Stir until the mixture is smooth. The paste is used to thicken sauces.

Plain rice

Use long-grain rice or patna rice, or better still, try fragrant Thai rice

SERVES 4

250 g/9 oz long-grain rice

about 250 ml/9 fl oz/1 cup cold water

pinch of salt

½ tsp oil (optional)

1 Wash and rinse the rice just once. Place the rice in a saucepan and add enough water so that there is no more than 2 cm/³/₄ /inch of water above the surface of the rice.

2 Bring to the boil, add salt and oil (if using), and stir to prevent the rice sticking to the bottom of the pan.

3 Reduce the heat to very, very low, cover and cook for 15-20 minutes.

4 Remove from the heat and let the pan stand, covered, for 10 minutes or so. Fluff up the rice with a fork or spoon before serving.

How to Use This Book

Each recipe contains a wealth of useful information, including a breakdown of nutritional quantites, preparation and cooking times, and level of difficulty. All of this information is explained in detail below.

The nutritional information provided for each recipe is per serving or per portion. Optional ingredients, variations or serving suggestions have not been included in the calculations.

The number of chef's hats represents the difficulty of each recipe, ranging from easy (1 chef's hat) to difficult (5 chef's hats).

This amount of time represents the preparation of ingredients, including cooling, chilling and soaking times.

This represents the cooking time.

The ingredients for each recipe are listed in the order that they are used.

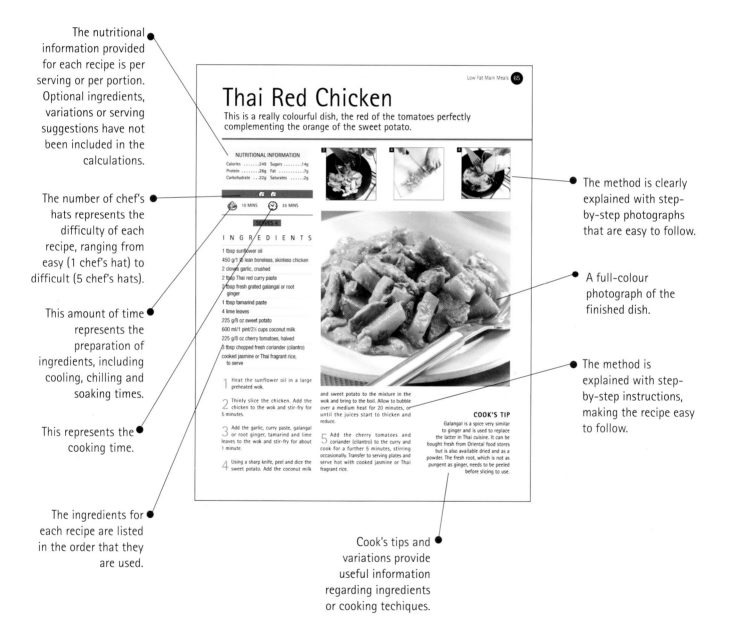

Low Fat Main Meals 65

Thai Red Chicken

This is a really colourful dish, the red of the tomatoes perfectly complementing the orange of the sweet potato.

NUTRITIONAL INFORMATION

Calories ....249 Sugars 14g
Protein ....26g Fat 7g
Carbohydrate ...22g Saturates 2g

10 MINS   35 MINS

SERVES 4

INGREDIENTS

1 tbsp sunflower oil

450 g/1 lb lean boneless, skinless chicken

2 cloves garlic, crushed

2 tbsp Thai red curry paste

2 tbsp fresh grated galangal or root ginger

1 tbsp tamarind paste

4 lime leaves

225 g/8 oz sweet potato

600 ml/1 pint/2½ cups coconut milk

225 g/8 oz cherry tomatoes, halved

3 tbsp chopped fresh coriander (cilantro)

cooked jasmine or Thai fragrant rice, to serve

1 Heat the sunflower oil in a large preheated wok.

2 Thinly slice the chicken. Add the chicken to the wok and stir-fry for 5 minutes.

3 Add the garlic, curry paste, galangal or root ginger, tamarind and lime leaves to the wok and stir-fry for about 1 minute.

4 Using a sharp knife, peel and dice the sweet potato. Add the coconut milk

and sweet potato to the mixture in the wok and bring to the boil. Allow to bubble over a medium heat for 20 minutes, or until the juices start to thicken and reduce.

5 Add the cherry tomatoes and coriander (cilantro) to the curry and cook for a further 5 minutes, stirring occasionally. Transfer to serving plates and serve hot with cooked jasmine or Thai fragrant rice.

COOK'S TIP

Galangal is a spice very similar to ginger and is used to replace the latter in Thai cuisine. It can be bought fresh from Oriental food stores but is also available dried and as a powder. The fresh root, which is not as pungent as ginger, needs to be peeled before slicing to use.

The method is clearly explained with step-by-step photographs that are easy to follow.

A full-colour photograph of the finished dish.

The method is explained with step-by-step instructions, making the recipe easy to follow.

Cook's tips and variations provide useful information regarding ingredients or cooking techiques.

Soups

Chicken soup has a long tradition of being comforting and good for us, and some cultures even think of it as a cure for all ills. It is certainly satisfying, full of flavour and easy to digest. For the best results, use a good homemade

chicken stock, although when time is at a premium, a good quality shop-bought bouillon cube can be used instead. Every cuisine in the world has its own favourite version of the chicken soup and in this section you'll find a selection of recipes from as far afield as Italy, Scotland and China.

Chicken Consommé

This is a very flavourful soup, especially if you make it from real chicken stock. Egg shells are used to give a crystal clear appearance.

NUTRITIONAL INFORMATION

Calories 96   Sugars 1g
Protein ....11g   Fat 1g
Carbohydrate ....1g   Saturates 0.4g

1¼ HOURS   15 MINS

SERVES 4

INGREDIENTS

1.75 litres/3 pints/8 cups chicken stock

150 ml/¼ pint/⅔ cup medium sherry

4 egg whites plus egg shells

125 g/4½ oz cooked lean chicken, sliced thinly

salt and pepper

1 Place the chicken stock and sherry in a large saucepan and heat gently for 5 minutes.

2 Add the egg whites and the egg shells to the chicken stock and whisk until the mixture begins to boil.

3 When the mixture boils, remove the pan from the heat and allow the mixture to subside for 10 minutes. Repeat this process three times.

4 This allows the egg white to trap the sediments in the chicken stock to clarify the soup.

5 Let the chicken consommé cool for 5 minutes.

6 Carefully place a piece of fine muslin (cheesecloth) over a clean saucepan.

Ladle the soup over the muslin and strain into the saucepan.

7 Repeat this process twice, then gently re-heat the consommé. Season with salt and pepper to taste, add the chicken slices to the consommé and serve immediately.

COOK'S TIP

For extra colour, add a garnish to the soup. Use a tablespoon each of finely diced carrot, celery and turnip or some finely chopped herbs, such as parsley or tarragon.

Hot & Sour Soup

This is the favourite soup in Chinese restaurants throughout the world.
Strain the soaking liquid and use in other soups, sauces and casseroles.

NUTRITIONAL INFORMATION

Calories 118   Sugar 0.3g
Protein ....14g   Fats 4g
Carbohydrates ....7g   Saturates 1g

4¹/₄ HOURS   10 MINS

SERVES 4

I N G R E D I E N T S

4-6 dried Chinese mushrooms (Shiitake),
    soaked

125 g/4½ oz cooked lean pork or chicken

1 cake tofu (bean curd)

60 g/2 oz canned sliced bamboo shoots,
    drained

600 ml/1 pint/2½ cups Chinese Stock (see
    page 14) or water

1 tbsp Chinese rice wine or dry sherry

1 tbsp light soy sauce

2 tbsp rice vinegar

1 tbsp cornflour (cornstarch) paste (see
    page 15)

salt, to taste

½ tsp ground white pepper

2-3 spring onions (scallions), thinly sliced,
    to serve

1 Drain the mushrooms, squeeze dry and discard the hard stalks. Thinly slice the mushrooms. Slice the meat, tofu (bean curd) and bamboo shoots into narrow shreds.

2 Bring the stock or water to a rolling boil in a wok or large pan and add the mushrooms, meat, tofu (bean curd) and bamboo shoots. Bring back to the boil then simmer for about 1 minute.

3 Add the wine, soy sauce and vinegar to the wok or pan.

4 Bring back to the boil once more, and add the cornflour (cornstarch) paste to thicken the soup. Season and gently stir the soup while it is thickening. Serve the soup hot, sprinkled with the sliced spring onions (scallions).

COOK'S TIP

There are many varieties of dried mushrooms, which add a particular flavour to Chinese cooking. Shiitake mushrooms are one of the best kinds. Soak in hot water for 25-30 minutes before use and cut off the hard stems.

Chicken & Asparagus Soup

This light, clear soup has a delicate flavour of asparagus and herbs. Use a good quality stock for best results.

NUTRITIONAL INFORMATION

Calories 224	Sugars 2g	
Protein 27g	Fat 5g	
Carbohydrate ...12g	Saturates 1g	

2³/4 HOURS   15 MINS

SERVES 4

INGREDIENTS

225 g/8 oz fresh asparagus

850 ml/1½ pints/3¾ cups Fresh Chicken Stock (see page 14)

150 ml/5 fl oz/⅔ cup dry white wine

1 sprig each fresh parsley, dill and tarragon

1 garlic clove

60 g/2 oz/⅓ cup vermicelli rice noodles

350 g/12 oz lean cooked chicken, finely shredded

salt and white pepper

1 small leek

1 Wash the asparagus and trim away the woody ends. Cut each spear into pieces 4 cm/1½ inches long.

2 Pour the stock and wine into a large saucepan and bring to the boil.

3 Wash the herbs and tie them with clean string. Peel the garlic clove and add, with the herbs, to the saucepan together with the asparagus and noodles. Cover and simmer for 5 minutes.

4 Stir in the chicken and plenty of seasoning. Simmer gently for a further 3-4 minutes until heated through.

5 Trim the leek, slice it down the centre and wash under running water to remove any dirt. Shake dry and shred finely.

6 Remove the herbs and garlic from the pan and discard. Ladle the soup into warm bowls, sprinkle with shredded leek and serve at once.

VARIATION

You can use any of your favourite herbs in this recipe, but choose those with a subtle flavour so that they do not overpower the asparagus. Small, tender asparagus spears give the best results and flavour.

Chicken & Leek Soup

This satisfying soup can be served as a main course. You can add rice and (bell) peppers to make it even more hearty, as well as colourful.

NUTRITIONAL INFORMATION

Calories 183	Sugar 4g
Protein 21g	Fats 9g
Carbohydrates 4g	Saturates 5g

5 MINS   1¹/₄ HOURS

SERVES 4–6

INGREDIENTS

25 g/1 oz/2 tbsp butter

350 g/12 oz boneless chicken

350 g/12 oz leeks, cut into 2.5-cm/ 1-inch pieces

1.2 litres/2 pints/5 cups Fresh Chicken Stock (see page 14)

1 bouquet garni sachet

8 pitted prunes, halved

salt and white pepper

cooked rice and diced (bell) peppers (optional)

1 Melt the butter in a large saucepan.

2 Add the chicken and leeks to the saucepan and fry for 8 minutes.

3 Add the chicken stock and bouquet garni sachet and stir well.

4 Season well with salt and pepper to taste.

5 Bring the soup to the boil and simmer for 45 minutes.

6 Add the prunes to the saucepan with some cooked rice and diced (bell) peppers (if using) and simmer for about 20 minutes.

7 Remove the bouquet garni sachet from the soup and discard. Serve

VARIATION

Instead of the bouquet garni sachet, you can use a bunch of fresh mixed herbs, tied together with string. Choose herbs such as parsley, thyme and rosemary.

Chicken & Pasta Broth

This satisfying soup makes a good lunch or supper dish and you can use any vegetables that you have at hand.

NUTRITIONAL INFORMATION

Calories 295   Sugar 8g
Protein . . . . .25g   Fats 10g
Carbohydrates . . .29g   Saturates 2g

5 MINS   20 MINS

SERVES 4

INGREDIENTS

350 g/12 oz boneless chicken breasts

2 tbsp sunflower oil

1 medium onion, diced

225 g/8 oz/1½ cups carrots, diced

225 g/8 oz cauliflower florets

900 ml/1½ pints/3¾ cups chicken stock

2 tsp dried mixed herbs

125 g/4½ oz small pasta shapes

salt and pepper

Parmesan cheese (optional) and crusty bread, to serve

1 Finely dice the chicken, discarding any skin.

2 Heat the oil and quickly sauté the chicken and vegetables until they are lightly coloured.

3 Stir in the stock and herbs. Bring to the boil and add the pasta. Return to the boil, cover and simmer for 10 minutes.

4 Season to taste and sprinkle with Parmesan cheese (if using). Serve with crusty bread.

Dickensian Chicken Broth

This soup is made with traditional Scottish ingredients. It should be left for at least two days before being re-heated.

NUTRITIONAL INFORMATION

Calories 357	Sugars 5g
Protein 53g	Fat 8g
Carbohydrate ...19g	Saturates 2g

48¼ HOURS   2¾ HOURS

SERVES 4

I N G R E D I E N T S

60 g/2 oz/⅓ cup pre-soaked dried peas

900 g/2 lb diced lean chicken, fat removed

1.2 litres/2 pints/5 cups chicken stock

600ml/1 pint/2½ cups water

60 g/2 oz/¼ cup barley

1 large carrot, peeled and diced

1 small turnip, peeled and diced

1 large leek, thinly sliced

1 red onion, chopped finely

salt and white pepper

oatmeal cakes or bread to serve

COOK'S TIP

Use either whole grain barley or pearl barley. Only the outer husk is removed from whole grain barley and when cooked it has a nutty flavour and a chewy texture.

1 Put the pre-soaked peas and diced chicken into a pan, then add the stock and water and bring slowly to the boil.

2 Skim the stock as it boils.

3 Wash the barley thoroughly and put to one side

4 When all the scum is removed, add the washed barley and salt and simmer for 35 minutes.

5 Add the rest of the ingredients and simmer for 2 hours and skim again.

6 Let the broth stand for at least 48 hours. Reheat, adjust the seasoning and serve with oatmeal cakes or bread.

Cock-a-Leekie Soup

A traditional Scottish soup in which a whole chicken is cooked with the vegetables to add extra flavour to the stock.

NUTRITIONAL INFORMATION

Calories	45	Sugars	........4g
Protein	.........5g	Fat	..........1g
Carbohydrate	....5g	Saturates	.....0.2g

2½ HOURS   2 HOURS

SERVES 4–6

I N G R E D I E N T S

1–1.5 kg/2lb 4 oz–3 lb 5 oz oven-ready chicken plus giblets, if available

1.75–2 litres/3–3½ pints/8–9 cups Chicken Stock (see page 14)

1 onion, sliced

4 leeks, sliced thinly

good pinch of ground allspice or ground coriander

1 Bouquet Garni

12 no-need-to-soak prunes, halved and pitted

salt and pepper

warm crusty bread, to serve

1 Put the chicken, giblets (if using) stock and onion in a large saucepan.

2 Bring to the boil and remove any scum from the surface.

3 Add the leeks, seasoning, allspice or coriander and bouquet garni to the pan, cover and simmer gently for about 1½ hours until the chicken is falling off the bones.

4 Remove the chicken and bouquet garni from the pan and skim any fat from the surface of the soup.

5 Chop some of the chicken flesh and return to the pan.

6 Add the prunes, bring back to the boil and simmer, uncovered, for about 20 minutes.

7 Adjust the seasoning and serve with warm crusty bread.

VARIATION

You can replace the chicken stock with 3 chicken stock cubes dissolved in the same amount of water, if you prefer.

Chicken & Bean Soup

This hearty and nourishing soup, combining chickpeas (garbanzo beans) and chicken, is an ideal starter for a family supper.

NUTRITIONAL INFORMATION

Calories 347   Sugars 2g
Protein ....28g   Fat 11g
Carbohydrate ...37g   Saturates 4g

5 MINS   1¾ HOURS

SERVES 4

INGREDIENTS

25 g/1 oz/2 tbsp butter

3 spring onions (scallions), chopped

2 garlic cloves, crushed

1 fresh marjoram sprig, finely chopped

350 g/12 oz boned chicken breasts, diced

1.2 litres/2 pints/5 cups chicken stock

350 g/12 oz can chickpeas (garbanzo beans), drained

1 bouquet garni

1 red (bell) pepper, diced

1 green (bell) pepper, diced

115 g/4 oz/1 cup small dried pasta shapes, such as elbow macaroni

salt and white pepper

croûtons, to serve

COOK'S TIP

If you prefer, you can use dried chickpeas (garbanzo beans). Cover with cold water and set aside to soak for 5–8 hours. Drain and add the beans to the soup, according to the recipe, and allow an additional 30 minutes– 1 hour cooking time.

1 Melt the butter in a large saucepan. Add the spring onions (scallions), garlic, sprig of fresh marjoram and the diced chicken and cook, stirring frequently, over a medium heat for 5 minutes.

2 Add the chicken stock, chickpeas (garbanzo beans) and bouquet garni and season with salt and white pepper.

3 Bring the soup to the boil, lower the heat and simmer for about 2 hours.

4 Add the diced (bell) peppers and pasta to the pan, then simmer for a further 20 minutes.

5 Transfer the soup to a warm tureen. To serve, ladle the soup into individual serving bowls and serve immediately, garnished with the croûtons.

Vegetable & Chickpea Soup

A tasty soup, full of vegetables, chicken and chickpeas (garbanzo beans), with just a hint of spiciness, to serve on any occasion.

NUTRITIONAL INFORMATION

Calories	271	Sugar	.........6g
Protein	........17g	Fats	..........13g
Carbohydrates	...24g	Saturates	......2g

10 MINS   55 MINS

SERVES 4–6

INGREDIENTS

3 tbsp olive oil

1 large onion, chopped finely

2–3 garlic cloves, crushed

½–1 red chilli, deseeded and chopped very finely

1 skinless, boneless chicken breast, about 150 g/5½ oz, sliced thickly

2 celery sticks (stalks), chopped finely

175 g/6 oz carrots, grated coarsely

1.25 litres/2¼ pints chicken stock

2 bay leaves

½ tsp dried oregano

¼ tsp ground cinnamon

400 g/14 oz can of chickpeas (garbanzo beans), drained

2 medium tomatoes, peeled, deseeded and chopped

1 tbsp tomato purée (paste)

salt and pepper

chopped fresh coriander (cilantro) or parsley, to garnish

corn or wheat tortillas, to serve

1 Heat the oil in a large saucepan and fry the onion, garlic and chilli very gently until they are softened but not coloured.

2 Add the chicken to the saucepan and continue to cook until well sealed and lightly browned.

3 Add the celery, carrots, stock, bay leaves, oregano, cinnamon, and salt and pepper. Bring to the boil, then cover and simmer gently for about 20 minutes, or until the chicken is tender and cooked throughout.

4 Remove the chicken from the soup and chop it finely, or cut it into narrow strips.

5 Return the chicken to the pan with the chickpeas (garbanzo beans), tomatoes and tomato purée (paste). Simmer, covered, for a further 15–20 minutes. Discard the bay leaves, then adjust the seasoning.

6 Serve very hot sprinkled with coriander (cilantro) or parsley and accompanied by warmed tortillas.

Lemon & Chicken Soup

This delicately flavoured summer soup is surprisingly easy to make, and tastes delicious.

NUTRITIONAL INFORMATION

Calories . . . . . . .506 Sugars 4g
Protein . . . . .19g Fat 31g
Carbohydrate . . .41g Saturates 19g

5-10 MINS 1¼ HOURS

SERVES 4

INGREDIENTS

60 g/2 oz/4 tbsp butter

8 shallots, thinly sliced

2 carrots, thinly sliced

2 celery sticks (stalks), thinly sliced

225 g/8 oz boned chicken breasts,
  finely chopped

3 lemons

1.2 litres/2 pints/5 cups chicken stock

225 g/8 oz dried spaghetti, broken into
  small pieces

150 ml/¼ pint/⅝ cup double (heavy) cream

salt and white pepper

TO GARNISH

fresh parsley sprig

3 lemon slices, halved

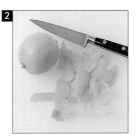

COOK'S TIP

You can prepare this soup
up to the end of step 3 in
advance, so that all you need do
before serving is heat it through
before adding the pasta and the
finishing touches.

1 Melt the butter in a large saucepan. Add the shallots, carrots, celery and chicken and cook over a low heat, stirring occasionally, for 8 minutes.

2 Thinly pare the lemons and blanch the lemon rind in boiling water for 3 minutes. Squeeze the juice from the lemons.

3 Add the lemon rind and juice to the pan, together with the chicken stock. Bring slowly to the boil over a low heat and simmer for 40 minutes, stirring occasionally.

4 Add the spaghetti to the pan and cook for 15 minutes. Season to taste with salt and white pepper and add the cream. Heat through, but do not allow the soup to boil or it will curdle.

5 Pour the soup into a tureen or individual bowls, garnish with the parsley and half slices of lemon and serve immediately.

Chicken & Sweetcorn Soup

A quick and satisfying soup, full of delicious flavours and many different textures.

NUTRITIONAL INFORMATION

Calories	200	Sugars	.........6g
Protein	........10g	Fat	..........12g
Carbohydrate	...13g	Saturates	......5g

10 MINS   40 MINS

SERVES 2

INGREDIENTS

2 tsp oil

15 g/½ oz/¼ cup butter or margarine

1 small onion, chopped finely

1 chicken leg quarter or 2–3 drumsticks

1 tbsp plain (all-purpose) flour

600 ml/1 pint/2½ cups chicken stock

½ small red, yellow or orange (bell) pepper, seeded and chopped finely

2 large tomatoes, peeled and chopped

2 tsp tomato purée (paste)

200 g/7 oz can of sweetcorn, drained

generous pinch of dried oregano

¼ tsp ground coriander

salt and pepper

chopped fresh parsley, to garnish

1 Heat the oil and butter or margarine in a saucepan and fry the onion until beginning to soften. Cut the chicken quarter (if using) into 2 pieces. Add the chicken and fry until golden brown.

2 Add the flour and cook for 1–2 minutes. Then add the stock, bring to the boil and simmer for 5 minutes.

3 Add the (bell) pepper, tomatoes, tomato purée (paste), sweetcorn, oregano, coriander and seasoning. Cover and simmer gently for about 20 minutes until the chicken is very tender.

4 Remove the chicken from the soup, strip off the flesh and chop finely. Return the chopped meat to the soup.

5 Adjust the seasoning and simmer for a further 2–3 minutes before sprinkling with parsley and serving very hot with crusty bread.

COOK'S TIP

If preferred, the chicken may be removed from the soup when tender to serve separately.

Chicken Noodle Soup

Quick to make, this hot and spicy soup is hearty and warming. If you like your food really fiery, add a chopped dried or fresh chilli with its seeds.

NUTRITIONAL INFORMATION

Calories 196   Sugars 4g
Protein . . . . .16g   Fat 11g
Carbohydrate . . . .8g   Saturates 2g

10 MINS   25 MINS

SERVES 4–6

INGREDIENTS

1 sheet of dried egg noodles
  from a 250 g/9 oz pack

1 tbsp oil

4 skinless, boneless
  chicken thighs, diced

1 bunch spring onions (scallions), sliced

2 garlic cloves, chopped

2 cm/¾ inch piece fresh
  ginger root, finely chopped

850 ml/1½ pints/3¾ cups chicken stock

200 ml/7 fl oz/scant 1 cup coconut milk

3 tsp red curry paste

3 tbsp peanut butter

2 tbsp light soy sauce

1 small red (bell) pepper, chopped

60 g/2 oz/½ cup frozen peas

salt and pepper

1 Put the noodles in a shallow dish and soak in boiling water as the packet directs.

2 Heat the oil in a large preheated saucepan or wok.

3 Add the diced chicken to the pan or wok and fry for 5 minutes, stirring until lightly browned.

4 Add the white part of the spring onions (scallions), the garlic and ginger and fry for 2 minutes, stirring.

5 Stir in the chicken stock, coconut milk, red curry paste, peanut butter and soy sauce.

6 Season with salt and pepper to taste. Bring to the boil, stirring, then simmer for 8 minutes, stirring occasionally.

7 Add the red (bell) pepper, peas and green spring onion (scallion) tops and cook for 2 minutes.

8 Add the drained noodles and heat through. Spoon the chicken noodle soup into warmed bowls and serve with a spoon and fork.

VARIATION

Green curry paste can be used instead of red curry paste for a less fiery flavour.

Chicken Wonton Soup

This Chinese-style soup is delicious as a starter to an oriental meal or as a light meal.

NUTRITIONAL INFORMATION

Calories . . . . .101 Sugars 0.3g
Protein . . . . .14g Fat 4g
Carbohydrate . . . .3g Saturates 1g

15 MINS   10 MINS

SERVES 4-6

INGREDIENTS

FILLING

350 g/12 oz minced (ground) chicken

1 tbsp soy sauce

1 tsp grated, fresh ginger root

1 garlic clove, crushed

2 tsp sherry

2 spring onions (scallions), chopped

1 tsp sesame oil

1 egg white

½ tsp cornflour (cornstarch)

½ tsp sugar

about 35 wonton wrappers

SOUP

1.5 litres/2¾ pints/6 cups chicken stock

1 tbsp light soy sauce

1 spring onion (scallion), shredded

1 small carrot, cut into very thin slices

1 Place all the ingredients for the filling in a large bowl and mix until thoroughly combined.

2 Place a small spoonful of the filling in the centre of each wonton wrapper.

3 Dampen the edges and gather up the wonton wrapper to form a small pouch enclosing the filling.

4 Cook the filled wontons in boiling water for 1 minute or until they float to the top. Remove with a slotted spoon and set aside.

5 Bring the chicken stock to the boil. Add the soy sauce, spring onion (scallion) and carrot.

6 Add the wontons to the soup and simmer gently for 2 minutes. Serve.

COOK'S TIP

Make double quantities of wonton skins and freeze the remainder. Place small squares of baking parchment in between each skin, then place in a freezer bag and freeze. Defrost thoroughly before using.

Chicken, Noodle & Corn Soup

The vermicelli gives this Chinese-style soup an Italian twist, but you can use egg noodles if you prefer.

NUTRITIONAL INFORMATION

Calories	.401	Sugars	.6g
Protein	.31g	Fat	.24g
Carbohydrate	.17g	Saturates	.13g

5 MINS   25 MINS

SERVES 4

INGREDIENTS

450 g/1 lb boned chicken breasts,
   cut into strips

1.2 litres/2 pints/5 cups chicken stock

150 ml/¼ pint/⅝ cup double (heavy)
   cream

100 g/3½ oz/¾ cup dried vermicelli

1 tbsp cornflour (cornstarch)

3 tbsp milk

175 g/6 oz sweetcorn (corn-on-the-cob)
   kernels

salt and pepper

finely chopped spring onion (scallions),
   to garnish (optional)

1 Put the chicken strips, chicken stock and double (heavy) cream into a large saucepan and bring to the boil over a low heat.

2 Reduce the heat slightly and simmer for about 20 minutes. Season the soup with salt and black pepper to taste.

3 Meanwhile, cook the vermicelli in lightly salted boiling water for 10-12 minutes, until just tender. Drain the pasta and keep warm.

4 In a small bowl, mix together the cornflour (cornstarch) and milk to make a smooth paste. Stir the cornflour

(cornstarch) paste into the soup until thickened.

5 Add the sweetcorn (corn-on-the-cob) and vermicelli to the pan and heat through.

6 Transfer the soup to a warm tureen or individual soup bowls, garnish with spring onions (scallions), if desired, and serve immediately.

VARIATION

For crab and sweetcorn soup, substitute 450 g/1 lb cooked crabmeat for the chicken breasts. Flake the crabmeat well before adding it to the saucepan and reduce the cooking time by 10 minutes.

Spicy Chicken Noodle Soup

This filling soup is filled with spicy flavours and bright colours for a really attractive and hearty dish.

NUTRITIONAL INFORMATION

Calories 286	Sugars 21g
Protein 22g	Fat 6g
Carbohydrate . . .37g	Saturates 1g

15 MINS   20 MINS

SERVES 4

INGREDIENTS

2 tbsp tamarind paste

4 red chillies, finely chopped

2 cloves garlic, crushed

2.5 cm/1-inch piece Thai ginger, peeled and very finely chopped

4 tbsp fish sauce

2 tbsp palm sugar or caster (superfine) sugar

8 lime leaves, roughly torn

1.2 litres/2 pints/5 cups chicken stock

350 g/12 oz boneless chicken breast

100 g/3½ oz carrots, very thinly sliced

350 g/12 oz sweet potato, diced

100 g/3½ oz baby corn cobs, halved

3 tbsp fresh coriander (cilantro), roughly chopped

100 g/3½ oz cherry tomatoes, halved

150 g/5½ oz flat rice noodles

fresh coriander (cilantro), chopped, to garnish

1 Preheat a large wok or frying pan (skillet). Place the tamarind paste, chillies, garlic, ginger, fish sauce, sugar, lime leaves and chicken stock in the wok and bring to the boil, stirring constantly. Reduce the heat and cook for about 5 minutes.

2 Using a sharp knife, thinly slice the chicken. Add the chicken to the wok and cook for a further 5 minutes, stirring the mixture well.

3 Reduce the heat and add the carrots, sweet potato and baby corn cobs to the wok. Leave to simmer, uncovered, for 5 minutes, or until the vegetables are just tender and the chicken is completely cooked through.

4 Stir in the chopped fresh coriander (cilantro), cherry tomatoes and flat rice noodles.

5 Leave the soup to simmer for about 5 minutes, or until the noodles are tender.

6 Garnish the spicy chicken noodle soup with chopped fresh coriander (cilantro) and serve hot.

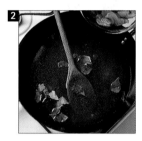

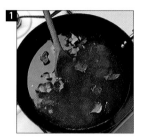

Clear Chicken & Egg Soup

This tasty chicken soup has the addition of poached eggs, making it both delicious and filling. Use fresh, home-made stock for a better flavour.

NUTRITIONAL INFORMATION

Calories ....138 Sugars 1g
Protein ....16g Fat 7g
Carbohydrate ....1g Saturates 2g

5 MINS   35 MINS

SERVES 4

INGREDIENTS

1 tsp salt

1 tbsp rice wine vinegar

4 eggs

850 ml/1½ pints/3¾ cups
    chicken stock

1 leek, sliced

125 g/4½ oz broccoli florets

125 g/4½ oz/1 cup shredded
    cooked chicken

2 open-cap mushrooms, sliced

1 tbsp dry sherry

dash of chilli sauce

chilli powder, to garnish

VARIATION

You could use 4 dried Chinese mushrooms, rehydrated according to the packet instructions, instead of the open-cap mushrooms, if you prefer.

1 Bring a large saucepan of water to the boil and add the salt and rice wine vinegar.

2 Reduce the heat so that it is just simmering and carefully break the eggs into the water, one at a time. Poach the eggs for 1 minute.

3 Remove the poached eggs with a slotted spoon and set aside.

4 Bring the chicken stock to the boil in a separate pan and add the leek, broccoli, chicken, mushrooms and sherry and season with chilli sauce to taste. Cook for 10–15 minutes.

5 Add the poached eggs to the soup and cook for a further 2 minutes. Carefully transfer the soup and poached eggs to 4 soup bowls. Dust with a little chilli powder and serve immediately.

Curried Chicken & Corn Soup

Tender cooked chicken strips and baby corn cobs are the main flavours in this delicious clear soup, with just a hint of ginger.

NUTRITIONAL INFORMATION

Calories . . . . . . .206 Sugars 5g
Protein . . . . .29g Fat 5g
Carbohydrate . . .13g Saturates 1g

🍲 5 MINS   🕐 30 MINS

SERVES 4

I N G R E D I E N T S

175 g/6 oz can sweetcorn
(corn), drained

850 ml/1½ pints/3¾ cups
chicken stock

350 g/12 oz cooked, lean chicken,
cut into strips

16 baby corn cobs

1 tsp Chinese curry powder

1-cm/½-inch piece fresh root ginger
(ginger root), grated

3 tbsp light soy sauce

2 tbsp chopped chives

1 Place the canned sweetcorn (corn) in a food processor, together with 150 ml/¼ pint/⅔ cup of the chicken stock and process until the mixture forms a smooth purée.

2 Pass the sweetcorn purée through a fine sieve (strainer), pressing with the back of a spoon to remove any husks.

3 Pour the remaining chicken stock into a large saucepan and add the strips of cooked chicken. Stir in the sweetcorn (corn) purée.

4 Add the baby corn cobs and bring the soup to the boil. Boil the soup for 10 minutes.

5 Add the Chinese curry powder, grated fresh root ginger and light soy sauce and stir well to combine. Cook for a further 10–15 minutes.

6 Stir the chopped chives into the soup.

7 Transfer the curried chicken and corn soup to warm soup bowls and serve immediately.

COOK'S TIP

Prepare the soup up to 24 hours in advance without adding the chicken, cool, cover and store in the refrigerator. Add the chicken and heat the soup through thoroughly before serving.

Chicken Soup with Almonds

This soup can also be made using pheasant breasts. For a really gamy flavour, make game stock from the carcass and use in the soup.

NUTRITIONAL INFORMATION

Calories . . . . .219 Sugars 2g
Protein . . . . .18g Fat 15g
Carbohydrate . . . .2g Saturates 2g

10 MINS   20 MINS

SERVES 4

INGREDIENTS

1 large or 2 small boneless skinned chicken breasts

1 tbsp sunflower oil

4 spring onions (scallions), thinly sliced diagonally

1 carrot, cut into julienne strips

700 ml/1¼ pints/3 cups chicken stock

finely grated rind of ½ lemon

40 g/1½ oz/⅓ cup ground almonds

1 tbsp light soy sauce

1 tbsp lemon juice

25 g/1 oz/¼ cup flaked almonds, toasted

salt and pepper

1 Cut each breast into 4 strips length-ways, then slice very thinly across the grain to give shreds of chicken.

2 Heat the oil in a wok, swirling it around until really hot.

3 Add the spring onions (scallions) and cook for 2 minutes, then add the chicken and toss it for 3-4 minutes until sealed and almost cooked through, stirring all the time. Add the carrot strips and stir.

4 Add the stock to the wok and bring to the boil. Add the lemon rind, ground almonds, soy sauce, lemon juice and plenty of seasoning. Bring back to the boil and simmer, uncovered, for 5 minutes, stirring from time to time.

5 Adjust the seasoning, add most of the toasted flaked almonds and continue to cook for a further 1-2 minutes.

6 Serve the soup very hot, in individual bowls, sprinkled with the remaining flaked almonds.

COOK'S TIP

To make game stock, break up a pheasant carcass and place in a pan with 2 litres/3½ pints/8 cups water. Bring to the boil slowly, skimming off any scum. Add 1 bouquet garni, 1 peeled onion and seasoning. Cover and simmer gently for 1½ hours. Strain, and skim any surface fat.

Appetizers

As chicken is so versatile and quick to cook, it is perfect for innovative and appetizing snacks. Its unassertive flavour means that it can be enlivened by exotic fruits and spices and Asian ingredients, such as soy sauce, sesame oil

and fresh ginger root. Here you will find fritters, salads and drumsticks that are stuffed and baked, or served with delicious fruity salsas. Because chicken pieces travel well and are easy to eat, many of the recipes are ideal to take on picnics or to pack in a lunch box.

Cranberry Turkey Burgers

This recipe is bound to be popular with children and is easy to prepare for their supper or tea.

NUTRITIONAL INFORMATION

Calories 209	Sugars 15g
Protein 22g	Fat 5g
Carbohydrate ...21g	Saturates 1g

45 MINS   25 MINS

SERVES 4

INGREDIENTS

350 g/12 oz/1½ cups lean minced (ground) turkey

1 onion, chopped finely

1 tbsp chopped fresh sage

6 tbsp dry white breadcrumbs

4 tbsp cranberry sauce

1 egg white, size 2, lightly beaten

2 tsp sunflower oil

salt and pepper

TO SERVE

4 toasted granary or wholemeal (whole wheat) burger buns

½ lettuce, shredded

4 tomatoes, sliced

4 tsp cranberry sauce

1 Mix together the turkey, onion, sage, seasoning, breadcrumbs and cranberry sauce, then bind with egg white.

2 Press into 4 x 10 cm/4 inch rounds, about 2 cm/¾ inch thick. Chill the burgers for 30 minutes.

3 Line a grill (broiler) rack with baking parchment, making sure the ends are secured underneath the rack to ensure they don't catch fire. Place the burgers on top and brush lightly with oil. Put under a preheated moderate grill (broiler) and cook for 10 minutes. Turn the burgers over, brush again with oil. Cook for a further 12–15 minutes until cooked through.

4 Fill the burger rolls with lettuce, tomato and a burger, and top with cranberry sauce.

COOK'S TIP

Look out for a variety of ready minced (ground) meats at your butchers or supermarket. If unavailable, you can mince (grind) your own by choosing lean cuts and processing them in a blender or food processor.

Turkey & Vegetable Loaf

This impressive-looking turkey loaf is flavoured with herbs and a layer of juicy tomatoes, and covered with courgette (zucchini) ribbons.

NUTRITIONAL INFORMATION

Calories 165   Sugars 1g
Protein ....36g   Fat 2g
Carbohydrate ....1g   Saturates 0.5g

10 MINS   1¼ HOURS

SERVES 6

INGREDIENTS

1 medium onion, finely chopped

1 garlic clove, crushed

900 g/2 lb lean turkey, minced (ground)

1 tbsp fresh parsley, chopped

1 tbsp fresh chives, chopped

1 tbsp fresh tarragon, chopped

1 medium egg white, lightly beaten

2 courgettes (zucchini), 1 medium, 1 large

2 medium tomatoes

salt and pepper

tomato and herb sauce, to serve

1 Preheat the oven to 190°C/ 375°F/Gas Mark 5 and line a non-stick loaf tin (pan) with baking parchment. Place the onion, garlic and turkey in a bowl, add the herbs and season well. Mix together with your hands, then add the egg white to bind.

2 Press half of the turkey mixture into the base of the tin (pan). Thinly slice the medium courgette (zucchini) and the tomatoes and arrange the slices over the meat. Top with the rest of the turkey and press down firmly.

3 Cover with a layer of kitchen foil and place in a roasting tin. Pour in enough boiling water to come half-way up the sides of the loaf tin. Bake in the oven for 1–1¼ hours, removing the foil for the last 20 minutes of cooking. Test the loaf is cooked by inserting a skewer into the centre – the juices should run clear. The loaf will also shrink away from the sides of the tin.

4 Meanwhile, trim the large courgette (zucchini). Using a vegetable peeler or hand-held metal cheese slicer, cut the courgette (zucchini) into thin slices. Bring a saucepan of water to the boil and blanch the courgette ribbons for 1–2 minutes until just tender. Drain and keep warm.

5 Remove the turkey loaf from the tin and transfer to a warm platter. Drape the courgette (zucchini) ribbons over the turkey loaf and serve with a tomato and herb sauce.

Parsley, Chicken & Ham Pâté

Pâté is easy to make at home, and this combination of lean chicken and ham mixed with herbs is especially straightforward.

NUTRITIONAL INFORMATION

Calories 119	Sugars 2g
Protein 20g	Fat 3g
Carbohydrate 2g	Saturates 1g

55 MINS   0 MINS

SERVES 4

INGREDIENTS

225 g/8 oz lean, skinless chicken, cooked

100 g/3½ oz lean ham, trimmed

small bunch fresh parsley

1 tsp lime rind, grated

2 tbsp lime juice

1 garlic clove, peeled

125 ml/4 fl oz/½ cup low-fat natural
    fromage frais (unsweetened yogurt)

salt and pepper

1 tsp lime zest, to garnish

TO SERVE

wedges of lime

crisp bread

green salad

VARIATION

This pâté can be made successfully
with other kinds of minced, lean,
cooked meat such as turkey, beef
and pork. Alternatively, replace the
meat with peeled prawns (shrimp)
and/or white crab meat, or with
canned tuna in brine, drained.

1 Dice the chicken and ham and place in a blender or food processor.

2 Add the parsley, lime rind and juice, and garlic to the chicken and ham, and process well until finely minced. Alternatively, finely chop the chicken, ham, parsley and garlic and place in a bowl. Mix gently with the lime rind and juice.

3 Transfer the mixture to a bowl and mix in the fromage frais (yogurt). Season with salt and pepper to taste, cover and leave to chill in the refrigerator for about 30 minutes.

4 Pile the pâté into individual serving dishes and garnish with lime zest. Serve the pâtés with lime wedges, crisp bread and a fresh green salad.

Sweet & Sour Drumsticks

Chicken drumsticks are marinated to impart a tangy, sweet and sour flavour and a shiny glaze before being cooked on a barbecue (grill).

NUTRITIONAL INFORMATION

Calories 171   Sugars 9g
Protein . . . . .23g   Fat 5g
Carbohydrate . . .10g   Saturates 1g

1¼ HOURS   20 MINS

SERVES 4

I N G R E D I E N T S

8 chicken drumsticks

4 tbsp red wine vinegar

2 tbsp tomato purée (paste)

2 tbsp soy sauce

2 tbsp clear honey

1 tbsp Worcestershire sauce

1 garlic clove

good pinch cayenne

salt and pepper

crisp salad leaves, to serve

1 Skin the chicken if desired and slash 2–3 times with a sharp knife.

2 Put the chicken drumsticks into a non-metallic container.

3 Mix all the remaining ingredients and pour over the chicken.

4 Leave to marinate in the refrigerator for 1 hour. Cook the drumsticks on a preheated barbecue (grill) for about 20 minutes, brushing with the glaze several times during cooking until the chicken is well browned and the juices run clear when pierced with a skewer. Serve with a crisp salad leaves.

COOK'S TIP

For a tangy flavour, add the juice of 1 lime to the marinade. While the drumsticks are grilling, check regularly to ensure that they are not burning.

Oat-Crusted Chicken Pieces

A very low-fat chicken recipe with a refreshingly light, mustard-spiced sauce, which is ideal for a healthy lunchbox or a light meal with salad.

NUTRITIONAL INFORMATION

Calories	120	Sugars	.........3g
Protein	........15g	Fat	...........3g
Carbohydrate	....8g	Saturates	......1g

5 MINS   40 MINS

SERVES 4

INGREDIENTS

25 g/1 oz/⅓ cup rolled oats

1 tbsp chopped fresh rosemary

4 skinless chicken quarters

1 egg white

150 g/5½ oz/½ cup natural low-fat fromage frais

2 tsp wholegrain mustard

salt and pepper

grated carrot salad, to serve

1 Mix together the rolled oats, chopped fresh rosemary and salt and pepper.

2 Brush each piece of chicken evenly with egg white, then coat in the oat mixture.

3 Place the chicken pieces on a baking tray (cookie sheet) and bake in a preheated oven, 200°C/400°F/Gas Mark 6, for about 40 minutes. Test to see if the chicken is cooked by inserted a skewer into the thickest part of the chicken – the juices should run clear without a trace of pink.

4 Mix together the fromage frais and mustard, season with salt and pepper to taste.

5 Serve the chicken, hot or cold, with the sauce and a grated carrot salad.

Sticky Chicken Drummers

The mango salsa contrasts well with the spicy chicken. Pack leftover chicken in lunchboxes for a tasty alternative to sandwiches.

NUTRITIONAL INFORMATION

Calories ....159 Sugars 3g
Protein ....22g Fat 6g
Carbohydrate ....4g Saturates 2g

10 MINS   40 MINS

SERVES 4

INGREDIENTS

8 skinless chicken drumsticks

3 tbsp mango chutney

2 tsp Dijon mustard

2 tsp oil

1 tsp paprika

1 tsp black mustard seeds, roughly crushed

½ tsp turmeric

2 garlic cloves, chopped

salt and pepper

SALSA

1 mango, diced

1 tomato, chopped finely

½ red onion, sliced thinly

2 tbsp chopped fresh coriander (cilantro)

1 Using a small, sharp knife, slash each drumstick three or four times then place in a roasting tin.

2 Mix together the mango chutney, mustard, oil, spices, garlic and salt and pepper and spoon over the chicken drumsticks, turning until they are coated all over with the glaze.

3 Cook in a preheated oven, 200°C/400°F/Gas Mark 6, for 40 minutes, brushing with the glaze several times during cooking until the chicken is well

browned and the juices run clear when pierced with a skewer.

4 Meanwhile, mix together the mango, tomato, onion and coriander (cilantro) for the mango salsa. Season to taste and chill until needed.

5 Arrange the chicken drumsticks on a serving plate and serve hot or cold with the mango salsa.

VARIATION

Use mild curry powder instead of the turmeric for a stronger flavour.

Spicy Chicken Tortillas

The chicken filling for these easy-to-prepare tortillas has a mild, mellow spicy heat and a fresh salad makes a perfect accompaniment.

NUTRITIONAL INFORMATION

Calories ....650 Sugars 15g
Protein ....48g Fat 31g
Carbohydrate ...47g Saturates 10g

10 MINS   35 MINS

SERVES 4

INGREDIENTS

2 tbsp oil

8 skinless, boneless chicken thighs, sliced

1 onion, chopped

2 garlic cloves, chopped

1 tsp cumin seeds, roughly crushed

2 large dried chillies, sliced

400 g/14 oz can tomatoes

400 g/14 oz can red kidney beans, drained

150 ml/¼ pint/⅔ cup chicken stock

2 tsp sugar

salt and pepper

lime wedges, to garnish

TO SERVE

1 large ripe avocado

1 lime

8 soft tortillas

225 ml/8 fl oz/1 cup thick yogurt

1 Heat the oil in a large frying pan or wok, add the chicken and fry for 3 minutes.

2 Add the chopped onion and fry for 5 minutes, stirring until browned.

3 Add the chopped garlic, cumin and chillies, with their seeds, and cook for about 1 minute.

4 Add the tomatoes, kidney beans, stock, sugar and salt and pepper. Bring to the boil, breaking up the tomatoes. Cover and simmer for 15 minutes. Remove the lid and cook for 5 minutes, stirring occasionally until the sauce has thickened.

5 Halve the avocado, discard the stone and scoop out the flesh onto a plate. Mash the avocado with a fork.

6 Cut half of the lime into 8 thin wedges. Now squeeze the juice from the remaining lime over the mashed avocado.

7 Warm the tortillas according to the directions on the pack. Put two tortillas on each serving plate, fill with the chicken mixture and top with spoonfuls of avocado and yogurt. Garnish the tortillas with lime wedges.

Chicken & Almond Rissoles

Cooked potatoes and cooked chicken are combined to make tasty rissoles rolled in chopped almonds then served with stir-fried vegetables.

NUTRITIONAL INFORMATION

Calories 161   Sugars 3g
Protein . . . . 12g   Fat 9g
Carbohydrate . . . .8g   Saturates 1g

🍳 🍳 🍳

35 MINS   20 MINS

SERVES 4

I N G R E D I E N T S

125 g/4½ oz par-boiled potatoes

90 g/3 oz/½ cup carrots

125 g/4½ oz/1 cup cooked chicken meat

1 garlic clove, crushed

½ tsp dried tarragon or thyme

generous pinch of ground allspice or ground coriander seeds

1 egg yolk, or ½ egg, beaten

about 25 g/1 oz/¼ cup flaked (slivered) almonds

salt and pepper

S T I R – F R I E D V E G E T A B L E S

1 celery stick (stalk)

2 spring onions (scallions), trimmed

1 tbsp oil

8 baby sweetcorn cobs (corn-on-the-cob)

about 10–12 mangetout (snow peas) or sugar snap peas, trimmed

2 tsp balsamic vinegar

salt and pepper

1 Grate the boiled potatoes and raw carrots coarsely into a bowl. Chop finely or mince (grind) the chicken. Add to the vegetables with the garlic, herbs and spices and plenty of salt and pepper.

2 Add the egg and bind the ingredients together. Divide in half and shape into sausages. Chop the almonds and then evenly-coat each rissole in the nuts. Place the rissoles in a greased ovenproof dish and cook in a preheated oven, 200°C/400°F/Gas Mark 6, for about 20 minutes until browned.

3 To prepare the stir-fried vegetables, cut the celery and spring onions (scallions) on the diagonal into narrow slices. Heat the oil in a frying pan (skillet) and toss in the vegetables. Cook over a high heat for 1–2 minutes, then add the sweetcorn cobs and peas, and cook for 2–3 minutes. Finally, add the balsamic vinegar and season well with salt and pepper .

4 Place the rissoles on to a platter and add the stir-fried vegetables.

Chicken & Cheese Jackets

Use the breasts from a roasted chicken to make these delicious potatoes and serve as a light lunch or supper dish.

NUTRITIONAL INFORMATION

Calories 417	Sugars 4g
Protein 28g	Fat 10g
Carbohydrate . . .57g	Saturates 5g

🥔 10 MINS 🕐 50 MINS

SERVES 4

I N G R E D I E N T S

4 large baking potatoes

225 g/8 oz cooked, boneless chicken breasts

4 spring onions (scallions)

250 g/9 oz/1 cup low-fat soft cheese or Quark

pepper

1 Scrub the potatoes and pat dry with absorbent kitchen paper (paper towels).

2 Prick the potatoes all over with a fork. Bake in a preheated oven, 200°C/400°F/Gas Mark 6, for about 50 minutes until tender, or cook in a microwave on HIGH/100% power for 12–15 minutes.

3 Using a sharp knife, dice the chicken and trim and thickly slice the spring onions (scallions). Place the chicken and spring onions (scallions) in a bowl.

4 Add the low-fat soft cheese or Quark to the chicken and spring onions (scallions) and stir well to combine.

5 Cut a cross through the top of each potato and pull slightly apart. Spoon the chicken filling into the potatoes and sprinkle with pepper.

6 Serve the chicken and cheese jackets immediately with coleslaw, green salad or a mixed salad.

COOK'S TIP

Look for Quark in the chilled section. It is a low-fat, white, fresh curd cheese made from cow's milk with a delicate, slightly sour flavour.

Crostini alla Fiorentina

Serve as a starter, or simply spread on small pieces of crusty fried bread (crostini) as an appetizer with drinks.

NUTRITIONAL INFORMATION

Calories 393   Sugars 2g
Protein . . . . .17g   Fat 25g
Carbohydrate . . .19g   Saturates 9g

🍴 🍴 🍴

10 MINS   40-45 MINS

SERVES 4

I N G R E D I E N T S

3 tbsp olive oil

1 onion, chopped

1 celery stalk, chopped

1 carrot, chopped

1–2 garlic cloves, crushed

125 g/4½ oz chicken livers

125 g/4½ oz calf's, lamb's or pig's liver

150 ml/¼ pint/⅔ cup red wine

1 tbsp tomato purée (paste)

2 tbsp chopped fresh parsley

3–4 canned anchovy fillets, chopped finely

2 tbsp stock or water

25–40 g/1–1½ oz/2–3 tbsp butter

1 tbsp capers

salt and pepper

small pieces of fried crusty bread, to serve

chopped parsley, to garnish

1 Heat the oil in a pan, add the onion, celery, carrot and garlic, and cook gently for 4–5 minutes or until the onion is soft, but not coloured.

2 Meanwhile, rinse and dry the chicken livers. Dry the calf's or other liver, and slice into strips. Add the liver to the pan and fry gently for a few minutes until the strips are well sealed on all sides.

3 Add half of the wine and cook until it has mostly evaporated. Then add the rest of the wine, tomato purée (paste), half of the parsley, the anchovy fillets, stock or water, a little salt and plenty of black pepper.

4 Cover the pan and leave to simmer, stirring occasionally, for 15–20 minutes or until tender and most of the liquid has been absorbed.

5 Leave the mixture to cool a little, then either coarsely mince or put into a food processor and process to a chunky purée.

6 Return to the pan and add the butter, capers and remaining parsley. Heat through gently until the butter melts. Adjust the seasoning and turn out into a bowl. Serve warm or cold spread on the slices of crusty bread and sprinkled with chopped parsley.

Spring Rolls

This classic Chinese dish is very popular in the West. Serve hot or chilled with a soy sauce or hoisin dip.

NUTRITIONAL INFORMATION

Calories 442   Sugars 4g
Protein . . . . .23g   Fat 21g
Carbohydrate . . .42g   Saturates 3g

45 MINS   45 MINS

SERVES 4

INGREDIENTS

175 g/6 oz cooked pork, chopped

75 g/2¾ oz cooked chicken, chopped

1 tsp light soy sauce

1 tsp light brown sugar

1 tsp sesame oil

1 tsp vegetable oil

225 g/8 oz bean sprouts

25 g/1 oz canned bamboo shoots, drained, rinsed and chopped

1 green (bell) pepper, seeded and chopped

2 spring onions (scallions), sliced

1 tsp cornflour (cornstarch)

2 tsp water

vegetable oil, for deep-frying

SKINS

125 g/4½ oz/1⅛ cups plain (all-purpose) flour

5 tbsp cornflour (cornstarch)

450 ml/16 fl oz/2 cups water

3 tbsp vegetable oil

1 Mix the pork, chicken, soy sauce, sugar and sesame oil. Cover and marinate for 30 minutes.

2 Heat the vegetable oil in a preheated wok. Add the bean sprouts, bamboo shoots, (bell) pepper and spring onions (scallions) to the wok and stir-fry for 2–3 minutes. Add the meat and the marinade to the wok and stir-fry for 2–3 minutes.

3 Blend the cornflour (cornstarch) with the water and stir the mixture into the wok. Set aside to cool completely.

4 To make the skins, mix the flour and cornflour (cornstarch) and gradually stir in the water, to make a smooth batter.

5 Heat a small, oiled frying pan (skillet). Swirl one-eighth of the batter over the base and cook for 2–3 minutes. Repeat with the remaining batter. Cover the skins with a damp tea towel (dish cloth) while frying the remaining skins.

6 Spread out the skins and spoon one-eighth of the filling along the centre of each. Brush the edges with water and fold in the sides, then roll up.

7 Heat the oil for deep-frying in a wok to 180°C/350°F. Cook the spring rolls, in batches, for 2–3 minutes, or until golden and crisp. Remove from the oil with a slotted spoon, drain and serve immediately.

Chicken Spring Rolls

A cucumber dipping sauce tastes perfect with these delicious spring rolls, filled with chicken and fresh, crunchy vegetables.

NUTRITIONAL INFORMATION

Calories 367   Sugars 18g
Protein ....13g   Fat 21g
Carbohydrate ...32g   Saturates 3g

10 MINS   25 MINS

SERVES 4

I N G R E D I E N T S

2 tbsp vegetable oil

4 spring onions (scallions), trimmed and sliced very finely

1 carrot, cut into matchstick pieces

1 small green or red (bell) pepper, cored, deseeded and sliced finely

60 g/2 oz/⅔ cup button mushrooms, sliced

60 g/2 oz/1 cup bean-sprouts

175 g/6 oz/1 cup cooked chicken, shredded

1 tbsp light soy sauce

1 tsp sugar

2 tsp cornflour (cornstarch), blended in 2 tbsp cold water

12 × 20 cm/8 inch spring roll wrappers

oil for deep-frying

salt and pepper

spring onion (scallion) brushes to garnish

S A U C E

50 ml/2 fl oz/¼ cup light malt vinegar

60 g/2 oz/¼ cup light muscovado sugar

½ tsp salt

5 cm/2 inch piece of cucumber, peeled and chopped finely

4 spring onions (scallions), trimmed and sliced finely

1 small red or green chilli, deseeded and chopped very finely

1 Stir-fry the spring onions (scallions), carrot and (bell) pepper for 2–3 minutes. Add the mushrooms, bean-sprouts and chicken and cook for 2 minutes. Season. Mix the soy sauce, sugar and blended cornflour (cornstarch). Add to the wok and stir-fry for 1 minute. Leave to cool slightly. Spoon the chicken and vegetable mixture on to the spring roll wrappers. Dampen the edges and roll them up to enclose the filling completely.

2 To make the sauce, heat the vinegar, water, sugar and salt in a pan. Boil for 1 minute. Combine the cucumber, spring onions (scallions) and chilli and pour over the vinegar mixture. Leave to cool.

3 Heat the oil and fry the rolls until crisp and golden brown. Drain on paper towels, garnish with spring onion (scallion) brushes and serve with the cucumber dipping sauce.

Pot Sticker Dumplings

These dumplings obtain their name from the fact that they would stick to the pot when steamed if they were not fried crisply enough initially.

NUTRITIONAL INFORMATION

Calories	345	Sugar	........3g
Protein	......13g	Fat	.........17g
Carbohydrate	...36g	Saturates	.......2g

50 MINS   25 MINS

SERVES 4

INGREDIENTS

DUMPLINGS

175 g/6 oz/1½ cups plain (all-purpose) flour

pinch of salt

3 tbsp vegetable oil

6–8 tbsp boiling water

oil, for deep-frying

125 ml/4 fl oz/½ cup water, for steaming

sliced spring onions (scallions) and chives, to garnish

soy sauce or hoisin sauce, to serve

FILLING

150 g/5½ oz lean chicken, very finely chopped

25 g/1 oz canned bamboo shoots, drained and chopped

2 spring onions (scallions), finely chopped

½ small red (bell) pepper, seeded and finely chopped

½ tsp Chinese curry powder

1 tbsp light soy sauce

1 tsp caster (superfine) sugar

1 tsp sesame oil

1 To make the dumplings, mix together the flour and salt in a bowl. Make a well in the centre, add the oil and water and mix well to form a soft dough. Knead the dough on a lightly floured surface, wrap in cling film (plastic wrap) and let stand for 30 minutes. Meanwhile, mix all of the filling ingredients together in a large bowl.

2 Divide the dough into 12 equal-sized pieces and roll each piece into a 12.5-cm/5-inch round. Spoon a portion of the filling on to one half of each round. Fold the dough over the filling to form a 'pasty', pressing the edges together to seal.

3 Pour a little oil into a frying pan (skillet) and cook the dumplings, in batches, until browned and slightly crisp.

4 Return all of the dumplings to the pan and add about 125 ml/4 fl oz/½ cup water. Cover and steam for 5 minutes, or until the dumplings are cooked through. Remove with a slotted spoon and garnish with spring onions (scallions) and chives. Serve with soy sauce or hoisin sauce.

Chinese Omelette

This is a fairly filling omelette, as it contains chicken and prawns (shrimp). It is cooked as a whole omelette and then sliced for serving.

NUTRITIONAL INFORMATION

Calories 309	Sugars 0g
Protein 34g	Fat 19g
Carbohydrate ...0.2g	Saturates 5g

5 MINS   5 MINS

SERVES 4

I N G R E D I E N T S

8 eggs

225 g/8 oz/2 cups cooked chicken, shredded

12 tiger prawns (jumbo shrimp), peeled and deveined

2 tbsp chopped chives

2 tsp light soy sauce

dash of chilli sauce

2 tbsp vegetable oil

1 Lightly beat the eggs in a large mixing bowl.

2 Add the shredded chicken and tiger prawns (jumbo shrimp) to the eggs, mixing well.

3 Stir in the chopped chives, light soy sauce and chilli sauce, mixing well to combine all the ingredients.

4 Heat the vegetable oil in a large preheated frying pan (skillet) over a medium heat.

5 Add the egg mixture to the frying pan (skillet), tilting the pan to coat the base completely.

6 Cook over a medium heat, gently stirring the omelette with a fork, until

the surface is just set and the underside is a golden brown colour.

7 When the omelette is set, slide it out of the pan, with the aid of a palette knife (spatula).

8 Cut the Chinese omelette into squares or slices and serve immediately. Alternatively, serve the omelette as a main course for two people.

VARIATION

You could add extra flavour to the omelette by stirring in 3 tablespoons of finely chopped fresh coriander (cilantro) or 1 teaspoon of sesame seeds with the chives in step 3.

Honeyed Chicken Wings

Chicken wings are ideal for a starter as they are small and perfect for eating with the fingers.

NUTRITIONAL INFORMATION

Calories 131	Sugars 4g	
Protein 10g	Fat 8g	
Carbohydrate 4g	Saturates 2g	

5 MINS   40 MINS

SERVES 4

INGREDIENTS

450 g/1 lb chicken wings

2 tbsp peanut oil

2 tbsp light soy sauce

2 tbsp hoisin sauce

2 tbsp clear honey

2 garlic cloves, crushed

1 tsp sesame seeds

MARINADE

1 dried red chilli

½–1 tsp chilli powder

½–1 tsp ground ginger

finely grated rind of 1 lime

1 To make the marinade, crush the dried chilli in a pestle and mortar. Mix together the crushed dried chilli, chilli powder, ground ginger and lime rind in a small mixing bowl.

2 Thoroughly rub the spice mixture into the chicken wings with your fingertips. Set aside for at least 2 hours to allow the flavours to penetrate the chicken wings.

3 Heat the peanut oil in a large wok or frying pan (skillet).

4 Add the chicken wings and fry, turning frequently, for about 10–12 minutes, until golden and crisp. Drain off any excess oil.

5 Add the soy sauce, hoisin sauce, honey, garlic and sesame seeds to the wok, turning the chicken wings to coat.

6 Reduce the heat and cook for 20–25 minutes, turning the chicken wings frequently, until completely cooked through. Serve hot.

COOK'S TIP

Make the dish in advance and freeze the chicken wings. Defrost thoroughly, cover with foil and heat right through in a moderate oven.

Bang-Bang Chicken

The cooked chicken meat is tenderized by being beaten with a rolling pin, hence the name for this very popular Szechuan dish.

NUTRITIONAL INFORMATION

Calories 82	Sugars 1g	
Protein 13g	Fat 3g	
Carbohydrate 2g	Saturates 1g	

1¼ HOURS   40 MINS

SERVES 4

INGREDIENTS

1 litre/1¾ pints/4 cups water

2 chicken quarters (breast half and leg)

1 cucumber, cut into matchstick shreds

SAUCE

2 tbsp light soy sauce

1 tsp sugar

1 tbsp finely chopped spring onions (scallions), plus extra to garnish

1 tsp red chilli oil

¼ tsp pepper

1 tsp white sesame seeds

2 tbsp peanut butter, creamed with a little sesame oil, plus extra to garnish

1 Bring the water to a rolling boil in a wok or a large saucepan. Add the chicken pieces, reduce the heat, cover and cook for 30–35 minutes.

2 Remove the chicken from the wok or pan and immerse in a bowl of cold water for at least 1 hour to cool it, ready for shredding.

3 Remove the chicken pieces, drain and dry on absorbent kitchen paper (paper towels). Take the meat off the bone.

4 On a flat surface, pound the chicken with a rolling pin, then tear the meat into shreds with 2 forks. Mix the chicken with the shredded cucumber and arrange in a serving dish.

5 To serve, mix together all the sauce ingredients until thoroughly combined and pour over the chicken and cucumber in the serving dish. Sprinkle some sesame seeds and chopped spring onions (scallions) over the sauce and serve.

COOK'S TIP

Take the time to tear the chicken meat into similar-sized shreds, to make an elegant-looking dish. You can do this quite efficiently with 2 forks, although Chinese cooks would do it with their fingers.

Steamed Duck Buns

The dough used in this recipe may also be wrapped around chicken, pork or prawns (shrimp), or sweet fillings as an alternative.

NUTRITIONAL INFORMATION

Calories 307	Sugars 11g
Protein 17g	Fat 6g
Carbohydrate . . .50g	Saturates 1g

1½ HOURS   1 HOUR

SERVES 4

INGREDIENTS

DUMPLING DOUGH

300 g/10½ oz/2⅔ cups plain (all-purpose) flour

15 g/½ oz dried yeast

1 tsp caster (superfine) sugar

2 tbsp warm water

175 ml/6 fl oz/¾ cup warm milk

FILLING

300 g/10½ oz duck breast

1 tbsp light brown sugar

1 tbsp light soy sauce

2 tbsp clear honey

1 tbsp hoisin sauce

1 tbsp vegetable oil

1 leek, finely chopped

1 garlic clove, crushed

1-cm/½-inch piece fresh root ginger (gingerroot), grated

1 Place the duck breast in a large bowl. Mix together the light brown sugar, soy sauce, honey and hoisin sauce. Pour the mixture over the duck and marinate for 20 minutes.

2 Remove the duck from the marinade and cook on a rack set over a roasting tin (pan) in a preheated oven, at 200°C/ 400°F/Gas Mark 6, for 35–40 minutes, or

until cooked through. Leave to cool, remove the meat from the bones and cut into small cubes.

3 Heat the vegetable oil in a preheated wok or frying pan (skillet) until really hot.

4 Add the leek, garlic and ginger to the wok and fry for 3 minutes. Mix with the duck meat.

5 Sift the plain (all-purpose) flour into a large bowl. Mix the yeast, caster (superfine) sugar and warm water in a separate bowl and leave in a warm place for 15 minutes.

6 Pour the yeast mixture into the flour, together with the warm milk, mixing to form a firm dough. Knead the dough on a floured surface for 5 minutes. Roll into a sausage shape, 2.5 cm/1 inch in diameter. Cut into 16 pieces, cover and let stand for 20–25 minutes.

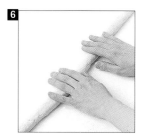

7 Flatten the dough pieces into 10-cm/4-inch rounds. Place a spoonful of filling in the centre of each, draw up the sides to form a 'moneybag' shape and twist to seal.

8 Place the dumplings on a clean, damp tea towel (dish cloth) in the base of a steamer, cover and steam for 20 minutes. Serve immediately.

Chicken or Beef Satay

In this dish, strips of chicken or beef are threaded on to skewers, grilled (broiled) and served with a spicy peanut sauce.

NUTRITIONAL INFORMATION

Calories	314	Sugars	.........8g
Protein	........32g	Fat	..........16g
Carbohydrate	...10g	Saturates	.......4g

2¼ HOURS   15 MINS

SERVES 6

I N G R E D I E N T S

4 boneless, skinned chicken breasts or 750 g/1 lb 10 oz rump steak, trimmed

M A R I N A D E

1 small onion, finely chopped

1 garlic clove, crushed

2.5 cm/1 inch piece ginger root, peeled and grated

2 tbsp dark soy sauce

2 tsp chilli powder

1 tsp ground coriander

2 tsp dark brown sugar

1 tbsp lemon or lime juice

1 tbsp vegetable oil

S A U C E

300 ml/½ pint/1¼ cups coconut milk

4 tbsp/⅓ cup crunchy peanut butter

1 tbsp fish sauce

1 tsp lemon or lime juice

salt and pepper

1 Using a sharp knife, trim any fat from the chicken or beef then cut into thin strips, about 7 cm/3 inches long.

2 To make the marinade, place all the ingredients in a shallow dish and mix well. Add the chicken or beef strips and turn in the marinade until well coated.

Cover with cling film (plastic wrap) and leave to marinate for 2 hours or overnight in the refrigerator.

3 Remove the meat from the marinade and thread the pieces, concertina style, on pre-soaked bamboo or thin wooden skewers.

4 Grill (broil) the chicken and beef satays for 8-10 minutes, turning and brushing occasionally with the marinade, until cooked through.

5 Meanwhile, to make the sauce, mix the coconut milk with the peanut butter, fish sauce and lemon or lime juice in a saucepan. Bring to the boil and cook for 3 minutes. Season to taste.

6 Transfer the sauce to a serving bowl and serve with the cooked satays.

Chicken Wontons

These deliciously crispy nibbles make an ideal introduction to a Chinese meal. Here they are filled with a chicken and mushroom mixture.

NUTRITIONAL INFORMATION

Calories ....285 Sugars 1g
Protein ....16g Fat 19g
Carbohydrate ...14g Saturates 5g

20 MINS   35 MINS

SERVES 4

INGREDIENTS

250 g/9 oz boneless chicken breast, skinned

60 g/2 oz/⅔ cup mushrooms

1 garlic clove

2 shallots

1 tbsp fish sauce or mushroom ketchup

1 tbsp chopped fresh coriander (cilantro)

2 tbsp vegetable oil

about 50 wonton wrappers

oil, for deep-frying

salt and pepper

sliced spring onion (scallion), to garnish

sweet chilli sauce, to serve

1 Put the chicken, mushrooms, garlic, shallots, fish sauce or mushroom ketchup and coriander (cilantro) into a blender or food processor. Blend for 10–15 seconds. Alternatively, chop all the ingredients finely and mix together well.

2 Heat the vegetable oil in a wok or frying pan (skillet) and add the chicken mixture. Stir-fry for about 8 minutes, breaking up the mixture as it cooks, until it browns. Transfer to a bowl and leave to cool for 10–15 minutes.

3 Place the wonton wrappers on a clean, damp tea towel (dish cloth).

Layering 2 wrappers together at a time, place teaspoonfuls of the chicken mixture into the middle. Dampen the edges with water, then make small pouches, pressing the edges together to seal. Repeat with the remaining wrappers until all the mixture is used.

4 Heat the oil for deep-frying in a wok or deep fat fryer. Fry the wontons, a few at a time, for about 2–3 minutes until golden brown. Remove the wontons from the oil with a perforated spoon and drain on kitchen paper (paper towels). Keep warm while frying the remaining wontons.

5 Transfer the wontons to a warmed serving platter and garnish with the sliced spring onion (scallion). Serve at once, accompanied by some sweet chilli sauce.

Sesame Ginger Chicken

Chunks of chicken breast are marinated in a mixture of lime juice, garlic, sesame oil and fresh ginger to give them a great flavour.

NUTRITIONAL INFORMATION

Calories	204	Sugars	.........0g
Protein	........28g	Fat	..........10g
Carbohydrate	....1g	Saturates	.......2g

2¼ HOURS   10 MINS

SERVES 4

INGREDIENTS

4 wooden satay sticks, soaked in warm water

500 g/1 lb 2 oz boneless chicken breasts

sprigs of fresh mint, to garnish

MARINADE

1 garlic clove, crushed

1 shallot, chopped very finely

2 tbsp sesame oil

1 tbsp fish sauce or light soy sauce

finely grated rind of 1 lime or ½ lemon

2 tbsp lime juice or lemon juice

1 tsp sesame seeds

2 tsp finely grated fresh ginger root

2 tsp chopped fresh mint

salt and pepper

1 To make the marinade, put the crushed garlic, chopped shallot, sesame oil, fish sauce or soy sauce, lime or lemon rind and juice, sesame seeds, grated ginger root and chopped mint into a large non-metallic bowl. Season with a little salt and pepper and mix together until all the ingredients are thoroughly combined.

2 Remove the skin from the chicken breasts and cut the flesh into chunks.

3 Add the chicken to the marinade, stirring to coat the chicken completely in the mixture. Cover with cling film (plastic wrap) and chill in the refrigerator for at least 2 hours so that the flavours are absorbed.

4 Thread the chicken on to wooden satay sticks. Place them on the rack of a grill (broiler) pan and baste with the marinade.

5 Place the kebabs under a preheated grill (broiler) for about 8–10 minutes. Turn them frequently, basting them with the remaining marinade.

6 Serve the chicken skewers at once, garnished with sprigs of fresh mint.

COOK'S TIP

The kebabs taste delicious if dipped into an accompanying bowl of hot chilli sauce.

Low-Fat Main Meals

Chicken and turkey contain less fat than red meats, and even less if you remove the skin first before cooking. Because chicken itself does not have a very strong flavour, it marries well with all manner of other ingredients, and the recipes in this chapter exploit that quality. Fruit

features heavily in low-fat diets and works especially well with chicken. Grilling (broiling) and barbecuing are very healthy ways to cook chicken as they require little or no fat and produce deliciously succulent meat with a crispy, tasty coating.

Chicken with a Yogurt Crust

A spicy, Indian-style coating is baked around lean chicken to give a full flavour. Serve with a tomato, cucumber and coriander (cilantro) relish.

NUTRITIONAL INFORMATION

Calories 176   Sugars 5g
Protein . . . . .30g   Fat 4g
Carbohydrate . . . .5g   Saturates 1g

10 MINS   35 MINS

SERVES 4

I N G R E D I E N T S

1 garlic clove, crushed

2.5 cm/1 inch piece root ginger, finely chopped

1 fresh green chilli, deseeded and finely chopped

6 tbsp low-fat natural (unsweetened) yogurt

1 tbsp tomato purée (paste)

1 tsp ground turmeric

1 tsp garam masala

1 tbsp lime juice

4 boneless, skinless chicken breasts, each 125 g/4½ oz

salt and pepper

wedges of lime or lemon, to serve

R E L I S H

4 medium tomatoes

¼ cucumber

1 small red onion

2 tbsp fresh coriander (cilantro), chopped

1 Preheat the oven to 190°C/375°F/Gas Mark 5.

2 Place the garlic, ginger, chilli, yogurt, tomato purée (paste), spices, lime juice and seasoning in a bowl and mix to combine all the ingredients.

3 Wash and pat dry the chicken breasts with absorbent kitchen paper (paper towels) and place them on a baking sheet.

4 Brush or spread the spicy yogurt mix over the chicken and bake in the oven for 30–35 minutes until the meat is tender and cooked through.

5 Meanwhile, make the relish. Finely chop the tomatoes, cucumber and onion and mix together with the coriander (cilantro). Season with salt and pepper to taste, cover and chill in the refrigerator until required.

6 Drain the cooked chicken on absorbent kitchen paper (paper towels) and serve hot with the relish and lemon or lime wedges. Alternatively, allow to cool, chill for at least 1 hour and serve sliced as part of a salad.

Sticky Chicken Wings

These tasty chicken wings should be eaten with your fingers so serve them at an informal supper or party.

NUTRITIONAL INFORMATION

Calories ....165 Sugars 12g
Protein ....14g Fat 7g
Carbohydrate ...12g Saturates 1g

3¹/₄ HOURS   1 HOUR

SERVES 4–6

INGREDIENTS

2 tbsp olive oil

1 small onion, finely chopped

2 garlic cloves, crushed

425 ml/¾ pint passata (sieved tomatoes)

2 tsp dried thyme

1 tsp dried oregano

pinch fennel seeds

3 tbsp red wine vinegar

2 tbsp Dijon mustard

pinch ground cinnamon

2 tbsp brown sugar

1 tsp chilli flakes

2 tbsp black treacle

16 chicken wings

salt and pepper

TO GARNISH

celery stalks

cherry tomatoes

1 Heat the olive oil in a large frying pan (skillet) and fry the onion and garlic for about 10 minutes.

2 Add the passata (sieved tomatoes), dried herbs, fennel, red wine vinegar, mustard and cinnamon to the frying pan (skillet) along with the sugar, chilli flakes, treacle, and salt and pepper. Bring to the boil, then reduce the heat and simmer gently for about 15 minutes, until the sauce is slightly reduced.

3 Put the chicken wings in a large dish, and coat liberally with the sauce. Leave to marinate for 3 hours or as long as possible, turning the wings over often in the marinade.

4 Transfer the wings to a clean baking sheet (cookie sheet), and roast in a preheated oven, 220°C/425°F/ Gas Mark 7, for 10 minutes. Reduce the heat to 190°C/375°F/Gas Mark 5 and cook for 20 minutes, basting often.

5 Serve the wings piping hot, garnished with celery stalks and cherry tomatoes.

Steamed Chicken Parcels

A healthy recipe with a delicate oriental flavour. Use large spinach leaves to wrap around the chicken, but make sure they are young leaves.

NUTRITIONAL INFORMATION

Calories 216   Sugars 7g
Protein . . . . .31g   Fat 7g
Carbohydrate . . . .7g   Saturates 2g

20 MINS   30 MINS

SERVES 4

INGREDIENTS

4 lean boneless, skinless chicken
  breasts

1 tsp ground lemon grass

2 spring onions (scallions), chopped finely

250 g/9 oz/1 cup young carrots

250 g/9 oz/1¾ cups young courgettes
  (zucchini)

2 sticks (stalks) celery

1 tsp light soy sauce

250 g/9 oz/¾ cup spinach leaves

2 tsp sesame oil

salt and pepper

1 With a sharp knife, make a slit through one side of each chicken breast, to open out a large pocket.

2 Sprinkle the inside of the pocket with lemon grass, salt and pepper. Tuck the spring onions (scallions) into the chicken pockets.

3 Trim the carrots, courgettes (zucchini) and celery, then cut into small matchsticks. Plunge them into a pan of boiling water for 1 minute, then drain and toss in the soy sauce

4 Pack the mixture into the pockets in each chicken breast and fold over firmly to enclose. Reserve the remaining vegetables. Wash and dry the spinach leaves then wrap the chicken breasts firmly in the leaves to enclose completely. If the leaves are too firm, steam them for a few seconds until they are softened and flexible.

5 Place the wrapped chicken in a steamer and steam over rapidly boiling water for 20–25 minutes, depending on size.

6 Stir-fry any leftover vegetable sticks and spinach for 1–2 minutes in the sesame oil and serve with the chicken.

Thai Red Chicken

This is a really colourful dish, the red of the tomatoes perfectly complementing the orange of the sweet potato.

NUTRITIONAL INFORMATION

Calories 249   Sugars 14g
Protein ....26g   Fat 7g
Carbohydrate ...22g   Saturates 2g

10 MINS   35 MINS

SERVES 4

INGREDIENTS

1 tbsp sunflower oil

450 g/1 lb lean boneless, skinless chicken

2 cloves garlic, crushed

2 tbsp Thai red curry paste

2 tbsp fresh grated galangal or root ginger

1 tbsp tamarind paste

4 lime leaves

225 g/8 oz sweet potato

600 ml/1 pint/2½ cups coconut milk

225 g/8 oz cherry tomatoes, halved

3 tbsp chopped fresh coriander (cilantro)

cooked jasmine or Thai fragrant rice, to serve

1 Heat the sunflower oil in a large preheated wok.

2 Thinly slice the chicken. Add the chicken to the wok and stir-fry for 5 minutes.

3 Add the garlic, curry paste, galangal or root ginger, tamarind and lime leaves to the wok and stir-fry for about 1 minute.

4 Using a sharp knife, peel and dice the sweet potato. Add the coconut milk and sweet potato to the mixture in the wok and bring to the boil. Allow to bubble over a medium heat for 20 minutes, or until the juices start to thicken and reduce.

5 Add the cherry tomatoes and coriander (cilantro) to the curry and cook for a further 5 minutes, stirring occasionally. Transfer to serving plates and serve hot with cooked jasmine or Thai fragrant rice.

COOK'S TIP

Galangal is a spice very similar to ginger and is used to replace the latter in Thai cuisine. It can be bought fresh from Oriental food stores but is also available dried and as a powder. The fresh root, which is not as pungent as ginger, needs to be peeled before slicing to use.

Teppanyaki

This simple, Japanese style of cooking is ideal for thinly-sliced breast of chicken. You can use thin turkey escalopes, if you prefer.

NUTRITIONAL INFORMATION

Calories ....206 Sugars 4g
Protein ....30g Fat 7g
Carbohydrate ....6g Saturates 2g

5 MINS   10 MINS

SERVES 4

INGREDIENTS

4 boneless chicken breasts

1 red (bell) pepper

1 green (bell) pepper

4 spring onions (scallions)

8 baby corn cobs (corn-on-the-cob)

100 g/3½ oz/½ cup bean sprouts

1 tbsp sesame or sunflower oil

4 tbsp soy sauce

4 tbsp mirin

1 tbsp grated fresh ginger root

1 Remove the skin from the chicken and slice at a slight angle, to a thickness of about 5 mm/¼ inch.

2 Deseed and thinly slice the (bell) peppers and trim and slice the spring onions (scallions) and corn cobs (corn-on-the-cob).

3 Arrange the (bell) peppers, spring onions (scallions), corn and bean sprouts on a plate with the sliced chicken.

4 Heat a large griddle or heavy frying pan then lightly brush with oil. Add the vegetables and chicken slices in small batches, allowing space between them so that they cook thoroughly.

5 Combine the soy sauce, mirin and ginger and serve as a dip with the chicken and vegetables.

COOK'S TIP

Mirin is a rich, sweet rice wine which you can buy in oriental shops, but if it is not available add one tablespoon of soft light brown sugar to the sauce instead.

Spiced Apricot Chicken

Spiced chicken legs are partially boned and packed with dried apricot.
A golden, spiced, low-fat yogurt coating keeps the chicken moist.

NUTRITIONAL INFORMATION

Calories 305   Sugars 21g
Protein . . . . .15g   Fat 8g
Carbohydrate . . .45g   Saturates 1g

10 MINS   40 MINS

SERVES 4

I N G R E D I E N T S

4 large, lean skinless chicken leg quarters

finely grated rind of 1 lemon

200 g/7 oz/1 cup ready-to-eat dried apricots

1 tbsp ground cumin

1 tsp ground turmeric

125 g/4½ oz/½ cup low-fat natural yogurt

salt and pepper

TO SERVE

250 g/9 oz/1½ cups brown rice

2 tbsp flaked hazelnuts, toasted

2 tbsp sunflower seeds, toasted

1 Remove any excess fat from the chicken legs. Use a small sharp knife to carefully cut the flesh away from the thigh bone. Scrape the meat away down as far as the knuckle. Grasp the thigh bone firmly and twist it to break it away from the drumstick.

2 Open out the boned part of the chicken and sprinkle with lemon rind and pepper. Pack the dried apricots into each piece of chicken.

3 Fold over to enclose, and secure with cocktail sticks. Mix together the cumin, turmeric, yogurt and salt and pepper, then brush this mixture over the

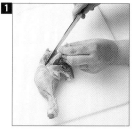

chicken to coat evenly. Place the chicken in an ovenproof dish and bake in a preheated oven, 190°C/375°F/Gas Mark 5, for 35–40 minutes, or until the chicken juices run clear, not pink, when pierced through the thickest part with a skewer.

4 Meanwhile, cook the rice in boiling, lightly salted water until just tender, then drain well. Stir the hazelnuts and sunflower seeds into the rice and serve.

VARIATION

For a change use dried herbs instead of spices to flavour the coating. Use dried oregano, tarragon or rosemary – but remember dried herbs are more powerful than fresh, so you will only need a little.

Sweet and Sour Chicken

This sweet-citrusy chicken is delicious hot or cold. Sesame-flavoured noodles are the ideal accompaniment for the hot version.

NUTRITIONAL INFORMATION

Calories 248	Sugars 8g
Protein 30g	Fat 8g
Carbohydrate ...16g	Saturates 2g

5 MINS   25 MINS

SERVES 4

INGREDIENTS

4 boneless chicken breasts, about 125 g/
   4½ oz each

2 tbsp clear honey

1 tbsp dark soy sauce

1 tsp lemon rind, finely grated

1 tbsp lemon juice

salt and pepper

TO GARNISH

1 tbsp fresh chives, chopped

lemon rind, grated

NOODLES

225 g/8 oz rice noodles

2 tsp sesame oil

1 tbsp sesame seeds

1 tsp lemon rind, finely grated

1 Preheat the grill (broiler) to medium. Skin and trim the chicken breasts to remove any excess fat, then wash and pat them dry with absorbent kitchen paper. Using a sharp knife, score the chicken breasts with a criss-cross pattern on both sides (making sure that you do not cut all the way through the meat).

2 Mix together the honey, soy sauce, lemon rind and juice in a small bowl, and then season well with black pepper.

3 Arrange the chicken breasts on the grill (broiler) rack and brush with half the honey mixture. Cook for 10 minutes, turn over and brush with the remaining mixture. Cook for a further 8–10 minutes or until cooked through.

4 Meanwhile, prepare the noodles according to the instructions on the packet. Drain well and transfer to a warm serving bowl. Mix the noodles with the sesame oil, sesame seeds and the lemon rind. Season and keep warm.

5 Drain the chicken and serve with a small mound of noodles, garnished with chopped chives and grated lemon rind.

VARIATION

For a different flavour, replace the lemon with orange or lime. If you prefer, serve the chicken with boiled rice or pasta, which you can flavour with sesame seeds and citrus rind in the same way.

Ginger Chicken & Corn

Chicken wings and corn in a sticky ginger marinade are designed to be eaten with the fingers – there's no other way!

NUTRITIONAL INFORMATION

Calories ....123 Sugars 3g
Protein ....14g Fat 6g
Carbohydrate ....3g Saturates 1g

10 MINS   20 MINS

SERVES 6

I N G R E D I E N T S

3 cobs fresh sweetcorn (corn-on-the-cob)

12 chicken wings

2.5cm/1 inch piece fresh ginger root

6 tbsp lemon juice

4 tsp sunflower oil

1 tbsp golden caster (superfine) sugar

jacket potatoes or salad, to serve

1 Remove the husks and silks from the corn. Using a sharp knife, cut each cob into 6 slices.

2 Place the corn in a large bowl with the chicken wings.

3 Peel and grate the ginger root or chop finely. Place in a bowl and add the lemon juice, sunflower oil and golden caster (superfine) sugar. Mix together until well combined.

4 Toss the corn and chicken in the ginger mixture to coat evely.

5 Thread the corn and chicken wings alternately on to metal or pre-soaked wooden skewers, to make turning easier.

6 Cook under a preheated moderately hot grill (broiler) or barbecue (grill) for 15–20 minutes, basting with the gingery glaze and turning frequently until the corn is golden brown and tender and the chicken is cooked. Serve with jacket potatoes or salad.

COOK'S TIP

Cut off the wing tips before grilling (broiling) as they burn very easily. Or you can cover them with small pieces of foil.

Poussin with Dried Fruits

Baby chickens are ideal for a one or two portion meal, and cook very easily and quickly for a special dinner – either in the oven or microwave.

NUTRITIONAL INFORMATION

Calories . . . . .316 Sugars 23g
Protein . . . . .23g Fat 15g
Carbohydrate . . .23g Saturates 2g

35 MINS   30 MINS

SERVES 2

I N G R E D I E N T S

125 g/4½ oz/¾ cup dried apples, peaches and prunes

120 ml/4 floz/½ cup boiling water

2 baby chickens

25 g/1 oz/⅓ cup walnut halves

1 tbsp honey

1 tsp ground allspice

1 tbsp walnut oil

salt and pepper

vegetables and new potatoes, to serve

1 Place the fruits in a bowl, cover with the water and leave to stand for about 30 minutes.

2 Cut the chickens in half down the breastbone using a sharp knife, or leave whole.

3 Mix the fruit and any juices with the walnuts, honey and allspice and divide between two small roasting bags or squares of foil.

4 Brush the chickens with walnut oil and sprinkle with salt and pepper then place on top of the fruits.

5 Close the roasting bags or fold the foil over to enclose the chickens and bake on a baking sheet in a preheated oven, 190°C/375°F/Gas Mark 5, for 25–30 minutes or until the juices run clear. To cook in a microwave, use microwave roasting bags and cook on high/100% power for 6–7 minutes each, depending on size.

6 Transfer the poussin to a warm plate and serve hot with fresh vegetables and new potatoes.

VARIATION

Alternative dried fruits that can be used in this recipe are cherries, mangoes or paw-paws (papayas).

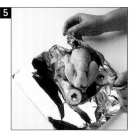

Harlequin Chicken

This colourful dish will tempt the appetites of all the family – it is ideal for toddlers, who enjoy the fun shapes of the multi-coloured peppers.

NUTRITIONAL INFORMATION

Calories 183	Sugar 8g	
Protein 24g	Fats 6g	
Carbohydrates 8g	Saturates 1g	

5 MINS   25 MINS

SERVES 4

INGREDIENTS

10 skinless, boneless chicken thighs

1 medium onion

1 each medium red, green and yellow (bell) peppers

1 tbsp sunflower oil

400 g/14 oz can chopped tomatoes

2 tbsp chopped fresh parsley

pepper

wholemeal bread and salad, to serve

1 Using a sharp knife, cut the chicken thighs into bite-sized pieces.

2 Peel and thinly slice the onion. Halve and deseed the (bell) peppers and cut into small diamond shapes.

3 Heat the sunflower oil in a shallow pan then quickly fry the chicken and onion until golden.

4 Add the (bell) peppers, cook for 2–3 minutes, then stir in the tomatoes and chopped fresh parsley and season with pepper.

5 Cover tightly and simmer for about 15 minutes, until the chicken and vegetables are tender. Serve hot with wholemeal (whole wheat) bread and a green salad.

COOK'S TIP

If you are making this dish for small children, the chicken can be finely chopped or minced (ground) first.

Chicken Tikka Kebabs

Chicken tikka is a low-fat Indian dish. Recipes vary but you can try your own combination of spices to suit your personal taste.

NUTRITIONAL INFORMATION

Calories 191   Sugars 8g
Protein . . . . .30g   Fat 4g
Carbohydrate . . . .8g   Saturates 2g

2¼ HOURS   15 MINS

SERVES 4

INGREDIENTS

4 × 125 g/4½ oz boneless, skinless chicken breasts,

1 garlic clove, crushed

1 tsp grated ginger root

1 fresh green chilli, seeded and chopped finely

6 tbsp low-fat natural yogurt

1 tbsp tomato purée (paste)

1 tsp ground cumin

1 tsp ground coriander

1 tsp ground turmeric

1 large ripe mango

1 tbsp lime juice

salt and pepper

fresh coriander (cilantro) leaves, to garnish

TO SERVE

boiled white rice

lime wedges

mixed salad

warmed naan bread

1 Cut the chicken into 2.5 cm/1 inch cubes and place in a shallow dish.

2 Mix together the garlic, ginger, chilli, yogurt, tomato purée (paste), spices and seasoning. Spoon over the chicken, cover and chill for 2 hours.

3 Using a vegetable peeler, peel the skin from the mango. Slice down either side of the stone (pit) and cut the mango flesh into cubes. Toss in lime juice, cover and chill until required.

4 Thread the chicken and mango pieces alternately on to 8 skewers. Place the skewers on a grill (broiler) rack and brush the chicken with the yogurt marinade and the lime juice left from the mango.

5 Place under a preheated moderate grill (broiler) for 6–7 minutes. Turn over, brush again with themarinade and lime juice and cook for a further 6–7 minutes until the chicken juices run clear when pierced with a sharp knife.

6 Serve on a bed of rice on a warmed platter, garnished with fresh coriander (cilantro) leaves and accompanied by lime wedges, salad and naan bread.

Chicken in Spicy Yogurt

Make sure the barbecue (grill) is really hot before you start cooking. The coals should be white and glow red when fanned.

NUTRITIONAL INFORMATION

Calories 74   Sugars 2g
Protein ....9g   Fat 4g
Carbohydrate ....2g   Saturates 1g

4³/₄ HOURS   25 MINS

SERVES 6

I N G R E D I E N T S

3 dried red chillies

2 tbsp coriander seeds

2 tsp turmeric

2 tsp garam masala

4 garlic cloves, crushed

½ onion, chopped

2.5cm/1 inch piece fresh ginger root, grated

2 tbsp lime juice

1 tsp salt

125 ml/4 fl oz/½ cup low-fat natural (unsweetened) yogurt

1 tbsp oil

2 kg/4 lb 8 oz lean chicken, cut into 6 pieces, or 6 chicken portions

TO SERVE

chopped tomatoes

diced cucumber

sliced red onion

cucumber and yogurt

1 Grind together the chillies, coriander seed, turmeric, garam masala, garlic, onion, ginger, lime juice and salt with a pestle and mortar or grinder.

2 Gently heat a frying pan (skillet) and add the spice mixture. Stir until fragrant, about 2 minutes, and turn into a shallow non-porous dish.

3 Add the natural (unsweetened) yogurt and the oil to the spice paste and mix well to combine.

4 Remove the skin from the chicken portions and make three slashes in the flesh of each piece. Add the chicken to the dish containing the yogurt and spice mixture and coat the pieces completely in the marinade. Cover with cling film (plastic wrap) and chill for at least 4 hours. Remove the dish from the refrigerator and leave covered at room temperature for 30 minutes before cooking.

5 Wrap the chicken pieces in foil, sealing well so the juices cannot escape.

6 Cook the chicken pieces over a very hot barbecue (grill) for about 15 minutes, turning once.

7 Remove the foil, with tongs, and brown the chicken on the barbecue (grill) for 5 minutes.

8 Serve the chicken with the chopped tomatoes, diced cucumber, sliced red onion and the yogurt and cucumber mixture.

Thai-Style Chicken Skewers

The chicken is marinated in an aromatic sauce before being cooked on the barbecue (grill). Use bay leaves if kaffir lime leaves are unavailable.

NUTRITIONAL INFORMATION

Calories 218   Sugars 4g
Protein . . . . .28g   Fat 10g
Carbohydrate . . . .5g   Saturates 2g

2¼ HOURS   20 MINS

SERVES 4

INGREDIENTS

lean chicken breasts, skinned and
  boned

1 onion, peeled and cut into wedges

1 large red (bell) pepper, deseeded

1 large yellow (bell) pepper deseeded

12 kaffir lime leaves

2 tbsp sunflower oil

2 tbsp lime juice

tomato halves, to serve

MARINADE

1 tbsp Thai red curry paste

150 ml/5 fl oz/⅔ cup canned coconut
  milk

1 To make the marinade, place the red curry paste in a small pan over medium heat and cook for 1 minute. Add half of the coconut milk to the pan and bring the mixture to the boil. Boil for 2–3 minutes until the liquid has reduced by about two-thirds.

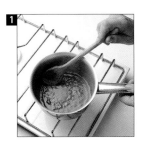

2 Remove the pan from the heat and stir in the remaining coconut milk. Set aside to cool.

3 Cut the chicken into 2.5 cm/1 inch pieces. Stir the chicken into the cold marinade, cover and leave to chill for at least 2 hours.

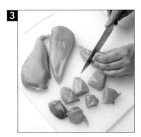

4 Cut the onion into wedges and the (bell) peppers into 2.5 cm/1 inch pieces.

5 Remove the chicken pieces from the marinade and thread them on to skewers, alternating the chicken with the vegetables and lime leaves.

6 Combine the oil and lime juice in a small bowl and brush the mixture over the kebabs. Barbecue (grill) the skewers over hot coals, turning and basting frequently for 10–15 minutes until the chicken is cooked through. Barbecue (grill) the tomato halves and serve with the chicken skewers.

COOK'S TIP

Cooking the marinade first intensifies the flavour. It is important to allow the marinade to cool before adding the chicken, or bacteria may breed in the warm temperature.

Chicken & Ginger Stir-Fry

The pomegranate seeds add a sharp Chinese flavour to this Indian stir-fry. Serve in the summer with a spicy rice salad or a mixed green salad.

NUTRITIONAL INFORMATION

Calories 291   Sugars 0g
Protein . . . . .41g   Fat 14g
Carbohydrate . . . .0g   Saturates 3g

10 MINS   25 MINS

SERVES 4

I N G R E D I E N T S

3 tbsp oil

700 g/1 lb 9 oz lean skinless, boneless chicken breasts, cut into 5 cm/2 inch strips

3 garlic cloves, crushed

3.5 cm/1½ inch piece fresh ginger root, cut into strips

1 tsp pomegranate seeds, crushed

½ tsp ground turmeric

1 tsp garam masala

2 fresh green chillies, sliced

½ tsp salt

4 tbsp lemon juice

grated rind of 1 lemon

6 tbsp chopped fresh coriander (cilantro)

125 ml/4 fl oz/½ cup chicken stock

naan bread, to serve

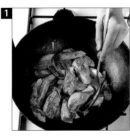

1 Heat the oil in a wok or large frying pan (skillet) and stir-fry the chicken until golden brown all over. Remove from the pan and set aside.

2 Add the garlic, ginger and pomegranate seeds to the pan and fry in the oil for 1 minute taking care not to let the garlic burn.

3 Stir in the turmeric, garam masala and chillies, and fry for 30 seconds.

4 Return the chicken to the pan and add the salt, lemon juice, lemon rind, coriander (cilantro) and stock. Stir the chicken well to make sure it is coated in the sauce.

5 Bring the mixture to the boil, then lower the heat and simmer for 10–15 minutes until the chicken is thoroughly cooked. Serve with warm naan bread.

COOK'S TIP

Stir-frying is perfect for low-fat diets as only a little oil is needed. Cooking the food over a high temperature ensures that food is sealed and cooked quickly to hold in the flavour.

Chicken with Two Sauces

With its red and yellow (bell) pepper sauces, this quick and simple dish is colourful and healthy, and perfect for an impromptu lunch or supper.

NUTRITIONAL INFORMATION

Calories 257	Sugars 7g	
Protein 29g	Fat 10g	
Carbohydrate 8g	Saturates 2g	

🕙 10 MINS   🕐 1½ HOURS

SERVES 4

INGREDIENTS

2 tbsp olive oil

2 medium onions, chopped finely

2 garlic cloves, crushed

2 red (bell) peppers, chopped

good pinch cayenne pepper

2 tsp tomato purée (paste)

2 yellow (bell) peppers, chopped

pinch of dried basil

4 lean skinless, boneless chicken breasts

150 ml/¼ pint/⅔ cup dry white wine

150 ml/¼ pint/⅔ cup chicken stock

bouquet garni

salt and pepper

fresh herbs, to garnish

1 Heat 1 tablespoon of olive oil in each of two medium saucepans. Place half the chopped onions, 1 of the garlic cloves, the red (bell) peppers, the cayenne pepper and the tomato purée (paste) in one of the saucepans. Place the remaining onion, garlic, yellow (bell) peppers and basil in the other pan.

2 Cover each pan and cook over a very low heat for 1 hour until the (bell) peppers are very soft. If either mixture becomes dry, add a little water. Process then sieve the contents of each pan separately.

3 Return to the pans and season with salt and pepper. Gently reheat the two sauces while the chicken is cooking.

4 Put the chicken breasts into a frying pan and add the wine and stock. Add the bouquet garni and bring the liquid to simmer. Cook the chicken for about 20 minutes until tender.

5 To serve, put a pool of each sauce on to four serving plates, slice the chicken breasts and arrange on the plates. Garnish with fresh herbs.

Pot-Roast Orange Chicken

This colourful, nutritious pot-roast could be served for a family meal or for a special dinner. Add more vegetables if you're feeding a crowd.

NUTRITIONAL INFORMATION

Calories 302	Sugar 17g	
Protein 29g	Fats 11g	
Carbohydrates ... 22g	Saturates 2g	

10 MINS   2 HOURS

SERVES 4

I N G R E D I E N T S

2 tbsp sunflower oil

1 chicken, weighing about 1.5 kg/3 lb 5 oz

2 large oranges

2 small onions, quartered

500 g/1 lb 2 oz/2 cups small whole carrots or thin carrots, cut into 5 cm/ 2 inch lengths

150ml/¼ pint/⅔ cup orange juice

2 tbsp brandy

2 tbsp sesame seeds

1 tbsp cornflour (cornstarch)

salt and pepper

1 Heat the oil in a large flameproof casserole and fry the chicken, turning occasionally until evenly browned.

2 Cut one orange in half and place half inside the cavity of the chicken. Place the chicken in a large, deep casserole. Arrange the onions and carrots around the chicken. Season with salt and pepper and pour over the orange juice.

3 Cut the remaining oranges into thin wedges and tuck around the chicken, among the vegetables.

4 Cover and cook in a preheated oven, 180°C/350°F/Gas Mark 4, for about 1½ hours, or until the chicken juices run clear when pierced, and the vegetables are tender. Remove the lid and sprinkle with the brandy and sesame seeds. Return to the oven for 10 minutes.

5 To serve, lift the chicken on to a large platter and add the vegetables. Skim any excess fat from the juices. Blend the cornflour (cornstarch) with 1 tablespoon of cold water, then stir into the juices and bring to the boil, stirring. Season to taste, then serve the sauce with the chicken.

Two-in-One Chicken

Cook four chicken pieces and serve two hot, topped with a crunchy herb mixture. Serve the remainder as a salad in a delicious curry sauce.

NUTRITIONAL INFORMATION

Calories . . . . .421　Sugars 20g
Protein . . . . .31g　Fat 18g
Carbohydrate . . .34g　Saturates 4g

2¹/₂ HOURS　45 MINS

SERVES 2

INGREDIENTS

4 lean chicken thighs

oil for brushing

garlic powder

½ dessert (eating) apple, grated coarsely

1½ tbsp dry parsley and thyme stuffing mix

salt and pepper

pasta shapes, to serve

SAUCE

15 g/½ oz/1 tbsp butter or margarine

2 tsp plain (all-purpose) flour

5 tbsp skimmed milk

2 tbsp dry white wine or stock

½ tsp dried mustard powder

1 tsp capers or chopped gherkins

SPICED CHICKEN SALAD

½ small onion, chopped finely

1 tbsp oil

1 tsp tomato purée (paste)

½ tsp curry powder

1 tsp apricot jam

1 tsp lemon juice

2 tbsp low-fat mayonnaise

1 tbsp low-fat natural fromage frais

90 g/3 oz/¾ cup seedless grapes, halved

60 g/2 oz ¼ cup white long-grain rice, cooked, to serve

1 Place the chicken in a shallow ovenproof dish. Brush with oil, sprinkle with garlic powder and season with salt and pepper. Place in a preheated oven, 200°C/400°F/Gas Mark 6, for 25 minutes, or until almost cooked through. Combine the apple with the stuffing mix. Baste the chicken, then spoon the mixture over two of the pieces. Return all the chicken pieces to the oven for about 10 minutes until the chicken is cooked.

2 To make the sauce, melt the magarine in a pan, stir in the flour and cook for 1–2 minutes. Add the milk gradually, then the wine or stock, and bring to the boil. Stir in the mustard, capers or gherkins, and seasoning. Simmer for 1 minute. Serve the two crunchy-topped pieces of chicken with the sauce and pasta shapes.

3 For the salad, fry the onion gently in the oil until barely coloured. Add the tomato purée (paste), curry powder and jam, and cook for 1 minute. Leave the mixture to cool. Blend the mixture in a food processor, or press through a sieve (strainer). Beat in the lemon juice, mayonnaise and fromage frais. Season to taste with salt and pepper.

4 Cut the chicken into strips and add to the sauce with the grapes. Mix well, and chill. Serve with the rice.

Karahi Chicken

A karahi is an extremely versatile two-handled metal pan, similar to a wok. Food is always cooked over a high heat in a karahi.

NUTRITIONAL INFORMATION

Calories	270	Sugars	.........1g
Protein	........41g	Fat	...........11g
Carbohydrate	....1g	Saturates	......2g

5 MINS   20 MINS

SERVES 4

I N G R E D I E N T S

2 tbsp ghee

3 garlic cloves, crushed

1 onion, chopped finely

2 tbsp garam masala

1 tsp coriander seeds, ground

½ tsp dried mint

1 bay leaf

750 g/1 lb 10 oz lean boneless chicken meat, diced

200 ml/7 fl oz/scant 1 cup chicken stock

1 tbsp fresh coriander (cilantro), chopped

salt

warm naan bread or chapatis, to serve

1 Heat the ghee in a karahi, wok or a large, heavy frying pan (skillet). Add the garlic and onion. Stir-fry for about 4 minutes until the onion is golden.

2 Stir in the garam masala, ground coriander, mint and bay leaf.

3 Add the chicken and cook over a high heat, stirring occasionally, for about 5 minutes. Add the stock and simmer for 10 minutes, until the sauce has thickened

and the chicken juices run clear when the meat is tested with a sharp knife.

4 Stir in the fresh coriander (cilantro) and salt to taste, mix well and serve immediately with warm naan bread or chapatis.

COOK'S TIP

Always heat a karahi or wok before you add the oil to help maintain the high temperature.

Lime Chicken Kebabs

These succulent chicken kebabs are coated in a sweet lime dressing and are served with a lime and mango relish. They make an ideal light meal.

NUTRITIONAL INFORMATION

Calories ....199 Sugars 14g
Protein ....28g Fat 4g
Carbohydrate ...14g Saturates 1g

15 MINS   10 MINS

SERVES 4

INGREDIENTS

4 lean boneless chicken breasts, skinned, about 125 g/4½ oz each

3 tbsp lime marmalade

1 tsp white wine vinegar

½ tsp lime rind, finely grated

1 tbsp lime juice

salt and pepper

TO SERVE

lime wedges

boiled white rice, sprinkled with chilli powder

SALSA

1 small mango

1 small red onion

1 tbsp lime juice

1 tbsp fresh coriander (cilantro), chopped

1 Slice the chicken breasts into thin pieces and thread on to 8 skewers so that the meat forms an S-shape down each skewer.

2 Preheat the grill (broiler) to medium. Arrange the chicken kebabs on the grill (broiler) rack. Mix together the lime marmalade, vinegar, lime rind and juice. Season with salt and pepper to taste. Brush the dressing generously over the chicken and grill (broil) for 5 minutes. Turn the chicken over, brush with the dressing again and grill (broil) for a further 4-5 minutes until the chicken is cooked through.

3 Meanwhile, prepare the salsa. Peel the mango and slice the flesh off the smooth, central stone. Dice the flesh into small pieces and place in a small bowl.

4 Peel and finely chop the onion and mix into the mango, together with the lime juice and chopped coriander (cilantro). Season, cover and chill until required.

5 Serve the chicken kebabs with the salsa, accompanied with wedges of lime and boiled rice sprinkled with chilli powder.

COOK'S TIP

To prevent sticking, lightly oil metal skewers or dip bamboo skewers in water before threading the chicken on to them.

Filipino Chicken

Tomato ketchup is a very popular ingredient in Asian dishes, as it imparts a zingy sweet-sour flavour.

NUTRITIONAL INFORMATION

Calories 197   Sugars 7g
Protein ....28g   Fat 4g
Carbohydrate ....8g   Saturates 1g

2³/₄ HOURS   20 MINS

SERVES 4

I N G R E D I E N T S

1 can lemonade or lime-and-lemonade

2 tbsp gin

4 tbsp tomato ketchup

2 tsp garlic salt

2 tsp Worcestershire sauce

4 lean chicken suprêmes or breast fillets

salt and pepper

T O   S E R V E

thread egg noodles

1 green chilli, chopped finely

2 spring onions (scallions), sliced

1 Combine the lemonade or lime-and-lemonade, gin, tomato ketchup, garlic salt, Worcestershire sauce and seasoning in a large non-porous dish.

2 Put the chicken supremes into the dish and make sure that the marinade covers them completely.

3 Leave to marinate in the refrigerator for 2 hours. Remove and leave covered at room temperature for 30 minutes.

4 Place the chicken over a medium barbecue (grill) and cook for 20 minutes.

5 Turn the chicken once, halfway through the cooking time.

6 Remove from the barbecue (grill) and leave to rest for 3–4 minutes before serving.

7 Serve with egg noodles, tossed with a little green chilli and spring onions (scallions).

COOK'S TIP

Cooking the meat on the bone after it has reached room temperature means that it cooks in a shorter time, which ensures that the meat remains moist right through to the bone.

Jerk Chicken

This is perhaps one of the best known Caribbean dishes. The 'jerk' in the name refers to the hot spicy coating.

NUTRITIONAL INFORMATION

Calories 158   Sugars 0.4g
Protein . . . . .29g   Fat 4g
Carbohydrate . . . .2g   Saturates 1g

24 HOURS   30 MINS

SERVES 4

INGREDIENTS

4 lean chicken portions

1 bunch spring onions (scallions), trimmed

1–2 Scotch Bonnet chillies, deseeded

1 garlic clove

5 cm/2 inch piece root ginger, peeled and roughly chopped

½ tsp dried thyme

½ tsp paprika

¼ tsp ground allspice

pinch ground cinnamon

pinch ground cloves

4 tbsp white wine vinegar

3 tbsp light soy sauce

pepper

 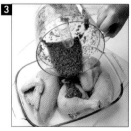 

1 Rinse the chicken portions and pat them dry on absorbent kitchen paper. Place them in a shallow dish.

2 Place the spring onions (scallions), chillies, garlic, ginger, thyme, paprika, allspice, cinnamon, cloves, wine vinegar, soy sauce and pepper to taste in a food processor and process until smooth.

3 Pour the spicy mixture over the chicken. Turn the chicken portions over so that they are well coated in the marinade.

4 Transfer the chicken portions to the refrigerator and leave to marinate for up to 24 hours.

5 Remove the chicken from the marinade and barbecue (grill) over medium hot coals for about 30 minutes, turning the chicken over and basting occasionally with any remaining marinade, until the chicken is browned and cooked through.

6 Transfer the chicken portions to individual serving plates and serve at once.

Chicken & Potato Bake

Make this when new potatoes are in season. A medium onion or a few shallots can be substituted for the spring onions (scallions).

NUTRITIONAL INFORMATION

Calories 323	Sugars 9g	
Protein 30g	Fat 10g	
Carbohydrate ...29g	Saturates 2g	

10 MINS   1¼ HOURS

SERVES 4

INGREDIENTS

2 tbsp olive oil

4 lean chicken breasts

1 bunch spring onions (scallions), trimmed and chopped

350 g/12 oz young spring carrots, scrubbed and sliced

125 g/4½ oz dwarf green beans, trimmed and sliced

600 ml/1 pint/2½ cups chicken stock

350 g/12 oz small new potatoes, scrubbed

1 small bunch mixed fresh herbs, such as thyme, rosemary, bay and parsley

salt and pepper

2 tbsp cornflour (cornstarch)

2–3 tbsp cold water

sprigs of fresh mixed herbs, to garnish

1 Heat the oil in a large flameproof casserole and add the chicken breasts. Gently fry for 5–8 minutes until browned on both sides. Lift from the casserole with a perforated spoon and set aside.

2 Add the spring onions (scallions), carrots and green beans and gently fry for 3–4 minutes.

3 Return the chicken to the casserole and pour in the stock. Add the potatoes and herbs. Season, bring to the boil, then cover the casserole and transfer to the oven. Bake in a preheated oven at 190°C/375°F/Gas Mark 5 for 40–50 minutes until the potatoes are tender.

4 Blend the cornflour (cornstarch) with the cold water. Add to the casserole, stirring until blended and thickened. Cover and cook for a further 5 minutes. Garnish with fresh herbs and serve.

COOK'S TIP

Use your favourite combination of herbs for this dish. If fresh herbs are unavailable, use half the quantity of dried mixed herbs. Alternatively, use a bouquet garni sachet which is usually a combination of bay, thyme and parsley.

Mexican Chicken

Chilli, tomatoes and corn are typical ingredients in a Mexican dish. This is a quick and easy meal for unexpected guests.

NUTRITIONAL INFORMATION

Calories 207	Sugars 8g
Protein 18g	Fat 9g
Carbohydrate . . .13g	Saturates 2g

5 MINS   35 MINS

SERVES 4

I N G R E D I E N T S

2 tbsp oil

8 chicken drumsticks

1 medium onion, finely chopped

1 tsp chilli powder

1 tsp ground coriander

425 g/15 oz can chopped tomatoes

2 tbsp tomato purée (paste)

125 g/4½ oz/⅔ cup frozen sweetcorn (corn-on-the-cob)

salt and pepper

TO SERVE

boiled rice

mixed (bell) pepper salad

1 Heat the oil in a large frying pan (skillet), add the chicken drumsticks and cook over a medium heat until lightly browned on all sides. Remove from the pan and set aside.

2 Add the onion to the pan and cook for 3–4 minutes until soft, then stir in the chilli powder and coriander and cook for a few seconds.

3 Add the chopped tomatoes with their juice and the tomato purée (paste).

4 Return the chicken to the pan and simmer gently for 20 minutes until the chicken is tender and thoroughly cooked. Add the sweetcorn (corn-on-the-cob) and cook a further 3–4 minutes. Season to taste.

5 Serve with boiled rice and mixed (bell) pepper salad.

COOK'S TIP

If you dislike the heat of the chillies, just leave them out – the chicken will still taste delicious.

Barbecued Chicken

These chicken wings are brushed with a simple barbecue (grill) glaze, which can be made in minutes, but will be enjoyed by all.

NUTRITIONAL INFORMATION

Calories 143   Sugars 6g
Protein ....14g   Fat 7g
Carbohydrate ....6g   Saturates 1g

5 MINS   20 MINS

SERVES 4

INGREDIENTS

8 chicken wings or 1 chicken cut into
  8 portions

3 tbsp tomato purée (paste)

3 tbsp brown fruity sauce

1 tbsp white wine vinegar

1 tbsp clear honey

1 tbsp olive oil

1 clove garlic, crushed (optional)

salad leaves, to serve

1 Remove the skin from the chicken if you want to reduce the fat in the dish.

2 To make the barbecue glaze, place the tomato purée (paste), brown fruity sauce, white wine vinegar, honey, oil and garlic in a small bowl. Stir all of the ingredients together until they are thoroughly blended.

3 Brush the barbecue (grill) glaze over the chicken and barbecue (grill) over hot coals for 15–20 minutes. Turn the chicken portions over occasionally and baste frequently with the barbecue (grill) glaze.

4 If the chicken begins to blacken before it is cooked, raise the rack if possible or move the chicken to a cooler part of the barbecue (grill) to slow down the cooking.

5 Transfer the barbecued (grilled) chicken to warm serving plates and serve with fresh salad leaves.

COOK'S TIP

When poultry is cooked over a very hot barbecue (grill) the heat immediately seals in all of the juices, leaving the meat succulent. For this reason make sure that the coals are hot enough before starting to barbecue (grill).

Festive Apple Chicken

The stuffing in this recipe is cooked under the breast skin so all the flavour sealed in, and the chicken stays really moist and succulent

NUTRITIONAL INFORMATION

Calories . . . . .219 Sugars 7g
Protein . . . . .29g Fat 8g
Carbohydrate . . . .9g Saturates 4g

10 MINS 2¹/₄ HOURS

SERVES 6

INGREDIENTS

1 chicken, weighing 2 kg/4½ lb

2 dessert apples

15 g/½ oz/1 tbsp butter

1 tbsp redcurrant jelly

parsley, to garnish

STUFFING

15 g/½ oz/1 tbsp butter

1 small onion, chopped finely

60 g/2 oz mushrooms, chopped finely

60 g/2 oz lean smoked ham, chopped finely

25 g/1 oz/½ cup fresh breadcrumbs

1 tbsp chopped fresh parsley

1 crisp eating apple

1 tbsp lemon juice

oil, to brush

salt and pepper

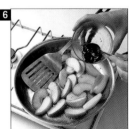

1 To make the stuffing, melt the butter and fry the onion gently, stirring until softened. Stir in the mushrooms and cook over a moderate heat for 2–3 minutes. Remove from the heat and stir in the ham, breadcrumbs and the chopped parsley.

2 Core the apple, leaving the skin on, and grate coarsely. Add the stuffing mixture to the apple with the lemon juice. Season to taste.

3 Loosen the breast skin of the chicken and carefully spoon the stuffing mixture under it, smoothing evenly with your hands.

4 Place the chicken in a roasting tin (pan) and brush lightly with oil.

5 Roast the chicken in a preheated oven, 190°C/375°F/Gas Mark 5, for 25 minutes per 500 g/1 lb 2 oz plus 25 minutes, or until there is no trace of pink in the juices when the chicken is pierced through the thickest part with a skewer. If the breast starts to brown too much, cover the chicken with foil.

6 Core and slice the remaining apples and sauté in the butter until golden. Stir in the redcurrant jelly and warm through until melted. Serve the chicken garnished with the apple and parsley.

Crispy Stuffed Chicken

An attractive main course of chicken breasts filled with mixed (bell) peppers and set on a sea of red (bell) peppers and tomato sauce.

NUTRITIONAL INFORMATION

Calories 196   Sugars 4g
Protein ....29g   Fat 6g
Carbohydrate ....6g   Saturates 2g

20 MINS   50 MINS

SERVES 4

INGREDIENTS

4 boneless chicken breasts, about 150 g/
5½ oz each, skinned

4 sprigs fresh tarragon

½ small orange (bell) pepper, deseeded and sliced

½ small green (bell) pepper, deseeded and sliced

15 g/½ oz wholemeal breadcrumbs

1 tbsp sesame seeds

4 tbsp lemon juice

1 small red (bell) pepper, halved and deseeded

200 g/7 oz can chopped tomatoes

1 small red chilli, deseeded and chopped

¼ tsp celery salt

salt and pepper

fresh tarragon, to garnish

1 Preheat the oven to 200°C/400°F/Gas Mark 6. Slit the chicken breasts with a small, sharp knife to create a pocket in each. Season inside each pocket.

2 Place a sprig of tarragon and a few slices of orange and green (bell) peppers in each pocket. Place the chicken breasts on a non-stick baking tray (cookie sheet) and sprinkle over the breadcrumbs and sesame seeds.

3 Spoon 1 tablespoon lemon juice over each chicken breast and bake in the oven for 35–40 minutes until the chicken is tender and cooked through.

4 Meanwhile, preheat the grill (broiler) to hot. Arrange the red (bell) pepper halves, skin side up, on the rack and cook for 5–6 minutes until the skin blisters. Leave to cool for 10 minutes, then peel off the skins.

5 Put the red (bell) pepper in a blender, add the tomatoes, chilli and celery salt and process for a few seconds. Season to taste. Alternatively, finely chop the red (bell) pepper and press through a sieve with the tomatoes and chilli.

6 When the chicken is cooked, heat the sauce, spoon a little on to a warm plate and arrange a chicken breast in the centre. Garnish with tarragon and serve.

Chicken with Whisky Sauce

After cooking with stock and vegetables, chicken breasts are served with a velvety sauce made from whisky and low-fat crème fraîche.

NUTRITIONAL INFORMATION

Calories 337	Sugars 6g	
Protein 37g	Fat 15g	
Carbohydrate 6g	Saturates 8g	

5 MINS   30 MINS

SERVES 4

INGREDIENTS

25 g/1 oz/2 tbsp butter

60 g/2 oz/½ cup shredded leeks

60 g/2 oz/⅓ cup diced carrot

60 g/2 oz/¼ cup diced celery

4 shallots, sliced

600 ml/1 pint/2½ cups chicken stock

6 chicken breasts

50 ml/2 fl oz/¼ cup whisky

200 ml/7 fl oz/1 cup low-fat crème fraîche

2 tbsp freshly grated horseradish

1 tsp honey, warmed

1 tsp chopped fresh parsley

salt and pepper

parsley, to garnish

TO SERVE

vegetable patty

mashed potato

fresh vegetables

1 Melt the butter in a large saucepan and add the leeks, carrot, celery and shallots. Cook for 3 minutes, add half the chicken stock and cook for about 8 minutes.

2 Add the remaining chicken stock, and bring to the boil. Add the chicken breasts and cook for about 10 minutes or until tender.

3 Remove the chicken with a perforated spoon and cut into thin slices. Place on a large, hot serving dish and keep warm.

4 In another saucepan, heat the whisky until reduced by half. Strain the chicken stock through a fine sieve, add to the pan and heat until the liquid is reduced by half.

5 Add the crème fraîche, the horseradish and the honey. Heat gently and add the chopped fresh parsley and salt and pepper to taste.

6 Pour a little of the whisky sauce around the chicken and pour the remaining sauce into a sauceboat to serve.

7 Serve with a vegetable patty made from the leftover vegetables, mashed potato and fresh vegetables. Garnish with fresh parsley.

Honeyed Citrus Chicken

This recipe is great when you are in a hurry. If you cut the chicken in half and press it flat, you can roast it in under an hour.

NUTRITIONAL INFORMATION

Calories ....288 Sugars 32g
Protein ....30g Fat 6g
Carbohydrate ...32g Saturates 1g

4¼ HOURS   55 MINS

SERVES 4

INGREDIENTS

2 kg/4 lb 8 oz chicken

salt and pepper

tarragon sprigs, to garnish

MARINADE

300 ml/½ pint/1¼ cups orange juice

3 tbsp cider vinegar

3 tbsp clear honey

2 tbsp chopped fresh tarragon

2 oranges, cut into wedges

SAUCE

handful of chopped tarragon

200 g/7 oz/1 cup fat-free fromage frais

2 tbsp orange juice

1 tsp clear honey

60 g/2 oz/½ cup stuffed olives, chopped

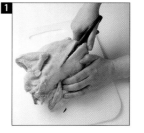

1 With the breast downwards, cut through the bottom part of the chicken using poultry shears or heavy kitchen scissors, making sure not to cut right through to the breast bone below.

2 Rinse the chicken with cold water, drain and place on a board with the skin side uppermost. Press the chicken flat, then cut off the leg ends. Thread two long wooden skewers through the bird to keep it flat and season with salt and pepper.

3 Put all the marinade ingredients, except the orange wedges, in a shallow non-metallic dish, then add the chicken. Cover and chill for 4 hours. Turn the chicken several times.

4 Mix all the sauce ingredients. Season, spoon into a dish, cover and chill.

5 Transfer the chicken and marinade to a roasting tin (pan), open out the chicken and place skin-side downwards. Tuck the orange wedges around the chicken and roast in a preheated oven, 200°C/400°F/Gas Mark 6, for 25 minutes.

6 Turn the chicken over and roast for another 20–30 minutes. Baste until the chicken is browned and the juices run clear when the thickest part of the leg is pierced with a skewer. Garnish with tarragon, slice and serve with the sauce.

Springtime Roast Chicken

This combination of baby vegetables and baby chickens with a tangy low-fat sauce makes a healthy meal.

NUTRITIONAL INFORMATION

Calories	280	Sugars	.........7g
Protein	........32g	Fat	..........7g
Carbohydrate	...16g	Saturates	......2g

🍗 🍗 🍗 🍗

⏲ 15 MINS 🕐 1 HOUR

SERVES 4

INGREDIENTS

5 tbsp fresh brown breadcrumbs

200 g/7 oz/½ cup low-fat fromage frais

5 tbsp chopped fresh parsley

5 tbsp chopped fresh chives

4 baby chickens

1 tbsp sunflower oil

675 g/1½ lb young spring vegetables such as carrots, courgettes (zucchini), sugar snap peas, corn (corn-on-the-cob) and turnips, cut into small chunks

125 ml/4 fl oz/½ cup boiling chicken stock

2 tsp cornflour (cornstarch)

150 ml/¼ pint/⅔ cup dry white wine

salt and pepper

1 Mix together the breadcrumbs, one-third of the fromage frais and 2 tablespoons each of parsley and chives. Season well then spoon into the neck ends of the baby chickens. Place the chickens on a rack in a roasting tin (pan), brush with oil and season well.

2 Roast in a preheated oven, 220°C/425°F/Gas Mark 7, for 30–35 minutes or until the juices run clear, not pink, when the chickens are pierced with a skewer.

3 Place the vegetables in a shallow ovenproof dish in one layer and add half the remaining herbs with the stock.

4 Cover and bake for 25–30 minutes until tender. Lift the chickens on to a serving plate and skim any fat from the juices in the tin. Add the vegetable juices.

5 Blend the cornflour (cornstarch) with the wine and whisk into the sauce with the remaining fromage frais. Whisk until boiling, then add the remaining herbs. Season to taste. Spoon the sauce over the chickens and serve with the vegetables.

COOK'S TIP

Baby chickens are simple to prepare, quick to cook and can be easily cut in half lengthways with a knife.

Baked Chicken & Chips

Traditionally, this dish is deep-fried, but the low-fat version is just as mouthwatering. Serve with chunky potato wedge chips.

NUTRITIONAL INFORMATION

Calories . . . . .361 Sugars 2g
Protein . . . . .24g Fat 8g
Carbohydrate . . .51g Saturates 2g

10 MINS   35 MINS

SERVES 4

I N G R E D I E N T S

4 baking potatoes, each 225 g/8 oz

1 tbsp sunflower oil

2 tsp coarse sea salt

2 tbsp plain (all-purpose) flour

pinch of cayenne pepper

½ tsp paprika

½ tsp dried thyme

8 chicken drumsticks, skin removed

1 medium egg, beaten

2 tbsp cold water

6 tbsp dry white breadcrumbs

salt and pepper

TO SERVE

low-fat coleslaw salad

sweetcorn relish

1 Preheat the oven to 200°C/400°F/Gas Mark 6. Wash and scrub the potatoes and cut each into 8 equal portions. Place in a clean plastic bag and add the oil. Seal and shake well to coat.

2 Arrange the potato wedges, skin side down, on a non-stick baking tray (cookie sheet), sprinkle over the sea salt and bake in the oven for 30–35 minutes until they are tender and golden.

3 Meanwhile, mix the flour, spices, thyme and seasoning together on a plate. Press the chicken drumsticks into the seasoned flour to lightly coat.

4 On one plate mix together the egg and water. On another plate sprinkle the breadcrumbs. Dip the chicken drumsticks first in the egg and then in the breadcrumbs. Place on a non-stick baking tray (cookie sheet).

5 Bake the chicken drumsticks along-side the potato wedges for 30 minutes, turning after 15 minutes, until both potatoes and chicken are tender and cooked through.

6 Drain the potato wedges thoroughly on absorbent kitchen paper (paper towels) to remove any excess fat and serve with the chicken, accompanied with low-fat coleslaw and sweetcorn relish.

Lime Fricassée of Chicken

The addition of lime juice and lime rind adds a delicious tangy flavour to this chicken stew.

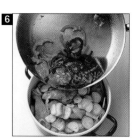

NUTRITIONAL INFORMATION

Calories	235	Sugars	.........3g
Protein	........20g	Fat	...........6g
Carbohydrate	...26g	Saturates	......1g

15 MINS   1¾ HOURS

SERVES 4

INGREDIENTS

2 tbsp oil

1 large chicken, cut into small portions

60 g/2 oz/½ cup flour, seasoned

500 g/1 lb 2 oz baby onions or shallots, sliced

1 each green and red (bell) pepper, sliced thinly

150 ml/¼ pint/⅔ cup chicken stock

juice and rind of 2 limes

2 chillies, chopped

2 tbsp oyster sauce

1 tsp Worcestershire sauce

salt and pepper

1 Heat the oil in a large frying pan (skillet). Coat the chicken pieces in the seasoned flour and cook for about 4 minutes until browned all over.

2 Transfer the chicken to a large casserole. Sprinkle with the onions.

3 Slowly fry the (bell) peppers in the juices in the frying pan.

4 Add the chicken stock, lime juice and rind and cook for a further 5 minutes.

5 Add the chillies, oyster sauce and Worcestershire sauce, mixing well.

6 Season to taste with salt and pepper, then pour the (bell) peppers and juices over the chicken and onions.

7 Cover the casserole with a lid or cooking foil.

8 Cook in the centre of a preheated oven, 190°C/375°F/Gas Mark 5, for 1½ hours until the chicken is very tender, then serve.

COOK'S TIP

Try this casserole with a cheese scone (biscuit) topping. About 30 minutes before the end of cooking time, simply top with rounds cut from cheese scone (biscuit) pastry.

Spicy Tomato Chicken

These low-fat, spicy skewers are cooked in a matter of minutes – assemble ahead of time and store in the fridge until you need them.

NUTRITIONAL INFORMATION

Calories 195   Sugars 11g
Protein . . . . .28g   Fat 4g
Carbohydrate . . .12g   Saturates 1g

10 MINS   10 MINS

SERVES 4

I N G R E D I E N T S

500 g/1 lb 2 oz skinless, boneless chicken
  breasts

3 tbsp tomato purée (paste)

2 tbsp clear honey

2 tbsp Worcestershire sauce

1 tbsp chopped fresh rosemary

250 g/9 oz cherry tomatoes

sprigs of rosemary, to garnish

couscous or rice, to serve

1 Cut the chicken into 2.5 cm/1 inch chunks and place in a bowl.

2 Mix together the tomato purée (paste), honey, Worcestershire sauce and rosemary. Add to the chicken, stirring to coat evenly.

3 Alternating the chicken pieces and cherry tomatoes, thread them on to eight wooden skewers.

4 Spoon over any remaining glaze. Cook under a preheated hot grill (broiler) for 8–10 minutes, turning occasionally, until the chicken is thoroughly cooked.

5 Serve on a bed of couscous or rice and garnish with sprigs of rosemary.

COOK'S TIP

Couscous is made from semolina that has been made into separate grains. It usually just needs moistening or steaming before serving.

Chicken & Plum Casserole

Full of the flavours of autumn (fall), this combination of lean chicken, shallots, garlic and fresh, juicy plums is a very fruity blend.

NUTRITIONAL INFORMATION

Calories 270   Sugars 9g
Protein . . . . .27g   Fat 7g
Carbohydrate . . .16g   Saturates 2g

2¼ HOURS   35 MINS

SERVES 4

I N G R E D I E N T S

2 rashers lean back bacon, rinds removed, trimmed and chopped

1 tbsp sunflower oil

450 g/1 lb skinless, boneless chicken thighs, cut into 4 equal strips

1 garlic clove, crushed

175 g/6 oz shallots, halved

225 g/8 oz plums, halved or quartered (if large) and stoned

1 tbsp light muscovado sugar

150 ml/5 fl oz/⅔ cup dry sherry

2 tbsp plum sauce

450 ml/16 fl oz/2 cups Fresh Chicken Stock (see page14)

2 tsp cornflour (cornstarch) mixed with 4 tsp cold water

2 tbsp flat-leaf parsley, chopped, to garnish

crusty bread, to serve

1 In a large, non-stick frying pan (skillet), dry fry the bacon for 2–3 minutes until the juices run out. Remove the bacon from the pan with a slotted spoon, set aside and keep warm.

2 In the same frying pan (skillet), heat the oil and fry the chicken with the garlic and shallots for 4–5 minutes, stirring occasionally, until well browned.

3 Return the bacon to the pan and stir in the plums, sugar, sherry, plum sauce and stock.

4 Bring to the boil and simmer for 20 minutes until the plums are soft and the chicken is cooked through. Add the cornflour (cornstarch) mixture to the pan and cook, stirring, for a further 2–3 minutes until thickened.

5 Spoon the casserole on to warm serving plates and garnish with chopped parsley. Serve the casserole with chunks of bread.

Chicken Tikka

Traditionally, chicken tikka is cooked in a clay tandoori oven, but it works well on the barbecue (grill), too.

NUTRITIONAL INFORMATION

Calories	173	Sugars	6g
Protein	28g	Fat	4g
Carbohydrate	6g	Saturates	2g

2¼ HOURS   15 MINS

SERVES 4

INGREDIENTS

4 chicken breasts, skinned and boned

½ tsp salt

4 tbsp lemon or lime juice

oil, for brushing

MARINADE

150 ml/5 fl oz/⅔ cup low-fat natural yogurt

2 cloves garlic, crushed

2.5 cm/1 inch piece root ginger, peeled and grated

1 tsp ground cumin

1 tsp chilli powder

½ tsp ground coriander

½ tsp ground turmeric

SAUCE

150 ml/5 fl oz/⅔ cup low-fat natural yogurt

1 tsp mint sauce

COOK'S TIP

Use the marinade to coat chicken portions, such as drumsticks, if you prefer. Barbecue (grill) over medium hot coals for 30–40 minutes, until the juices run clear when the chicken is pierced with a skewer.

1 Cut the chicken into 2.5 cm/1 inch cubes. Sprinkle with the salt and the citrus juice. Set aside for 10 minutes.

2 To make the marinade, combine all the ingredients together in a small bowl until well mixed.

3 Thread the cubes of chicken on to skewers. Brush the marinade over the

chicken. Cover and leave to marinate in the refrigerator for at least 2 hours, preferably overnight. Barbecue (grill) the chicken skewers over hot coals, brushing with oil and turning frequently, for 15 minutes or until cooked through.

4 Meanwhile, combine the yogurt and mint to make the sauce and serve with the chicken.

Mediterranean Chicken

This recipe uses ingredients found in the Languedoc area of France, where cooking over hot embers is a way of life.

NUTRITIONAL INFORMATION

Calories ....143 Sugars 4g
Protein ....13g Fat 8g
Carbohydrate ....4g Saturates 2g

2³/₄ HOURS   40 MINS

SERVES 4

INGREDIENTS

4 tbsp low-fat natural yogurt

3 tbsp sun-dried tomato paste

1 tbsp olive oil

15 g/½ oz/¼ cup fresh basil leaves, lightly crushed

2 garlic cloves, chopped roughly

4 chicken quarters

green salad, to serve

1 Combine the yogurt, tomato paste, olive oil, basil leaves and garlic in a small bowl and stir well to mix.

2 Put the marinade into a bowl large enough to hold the chicken quarters in a single layer. Add the chicken quarters. Make sure that the chicken pieces are thoroughly coated in the marinade.

3 Leave to marinate in the refrigerator for 2 hours. Remove and leave covered at room temperature for 30 minutes.

4 Place the chicken over a medium barbecue and cook for 30–40 minutes, turning frequently. Test for readiness by piercing the flesh at the thickest part – usually at the top of the drumstick. If the juices that run out are clear, it is cooked through.

5 Serve hot with a green salad. It is also delicious eaten cold.

VARIATION

For a marinade with an extra zingy flavour combine 2 garlic cloves, coarsely chopped, the juice of 2 lemons and 3 tbsp olive oil, and cook in the same way.

Whisky Roast Chicken

An unusual change from a plain roast, with a distinctly warming
Scottish flavour and a delicious oatmeal stuffing.

NUTRITIONAL INFORMATION

Calories ....254 Sugars 6g
Protein ....27g Fat 8g
Carbohydrate ....11g Saturates 2g

5 MINS   1¹/₂ HOURS

SERVES 6

I N G R E D I E N T S

1 chicken, weighing 2 kg/4 lb 8 oz

1 tbsp heather honey

2 tbsp Scotch whisky

2 tbsp plain (all-purpose) flour

300 ml/½ pint/1¼ cups chicken stock

vegetables and sauté potatoes,
    to serve

S T U F F I N G

1 medium onion, finely chopped

1 stick (stalk) celery, sliced thinly

1 tbsp sunflower oil

1 tsp dried thyme

4 tbsp porridge oats

4 tbsp chicken stock

salt and pepper

1 To make the stuffing, fry the onion
and celery in the sunflower oil,
stirring over a moderate heat until
softened and lightly browned.

2 Remove from the heat and stir in the
thyme, oats, stock, salt and pepper.

3 Stuff the neck end of the chicken
with the mixture and tuck the neck
flap under. Place in a roasting tin, (pan)
brush lightly with oil, and roast in a

preheated oven, 190°C/375°F/Gas Mark 5,
for about 1 hour.

4 Mix the honey with 1 tablespoon
whisky and brush the mixture over
the chicken. Return to the oven for a
further 20 minutes, or until the chicken is
golden brown and the juices run clear
when pierced through the thickest part
with a skewer.

5 Lift the chicken on to a serving plate.
Skim the fat from the juices then stir
in the flour. Stir over a moderate heat
until the mixture bubbles, then gradually
add the stock and remaining whisky to the
pan.

6 Bring to the boil, stirring, then
simmer for 1 minute and serve the
chicken with the sauce, green vegetable
and sauté potatoes.

Chicken with Vermouth

The aromatic flavours of vermouth makes a good base for the sauce, and when partnered with refreshing grapes ensures a delicious meal.

NUTRITIONAL INFORMATION

Calories 271   Sugars 5g
Protein . . . . .31g   Fat 4g
Carbohydrate . . .22g   Saturates 1g

2¼ HOURS   45 MINS

SERVES 4

I N G R E D I E N T S

4 × 175 g/6 oz 'part-boned' chicken breasts, skinned

150 ml/¼ pint/⅔ cup dry white vermouth

150 ml/¼ pint/⅔ cup Fresh Chicken Stock (see page 14)

2 shallots, sliced thinly

about 400 g/13 oz can artichoke hearts, drained and halved

125 g/4½ oz/¾ cup seedless green grapes

1 tbsp cornflour (cornstarch) mixed with tbsp cold water

salt and pepper

watercress sprigs to garnish

freshly cooked vegetables to serve

1 Cook the chicken in a heavy-based non-stick frying pan (skillet) for 2–3 minutes on each side until sealed. Drain on kitchen paper (paper towels).

2 Rinse out the pan, then add the dry vermouth and stock. Bring to the boil and add the shallots and chicken.

3 Cover and simmer for 35 minutes. Season to taste.

4 Stir in the artichokes and grapes and heat through for 2–3 minutes.

5 Stir in the cornflour (cornstarch) mixture until thickened. Garnish the chicken with watercress sprigs and serve with freshly cooked vegetables.

COOK'S TIP

Vermouth is a mixture of wines. It is fortified, and enriched with a secret blend of herbs and spices. It is available in sweet and dry forms. Dry white wine would make a suitable substitute in this recipe.

Chicken Tikka Masala

Try serving the chicken with mango chutney, lime pickle and cucumber raita (see page 207). Add poppadoms and rice to make a delicious meal.

NUTRITIONAL INFORMATION

Calories	353	Sugars	.........8g
Protein	........44g	Fat	..........16g
Carbohydrate	....8g	Saturates	......2g

2¼ HOURS · 50 MINS

SERVES 4

INGREDIENTS

½ onion, chopped coarsely

60 g/2 oz/3 tbsp tomato purée (paste)

1 tsp cumin seeds

2.5 cm/1 inch piece ginger root, chopped

3 tbsp lemon juice

2 garlic cloves, crushed

2 tsp chilli powder

750 g/1 lb 10 oz boneless chicken

salt and pepper

fresh mint sprigs, to garnish

MASALA SAUCE

2 tbsp ghee

1 onion, sliced

1 tbsp black onion seeds

3 garlic cloves, crushed

2 fresh green chillies, chopped

200 g/7 oz can tomatoes

125 ml/4 fl oz/½ cup low-fat natural yogurt

125 ml/4 fl oz/½ cup coconut milk

1 tbsp chopped fresh coriander (cilantro)

1 tbsp chopped fresh mint

2 tbsp lemon or lime juice

½ tsp garam masala

sprigs of fresh mint, to garnish

1 Combine the first seven ingredients and seasoning in a food processor or blender and then transfer to a bowl. Cut the chicken into 4 cm/1½ inch cubes. Stir into the bowl and leave for 2 hours.

2 Make the masala sauce. Heat the ghee in a saucepan, add the onion and stir over a medium heat for 5 minutes. Add the spices and garlic. Add the tomatoes, yogurt and coconut milk, bring to the boil, then simmer for 20 minutes.

3 Divide the chicken evenly between 8 oiled skewers and cook under a preheated very hot grill (broiler) for 15 minutes, turning frequently. Remove the chicken and add to the sauce. Stir in the herbs, lemon or lime juice, and garam masala. Serve garnished with mint sprigs.

Chicken & Lemon Skewers

A tangy lemon yogurt is served with these tasty lemon- and coriander (cilantro)-flavoured chicken skewers.

NUTRITIONAL INFORMATION

Calories 181   Sugars 6g
Protein . . . . .30g   Fat 4g
Carbohydrate . . . .6g   Saturates 2g

2¼ HOURS   15 MINS

SERVES 4

INGREDIENTS

4 chicken breasts, skinned and boned

1 tsp ground coriander

2 tsp lemon juice

300 ml/½ pint/1¼ cups low-fat natural yogurt

1 lemon

2 tbsp chopped, fresh coriander (cilantro)

oil for brushing

salt and pepper

1 Cut the chicken into 2.5 cm/1 inch pieces and place them in a shallow, non-metallic dish.

2 Add the coriander, lemon juice, salt and pepper to taste and 4 tbsp of the yogurt to the chicken and mix together until thoroughly combined. Cover and chill for at least 2 hours, preferably overnight.

3 To make the lemon yogurt, peel and finely chop the lemon, discarding any pips. Stir the lemon into the yogurt together with the fresh coriander (cilantro). Refrigerate until required.

4 Thread the chicken pieces on to skewers. Brush the rack with oil and

barbecue (grill) the chicken over hot coals for about 15 minutes, basting with the oil.

5 Transfer the chicken kebabs to warm serving plates and garnish with a sprig of fresh coriander (cilantro), lemon wedges and fresh salad leaves. Serve with the lemon yogurt.

COOK'S TIP

These kebabs are delicious served on a bed of blanched spinach, which has been seasoned with salt, pepper and nutmeg.

Cheesy Baked Chicken

Cheese and mustard, and a simple, crispy coating, make a delicious combination for this healthy dish.

NUTRITIONAL INFORMATION

Calories 225	Sugars 1g
Protein 32g	Fat 7g
Carbohydrate 9g	Saturates 3g

5 MINS   35 MINS

SERVES 4

I N G R E D I E N T S

1 tbsp skimmed milk

2 tbsp prepared English mustard

60 g/2oz/1 cup grated low-fat mature (sharp) Cheddar cheese

3 tbsp plain (all-purpose) flour

2 tbsp chopped fresh chives

4 skinless, boneless chicken breasts

TO SERVE

jacket potatoes and fresh vegetables

crisp salad

1 Mix together the milk and mustard in a bowl. Mix the cheese with the flour and chives on a plate.

2 Dip the chicken into the milk and mustard mixture, brushing with a pastry brush to coat evenly.

3 Dip the chicken breasts into the cheese mixture, pressing to coat them evenly all over.

4 Place on a baking tray (cookie sheet) and spoon any spare cheese coating on top.

5 Bake the chicken in a preheated oven, 200°C/400°F/ Gas Mark 6, for 30–35 minutes, or until golden brown and the juices run clear, not pink, when pierced with a skewer.

6 Serve the chicken hot, with jacket potatoes and fresh vegetables, or serve cold, with a crisp salad.

COOK'S TIP

Part-boned chicken breasts are very suitable for pan-cooking and casseroling, as they stay moist and tender. Try using chicken quarters if part-boned breasts are unavailable.

Spanish Chicken Casserole

Tomatoes, olives, peppers and potatoes, with a splash of Spanish red wine, make this a marvellous peasant-style dish.

NUTRITIONAL INFORMATION

Calories 293	Sugar 6g
Protein 15g	Fats 12g
Carbohydrates ...26g	Saturates 2g

10 MINS   1¼ HOURS

SERVES 4

INGREDIENTS

25 g/1 oz/¼ cup plain (all-purpose) flour

1 tsp salt

pepper

1 tbsp paprika

4 chicken portions

3 tbsp olive oil

1 large onion, chopped

2 garlic cloves, crushed

6 tomatoes, chopped, or 425 g/15 oz can chopped tomatoes

1 green (bell) pepper, cored, deseeded and chopped

150 ml/¼ pint/⅔ cup Spanish red wine

300 ml/½ pint/1¼ cups chicken stock

3 medium potatoes, peeled and quartered

12 pitted black olives

1 bay leaf

crusty bread, to serve

1 Put the plain (all-purpose) flour, salt, pepper and paprika into a large polythene bag.

2 Rinse the chicken portions and pat dry with kitchen paper (paper towels). Put them into the bag and shake to coat in the seasoned flour.

3 Heat the oil in a large flameproof casserole dish. Add the chicken portions and cook over a medium–high heat for 5–8 minutes until well-browned on each side. Lift out of the casserole with a perforated spoon and set aside.

4 Add the onion and garlic to the casserole and cook for a few minutes until browned. Add the tomatoes and (bell) pepper and cook for 2–3 minutes.

5 Return the chicken to the casserole. Add the wine, stock and potatoes, and then the olives and bay leaf. Cover and bake in a preheated oven at 190°C/375°F/ Gas Mark 5 for 1 hour until the chicken is tender.

6 Check the seasoning, adding more salt and pepper if necessary. Serve the chicken casserole hot with chunks of crusty bread.

Spicy Sesame Chicken

This is a quick and easy recipe for the grill, perfect for lunch or to eat outdoors on a picnic.

NUTRITIONAL INFORMATION

Calories 110   Sugars 3g
Protein . . . . .15g   Fat 4g
Carbohydrate . . . .3g   Saturates 1g

5 MINS   15 MINS

SERVES 4

I N G R E D I E N T S

4 chicken quarters

150 g/5½ oz/½ cup low-fat natural yogurt

finely grated rind and juice of 1 small lemon

2 tsp medium-hot curry paste

1 tbsp sesame seeds

T O   S E R V E

salad

naan bread

lemon wedges

1 Remove the skin from the chicken and slash the flesh at intervals with a sharp knife.

2 Mix together the yogurt, lemon rind, lemon juice and curry paste.

3 Spread the mixture over the chicken and arrange on a foil-lined grill (broiler) pan or baking tray (cookie sheet).

4 Place under a preheated moderately hot grill (broiler) and grill (broil) for 12–15 minutes, turning once. Grill (broil) until golden brown and thoroughly cooked. Just before the end of the cooking time, sprinkle the chicken with the sesame seeds.

5 Serve with a salad, naan bread and lemon wedges.

VARIATION

Poppy seeds, fennel seeds or cumin seeds, or a mixture of all three, can also be used to sprinkle over the chicken.

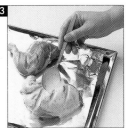

Marmalade Chicken

Marmalade lovers will enjoy this festive recipe. You can use any favourite marmalade, such as lemon or grapefruit.

NUTRITIONAL INFORMATION

Calories	304	Sugars	........20g
Protein	........29g	Fat	...........7g
Carbohydrate	...30g	Saturates	......2g

10 MINS   2 HOURS

SERVES 6

I N G R E D I E N T S

1 chicken, weighing about 2.25 kg/5 lb

bay leaves

2 tbsp marmalade

S T U F F I N G

1 stick (stalk) celery, chopped finely

1 small onion, chopped finely

1 tbsp sunflower oil

125 g/4½ oz/2 cups fresh wholemeal (whole wheat) breadcrumbs

4 tbsp marmalade

2 tbsp chopped fresh parsley

1 egg, beaten

salt and pepper

S A U C E

2 tsp cornflour (cornstarch)

2 tbsp orange juice

3 tbsp marmalade

150 ml/¼ pint/⅔ cup chicken stock

1 medium orange

2 tbsp brandy

1 Lift the neck flap of the chicken and remove the wishbone. Place a sprig of bay leaves inside the body cavity.

2 To make the stuffing, sauté the celery and onion in the oil. Add the the other ingredients. Season with salt and pepper to taste. Stuff the neck cavity of the chicken.

3 Place the chicken in a roasting tin (pan) and brush lightly with oil. Roast in a preheated oven, 190°C/375°F/Gas Mark 5 for 20 minutes per 500 g/1 lb 2 oz plus 20 minutes or until the juices run clear when the chicken is pierced with a knife. Glaze the chicken with the remaining marmalade.

4 For the sauce, blend the cornflour (cornstarch) in a pan with the orange juice, then add the marmalade and stock. Heat gently, stirring, until thickened. Remove from the heat.

5 Cut the segments from the orange, discarding all white pith and membrane, add to the sauce with the brandy and bring to the boil. Serve with the roast chicken.

Springtime Chicken Cobbler

Fresh spring vegetables are the basis of this colourful casserole, which is topped with hearty wholemeal (whole wheat) dumplings.

NUTRITIONAL INFORMATION

Calories 560   Sugars 10g
Protein . . . . .39g   Fat 18g
Carbohydrate . . .64g   Saturates 4g

15 MINS   1½ HOURS

SERVES 4

INGREDIENTS

8 skinless chicken drumsticks

1 tbsp oil

1 small onion, sliced

350 g/12 oz/1½ cups baby carrots

2 baby turnips

125 g/4½ oz/1 cup broad (fava) beans or peas

1 tsp cornflour (cornstarch)

300ml/½ pint/1¼ cups chicken stock

2 bay leaves

salt and pepper

COBBLER TOPPING

250 g/9 oz/2 cups wholemeal (whole wheat) plain (all-purpose) flour

2 tsp baking powder

25 g/1 oz/2 tbsp sunflower soft margarine

2 tsp dry wholegrain mustard

60 g/2 oz/½ cup low-fat mature (sharp) Cheddar cheese, grated

skimmed milk, to mix

sesame seeds, to sprinkle

1 Fry the chicken in the oil, turning, until golden brown. Drain well and place in an ovenproof casserole. Sauté the onion for 2–3 minutes to soften.

2 Wash and trim the carrots and turnips and cut into equal-sized pieces. Add to the casserole with the onions and beans or peas.

3 Blend the cornflour with a little of the stock, then stir in the rest and heat gently, stirring until boiling. Pour into the casserole and add the bay leaves, salt and pepper.

4 Cover tightly and bake in a preheated oven, 200°C/400°F/Gas Mark 6, for 50–60 minutes, or until the chicken juices run clear when pierced with a skewer.

5 For the topping, sift the flour and baking powder. Mix in the margarine with a fork. Stir in the mustard, the cheese and enough milk to mix to a fairly soft dough.

6 Roll out and cut 16 rounds with a 4 cm/1½ inch cutter. Uncover the casserole, arrange the scone (biscuit) rounds on top, then brush with milk and sprinkle with sesame seeds. Bake in the oven for 20 minutes or until the topping is golden and firm.

Chilli Chicken Meatballs

These tender chicken and sweetcorn nuggets are served with a sweet and sour sauce.

NUTRITIONAL INFORMATION

Calories 196	Sugars 12g
Protein 26g	Fat 4g
Carbohydrate ...15g	Saturates 1g

2½ HOURS   25 MINS

SERVES 4

INGREDIENTS

450 g/1 lb lean chicken, minced (ground)

4 spring onions (scallions), trimmed and finely chopped, plus extra to garnish

1 small red chilli, deseeded and finely chopped

2.5 cm/1 inch piece root ginger, finely chopped

100 g/3½ oz can sweetcorn (no added sugar or salt), drained

salt and white pepper

boiled jasmine rice, to serve

SAUCE

150 ml/5 fl oz/⅔ cup Fresh Chicken Stock (see page 14)

100 g/3½ oz cubed pineapple in natural juice, drained, with 4 tbsp reserved juice

1 medium carrot, cut into thin strips

1 small red (bell) pepper, deseeded and diced, plus extra to garnish

1 small green (bell) pepper, deseeded and diced

1 tbsp light soy sauce

2 tbsp rice vinegar

1 tbsp caster (superfine) sugar

1 tbsp tomato purée (paste)

2 tsp cornflour (cornstarch) mixed to a paste with 4 tsp cold water

1 To make the meatballs, place the chicken in a bowl and mix with the spring onions (scallions), chilli, ginger, seasoning and sweetcorn.

2 Divide into 16 portions and form each into a ball. Bring a saucepan of water to the boil. Arrange the meatballs on baking parchment in a steamer or large sieve (strainer), place over the water, cover and steam for 10–12 minutes.

3 To make the sauce, pour the stock and pineapple juice into a pan and bring to the boil. Add the carrot and (bell) peppers, cover and simmer for 5 minutes. Add the remaining ingredients, stirring until thickened. Season and set aside.

4 Drain the meatballs and transfer to a serving plate. Garnish with snipped chives and serve with boiled rice and the sauce (re-heated if necessary).

Minty Lime Chicken

These tangy lime and honey-coated pieces have a matching sauce or dip based on creamy natural yogurt.

NUTRITIONAL INFORMATION

Calories 170   Sugars 12g
Protein . . . . .23g   Fat 3g
Carbohydrate . . .12g   Saturates 1g

35 MINS   15 MINS

SERVES 6

INGREDIENTS

3 tbsp finely chopped mint

4 tbsp clear honey

4 tbsp lime juice

12 boneless chicken thighs

salt and pepper

salad, to serve

SAUCE

150 g/5½ oz/½ cup low-fat natural thick yogurt

1 tbsp finely chopped mint

2 tsp finely grated lime rind

1 Combine the mint, honey and lime juice in a bowl and season with salt and pepper to taste.

2 Use cocktail sticks (toothpicks) to keep the chicken thighs in neat shapes and add the chicken to the marinade, turning to coat evenly.

3 Leave the chicken to marinate for at least 30 minutes, longer if possible

4 Cook the chicken on a preheated moderately hot barbecue (grill) or grill

(broiler), turning frequently and basting with the marinade.

5 The chicken is cooked if the juices run clear when the chicken is pierced with a skewer.

6 Meanwhile, mix together the sauce ingredients.

7 Remove the cocktail sticks and serve the chicken with a salad and the sauce for dipping or pouring.

Chicken Fajitas

This spicy chicken filling, made up of mixed peppers, chillies and mushrooms, is put into folded tortillas and topped with soured cream.

NUTRITIONAL INFORMATION

Calories 303	Sugars 8g	
Protein 23g	Fat 18g	
Carbohydrate ...13g	Saturates 7g	

15 MINS   25 MINS

SERVES 4

INGREDIENTS

2 red (bell) peppers

2 green (bell) peppers

2 tbsp olive oil

2 onions, chopped

3 garlic cloves, crushed

1 chilli, deseeded and chopped finely

2 boneless chicken breasts (about 350 g/ 12 oz)

60 g/2 oz button mushrooms, sliced

2 tsp freshly chopped coriander (cilantro)

grated rind of ½ lime

2 tbsp lime juice

salt and pepper

4 wheat or corn tortillas

4–6 tbsp soured cream

TO GARNISH

Tomato salsa

lime wedges

1 Halve the (bell) peppers, remove the seeds and place skin-side upwards under a preheated moderate grill until well charred. Leave to cool slightly and then peel off the skin; cut the flesh into thin slices.

2 Heat the oil in a pan, add the onions, garlic and chilli, and fry them for a few minutes just until the onion has softened.

3 Cut the chicken into narrow strips, add to the vegetable mixture in the pan and fry for 4–5 minutes until almost cooked through, stirring occasionally.

4 Add the peppers, mushrooms, coriander, lime rind and juice, and continue to cook for 2–3 minutes. Season to taste.

5 Heat the tortillas, wrapped in foil, in a preheated oven at 180°C/350°F/Gas Mark 4 for a few minutes. Bend them in half and divide the chicken mixture between them.

6 Top the chicken filling in each tortilla with a spoonful of soured cream and serve garnished with tomato salsa and lime wedges.

Citrus Duckling Skewers

The tartness of citrus fruit goes well with the rich meat of duckling. Duckling makes a change from chicken for the barbecue (grill).

NUTRITIONAL INFORMATION

Calories	205	Sugars	.........5g
Protein	........24g	Fat	..........10g
Carbohydrate	....5g	Saturates	......2g

45 MINS   20 MINS

SERVES 12

I N G R E D I E N T S

3 duckling breasts, skinned, boned and cut into bite-size pieces

1 small red onion, cut into wedges

1 small aubergine (eggplant), cut into cubes

lime and lemon wedges, to garnish (optional)

M A R I N A D E

grated rind and juice of 1 lemon

grated rind and juice of 1 lime

grated rind and juice of 1 orange

1 clove garlic, crushed

1 tsp dried oregano

2 tbsp olive oil

dash of Tabasco sauce

1 Cut the duckling into bite-sized pieces. Place in a non-metallic bowl together with the prepared vegetables.

2 To make the marinade, place the lemon, lime and orange rinds and juices, garlic, oregano, oil and Tabasco sauce in a screw-top jar and shake until well combined. Pour the marinade over the duckling and vegetables and toss to coat. Leave to marinate for 30 minutes.

3 Remove the duckling and vegetables from the marinade and thread them on to skewers, reserving the marinade.

4 Barbecue (grill) the skewers on an oiled rack over medium hot coals, turning and basting frequently with the reserved marinade, for 15-20 minutes until the meat is cooked through. Serve the kebabs garnished with lemon and lime wedges for squeezing (if using).

Golden Glazed Chicken

A glossy glaze with sweet and fruity flavours coats chicken breasts in this tasty recipe.

NUTRITIONAL INFORMATION

Calories 427	Sugars 11g	
Protein 39g	Fat 12g	
Carbohydrate ...42g	Saturates 3g	

5 MINS   35 MINS

SERVES 4

I N G R E D I E N T S

6 boneless chicken breasts

1 tsp turmeric

1 tbsp wholegrain (whole-grain) mustard

300 ml/½ pint/1¼ cups orange juice

2 tbsp clear honey

2 tbsp sunflower oil

350 g/12 oz/1½ cups long grain rice

1 orange

3 tbsp chopped mint

salt and pepper

mint sprigs, to garnish

1 With a sharp knife, mark the surface of the chicken breasts in a diamond pattern.

2 Mix together the turmeric, mustard, orange juice and honey and pour over the chicken. Season with salt and pepper to taste. Chill until required.

3 Lift the chicken from the marinade and pat dry on kitchen paper (paper towels).

4 Heat the oil in a wide pan, add the chicken and sauté until golden, turning once. Drain off any excess oil. Pour over the marinade, cover and simmer for 10–15 minutes until the chicken is tender.

5 Boil the rice in lightly salted water until tender and drain well. Finely grate the rind from the orange and stir into the rice with the mint.

6 Remove the peel and white pith from the orange and cut into segments.

7 Serve the chicken with the orange and mint rice, garnished with orange segments and mint sprigs.

COOK'S TIP

To make a slightly sharper sauce, use small grapefruit instead of the oranges.

Chicken with Lime Stuffing

A cheesy stuffing is tucked under the breast skin of the chicken to give added flavour and moistness to the meat.

NUTRITIONAL INFORMATION

Calories . . . . . . .236 Sugars 1g
Protein . . . . .28g Fat 12g
Carbohydrate . . . .3g Saturates 7g

10 MINS   2 HOURS

SERVES 4

I N G R E D I E N T S

1 chicken, weighing 2.25 kg/5 lb

oil for brushing

225 g/8 oz/1⅓ cups courgette (zucchini)

25 g/1 oz/2 tbsp butter

juice of 1 lime

lime slices and shreds of lime rind,
   to garnish

S T U F F I N G

90 g/3 oz/½ cup courgette (zucchini)

90 g/3 oz/¾ cup low-fat soft cheese

finely grated rind of 1 lime

2 tbsp fresh breadcrumbs

salt and pepper

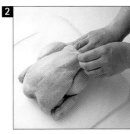 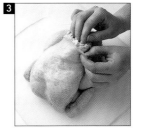 

1 To make the stuffing, trim and coarsely grate the courgette (zucchini) and mix with the cheese, lime rind, breadcrumbs, salt and pepper.

2 Carefully ease the skin away from the breast of the chicken with the fingertips, taking care not to split it.

3 Push the stuffing under the skin, to cover the breast evenly.

4 Place in a baking tin (pan), brush with oil and roast in a preheated oven, 190°C/ 375°F/Gas Mark 5, for 20 minutes per 500 g/1 lb 2 oz plus 20 minutes, or until the chicken juices run clear when pierced with a skewer.

5 Meanwhile, trim the remaining courgettes (zucchini) and cut into long, thin strips with a potato peeler or sharp knife. Sauté in the butter and lime juice until just tender, then serve with the chicken. Garnish the chicken with lime slices and shreds of lime rind and serve immediately.

COOK'S TIP

For quicker cooking,
finely grate the courgettes (zucchini)
rather than cutting them into strips.

Rustic Chicken & Orange Pot

Low in fat and high in fibre, this colourful casserole makes a healthy and hearty meal.

NUTRITIONAL INFORMATION

Calories 345   Sugars 6g
Protein . . . . .29g   Fat 10g
Carbohydrate . . .39g   Saturates 2g

5 MINS   1 HOUR

SERVES 4

INGREDIENTS

8 chicken drumsticks, skinned

1 tbsp wholemeal (whole wheat) flour

1 tbsp olive oil

2 medium red onions

1 garlic clove, crushed

1 tsp fennel seeds

1 bay leaf

finely grated rind and juice of 1 small
   orange

400 g/14 oz can chopped tomatoes

400 g/14 oz can cannellini or flageolet
   beans, drained

salt and black pepper

TOPPING

3 thick slices wholemeal (whole wheat)
   bread

2 tsp olive oil

1 Toss the chicken in the flour to coat evenly. Heat the oil in a non-stick pan and fry the chicken over a fairly high heat, turning often until golden brown. Transfer to a large ovenproof casserole.

2 Slice the red onions into thin wedges. Add to the pan and cook for a few minutes until lightly browned. Stir in the garlic, then add the onions and garlic to the casserole.

3 Add the fennel seeds, bay leaf, orange rind and juice, tomatoes, beans and salt and pepper.

4 Cover tightly and cook in a preheated oven, 190°C/375°F/Gas Mark 5, for 30–35 minutes until the chicken juices are clear and not pink when pierced through the thickest part with a skewer.

5 Cut the bread into small dice and toss in the oil. Remove the lid from the casserole and top with the bread cubes. Bake for a further 15–20 minutes until the bread is golden and crisp.

Marinated Chicken Kebabs

Pieces of chicken marinated in yogurt, chutney and spices make meltingly tender kebabs, and are cooked quickly in the microwave.

NUTRITIONAL INFORMATION

Calories	180	Sugars	........11g
Protein	........24g	Fat	..........5g
Carbohydrate	....11g	Saturates	......1g

🍴🍴

🍲 1¹/₄ HOURS   🕐 15 MINS

SERVES 4

INGREDIENTS

1 tbsp peach chutney

3 tbsp low-fat natural yogurt

½ tsp ground cumin

pinch of mixed (apple pie) spice

squeeze of lemon juice

3 chicken breast fillets, cut into even pieces

½ red (bell) pepper, cut into 16 even chunks

1 courgette (zucchini), cut into 16 slices

8 button mushrooms

salt and pepper

CHIVE & MINT DRESSING

150 ml/¼ pint/⅔ cup low-fat natural yogurt

2 tbsp low-fat mayonnaise

skimmed milk

1 tbsp chopped fresh chives

1 tbsp chopped fresh mint

mixed salad, to serve

TO GARNISH

sprigs of fresh mint

fresh chives

mixed salad, to serve

1 Mix the chutney, yogurt, spices and lemon juice together in a bowl. Season to taste.

2 Add the chicken to the bowl. Mix well and leave in a cool place to marinate for 1 hour.

3 Thread the red (bell) pepper, courgette (zucchini), chicken and mushrooms on to 8 long wooden skewers.

4 Arrange 4 skewers on a large plate or microwave rack. Cook on HIGH power for 6 minutes, turning over and rearranging halfway through. Repeat with the remaining 4 kebabs.

5 To make the chive and mint dressing, mix together all the ingredients and season with salt and pepper to taste. Spoon the dressing over the kebabs and garnish with mint and chives. Serve with a mixed salad.

Chicken with Bramble Sauce

This autumnal recipe can be made with fresh-picked wild blackberries from the hedgerow if you're lucky enough to live near a good supply.

NUTRITIONAL INFORMATION

Calories ....174 Sugars 5g
Protein ....27g Fat 4g
Carbohydrate ....5g Saturates 1g

1¼ HOURS   20 MINS

SERVES 4

INGREDIENTS

4 chicken breasts or 8 thighs

4 tbsp dry white wine or cider

2 tbsp chopped fresh rosemary

pepper

rosemary sprigs and blackberries,
   to garnish

SAUCE

200 g/7 oz/scant 2 cups blackberries

1 tbsp cider vinegar

2 tbsp redcurrant jelly

¼ tsp grated nutmeg

1 Cut the chicken into 2.5 cm/1 inch pieces and place in a bowl. Sprinkle over the wine or cider and rosemary, and season well with pepper. Cover and leave to marinate for at least an hour.

2 Drain the marinade from the chicken and thread the meat on to 8 metal or wooden skewers.

3 Cook under a preheated moderately hot grill (broiler) for 8–10 minutes, turning occasionally, until golden.

4 To make the sauce, place the marinade in a saucepan with the blackberries and simmer gently until soft. Press though a sieve (strainer).

5 Return the blackberry purée to the saucepan with the cider vinegar and redcurrant jelly and bring to the boil. Boil the sauce uncovered until it is reduced by about one-third.

6 Spoon a little bramble sauce on to each plate and place a chicken skewer on top. Sprinkle with nutmeg. Garnish each skewer with rosemary and blackberries.

COOK'S TIP

If you use canned fruit, omit the redcurrant jelly.

Chicken Jalfrezi

This is a quick and tasty way to use leftover roast chicken. The sauce can also be used for any cooked poultry, lamb or beef.

NUTRITIONAL INFORMATION

Calories . . . . .270 Sugars 3g
Protein . . . . .36g Fat 11g
Carbohydrate . . . .7g Saturates 2g

25 MINS   15 MINS

SERVES 4

I N G R E D I E N T S

1 tsp mustard oil

3 tbsp vegetable oil

1 large onion, chopped finely

3 garlic cloves, crushed

1 tbsp tomato purée (paste)

2 tomatoes, skinned and chopped

1 tsp ground turmeric

½ tsp cumin seeds, ground

½ tsp coriander seeds, ground

½ tsp chilli powder

½ tsp garam masala

1 tsp red wine vinegar

1 small red (bell) pepper, chopped

125 g/4½ oz/1 cup frozen broad (fava) beans

500 g/1 lb 2 oz cooked chicken, cut into bite-sized pieces

salt

sprigs of fresh coriander (cilantro), to garnish

1 Heat the mustard oil in a large, frying pan (skillet) set over a high heat for about 1 minute until it begins to smoke.

2 Add the vegetable oil, reduce the heat and then add the onion and the garlic. Fry the garlic and onion until they are golden.

3 Add the tomato purée (paste), chopped tomatoes, turmeric, ground cumin and coriander seeds, chilli powder, garam masala and wine vinegar to the frying pan (skillet). Stir the mixture until fragrant.

4 Add the red (bell) pepper and broad (fava) beans and stir for 2 minutes until the pepper is softened. Stir in the chicken, and salt to taste.

5 Simmer gently for 6–8 minutes until the chicken is heated through and the beans are tender.

6 Serve garnished with sprigs of coriander (cilantro).

Jamaican Hot Pot

A tasty way to make chicken joints go a long way, this hearty casserole is spiced with the warm, subtle flavour of ginger.

NUTRITIONAL INFORMATION

Calories 277	Sugars 6g
Protein 33g	Fat 7g
Carbohydrate . . .22g	Saturates 1g

5 MINS   1¼ HOURS

SERVES 4

I N G R E D I E N T S

2 tsp sunflower oil

4 chicken drumsticks

4 chicken thighs

1 medium onion

750 g/1 lb 10 oz piece squash or pumpkin, peeled

1 green (bell) pepper

2.5 cm/1 inch fresh ginger root, chopped finely

425 g/15 oz can chopped tomatoes

300ml/½ pint/1¼ cups chicken stock

60 g/2 oz/¼ cup split lentils

garlic salt and cayenne pepper

350 g/12 oz can sweetcorn (corn-on-the-cob)

1 Heat the oil in a large flameproof casserole and fry the chicken joints, turning frequently, until they are golden all over.

2 Peel and slice the onion.

3 Using a sharp knife, cut the squash or pumpkin into dice.

4 Deseed and slice the green (bell) pepper.

5 Drain any excess fat from the pan and add the onion, pumpkin and pepper. Gently fry for a few minutes. Add the ginger, tomatoes, stock and lentils. Season with garlic salt and cayenne.

6 Cover and place in a preheated oven, 190°C/375°F/Gas Mark 5, for about 1 hour, until the vegetables are tender and the juices from the chicken run clear.

7 Add the drained corn and cook for a further 5 minutes. Season to taste and serve with crusty bread.

Tasmanian Duck

Some of the best cherries in the world are grown in Tasmania, hence the title for this recipe, although dried cherries from any country can be used.

NUTRITIONAL INFORMATION

Calories	259	Sugars	........12g
Protein	........24g	Fat	..........12g
Carbohydrate	...12g	Saturates	......2g

5 MINS   35 MINS

SERVES 4

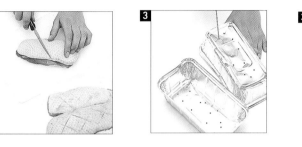

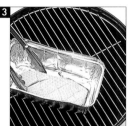

INGREDIENTS

4 duck breasts

60 g/2 oz/½ cup dried cherries

125 ml/4 fl oz/½ cup water

4 tbsp lemon juice

2 large leeks, quartered, or 8 baby leeks

2 tbsp olive oil

2 tbsp balsamic vinegar

2 tbsp port

2 tsp pink peppercorns

1 Using a sharp knife, make 3 slashes in the fat of the duck breasts in one direction, and 3 in the other.

2 Put the dried cherries, water and lemon juice into a small saucepan. Bring to the boil. Remove from the heat and leave to cool.

3 Turn a large foil tray upside-down, make several holes in the bottom with a skewer and put it over a hot barbecue (grill). Put the duck into the tray. Cover with foil and cook for 20 minutes.

4 Brush the leeks with olive oil and cook on the open barbecue (grill) for 5–7 minutes, turning constantly.

5 Remove the duck from the tray and cook on the open barbecue (grill) for 5 minutes, skin-side down, while you make the sauce.

6 Stir the balsamic vinegar into the cooking sauces in the tray, scraping any bits from the bottom. Add to the cherries in the saucepan. Return to the

heat – either the hob (stove top) or barbecue (grill) – and stir in the port and pink peppercorns. Bring to the boil and cook for 5 minutes, until the sauce has thickened slightly.

7 Serve the duck piping hot, pour over the cherry sauce, and accompany with the leeks.

Sticky Chicken Drumsticks

These drumsticks are always popular - provide plenty of napkins for wiping sticky fingers or provide finger bowls with a slice of lemon.

NUTRITIONAL INFORMATION

Calories	.213	Sugars	.14g
Protein	.27g	Fat	.6g
Carbohydrate	.14g	Saturates	.2g

5 MINS   30 MINS

SERVES 4

INGREDIENTS

10 chicken drumsticks

4 tbsp fine-cut orange marmalade

1 tbsp Worcestershire sauce

grated rind and juice of ½ orange

salt and pepper

TO SERVE

cherry tomatoes

salad leaves

1 Using a sharp knife, make 2–3 slashes in the flesh of each chicken drumstick.

2 Bring a large saucepan of water to the boil and add the chicken drumsticks. Cover the pan, return to the boil and cook for 5–10 minutes. Remove the chicken and drain thoroughly.

3 Meanwhile, make the baste. Place the orange marmalade, Worcestershire sauce, orange rind and juice and salt and pepper to taste in a small saucepan. Heat gently, stirring continuously, until the marmalade melts and all of the ingredients are well combined.

4 Brush the baste over the par-cooked chicken drumsticks and transfer them to the barbecue (grill) to complete cooking. Barbecue (grill) over hot coals for about 10 minutes, turning and basting frequently with the remaining baste.

5 Carefully thread 3 cherry tomatoes on to a skewer and transfer to the barbecue (grill) for 1–2 minutes.

6 Transfer the chicken drumsticks to serving plates. Serve with the cherry tomato skewers and a selection of fresh salad leaves.

COOK'S TIP

Par-cooking the chicken is an ideal way of making sure that it is cooked through without becoming overcooked and burned on the outside.

Duck with Berry Sauce

Duck is a rich meat and is best accompanied with fruit, as in this sophisticated dinner dish.

NUTRITIONAL INFORMATION

Calories 293   Sugars 10g
Protein ....28g   Fat 8g
Carbohydrate ...13g   Saturates 2g

1¼ HOURS   30 MINS

SERVES 4

INGREDIENTS

450 g/1 lb boneless duck breasts, skin removed

2 tbsp raspberry vinegar

2 tbsp brandy

1 tbsp clear honey

1 tsp sunflower oil, to brush

salt and pepper

TO SERVE

2 kiwi fruit, peeled and sliced thinly

assorted vegetables

SAUCE

225 g/8 oz raspberries, thawed if frozen

300 ml/½ pint/1¼ cups rosé wine

2 tsp cornflour (cornstarch) blended with 4 tsp cold water

1 Preheat the grill (broiler) to medium. Skin and trim the duck breasts to remove any excess fat. Using a sharp knife, score the flesh in diagonal lines and pound it with a meat mallet or a covered rolling pin until it is 1.5 cm/¾ inch thick.

2 Place the duck breasts in a shallow dish. Mix together the vinegar, brandy and honey in a small bowl and spoon it over the duck. Cover and leave to chill in the refrigerator for about 1 hour. Drain the duck, reserving the marinade, and place on the grill (broiler) rack. Season and brush with a little oil. Cook for 10 minutes, turn over, season and brush with oil again. Cook for a further 8–10 minutes until the meat is cooked through.

3 Meanwhile, make the sauce. Reserving about 60 g/2 oz raspberries, place the rest in a pan. Add the reserved marinade and the wine. Bring to the boil and simmer for 5 minutes until slightly reduced. Strain the sauce through a sieve, pressing the raspberries with the back of a spoon. Return the liquid to the saucepan and add the cornflour (cornstarch) paste. Heat through, stirring, until thickened. Add the reserved raspberries and season to taste.

4 Thinly slice the duck breast and alternate with slices of kiwi fruit. on warm serving plates. Spoon over the sauce and serve with a selection of vegetables.

Turkey with Redcurrant

Prepare these steaks the day before they are needed and serve in toasted ciabatta bread, accompanied with crisp salad leaves.

NUTRITIONAL INFORMATION

Calories 219	Sugars 4g	
Protein 28g	Fat 10g	
Carbohydrate 4g	Saturates 1g	

12 HOURS   15 MINS

SERVES 4

INGREDIENTS

100 g/ 3½ oz redcurrant jelly

2 tbsp lime juice

3 tbsp olive oil

2 tbsp dry white wine

¼ tsp ground ginger

pinch grated nutmeg

4 turkey breast steaks

salt and pepper

TO SERVE

mixed salad leaves

vinaigrette dressing

1 ciabatta loaf

cherry tomatoes

1 Place the redcurrant jelly and lime juice in a saucepan and heat gently until the jelly melts. Add the oil, wine, ginger and nutmeg.

2 Place the turkey steaks in a shallow, non-metallic dish and season with salt and pepper. Pour over the marinade, turning the meat so that it is well coated. Cover and refrigerate overnight.

3 Remove the turkey from the marinade, reserving the marinade for basting, and barbecue (grill) on an oiled rack over hot coals for about 4 minutes on each side. Baste the turkey steaks frequently with the reserved marinade.

4 Meanwhile, toss the salad leaves in the vinaigrette dressing. Cut the ciabatta loaf in half lengthwise and place, cut-side down, at the side of the barbecue. Barbecue (grill) until golden. Place each steak on top of a salad leaf, sandwich between 2 pieces of bread and serve with cherry tomatoes.

COOK'S TIP

Turkey and chicken escalopes are also ideal for cooking on the barbecue (grill). Because they are thin, they cook through without burning on the outside. Leave them overnight in a marinade of your choice and cook, basting with a little lemon juice and oil.

Roast Duck with Apple

The richness of the duck meat contrasts well with the apricot sauce. If duckling portions are unavailable, use a whole bird cut into joints.

NUTRITIONAL INFORMATION

Calories 316	Sugars 38g
Protein 25g	Fat 6g
Carbohydrate . . .40g	Saturates 1g

10 MINS   1¹/₂ HOURS

SERVES 4

I N G R E D I E N T S

4 duckling portions, 350 g/12 oz each

4 tbsp dark soy sauce

2 tbsp light muscovado sugar

2 red-skinned apples

2 green-skinned apples

juice of 1 lemon

2 tbsp clear honey

few bay leaves

salt and pepper

assorted fresh vegetables, to serve

S A U C E

400 g/14 oz can apricots, in natural juice

4 tbsp sweet sherry

1 Preheat the oven to 190°C/375°F/Gas Mark 5. Wash the duck and trim away any excess fat. Place on a wire rack over a roasting pan and prick all over with a fork.

2 Brush the duck with the soy sauce. Sprinkle over the sugar and season with pepper. Cook in the oven, basting occasionally, for 50–60 minutes until the meat is cooked through – the juices should run clear when a skewer is inserted into the thickest part of the meat.

3 Meanwhile, core the apples and cut each into 6 wedges. Place in a small roasting tin and mix with the lemon juice and honey. Add a few bay leaves and season. Cook alongside the duck, basting occasionally, for 20–25 minutes until tender. Discard the bay leaves.

4 To make the sauce, place the apricots in a blender or food processor together with the juice from the can and the sherry. Process for a few seconds until smooth. Alternatively, mash the apricots with a fork until smooth and mix with the juice and sherry.

5 Just before serving, heat the apricot purée (paste) in a small pan. Remove the skin from the duck and pat the flesh with kitchen paper to absorb any fat. Serve the duck with the apple wedges, apricot sauce and fresh vegetables.

VARIATION

Fruit complements duck perfectly. Use canned pineapple in natural juice for a delicious alternative.

Italian Dishes

Poulty dishes provide some of Italy's finest food. Every part of the chicken is used, including the feet and innards for making up soup. Spit-roasting chicken, flavoured strongly

with aromatic rosemary, has become almost a national dish. This chapter contains a superb collection of mouth-watering recipes. Along with old family favourites such as chicken lasagne, discover modern ideas such as chicken flavoured with balsamic vinegar. You will be astonished at how quickly you can prepare some of

these gourmet dishes.

Garlicky Chicken Cushions

Stuffed with creamy ricotta, spinach and garlic, then gently cooked in a rich tomato sauce, this is a suitable dish to make ahead of time.

NUTRITIONAL INFORMATION

Calories 316   Sugars 6g
Protein . . . . .40g   Fat 13g
Carbohydrate . . . .6g   Saturates 5g

10 MINS   40 MINS

SERVES 4

INGREDIENTS

4 part-boned chicken breasts

125 g/4½ oz/½ cup frozen spinach, defrosted

150 g/5½ oz/½ cup low-fat ricotta cheese

2 garlic cloves, crushed

1 tbsp olive oil

1 onion, chopped

1 red (bell) pepper, sliced

425 g/15 oz can chopped tomatoes

6 tbsp wine or chicken stock

10 stuffed olives, sliced

salt and pepper

flat leaf parsley sprigs, to garnish

pasta, to serve

1 Make a slit between the skin and meat on one side of each chicken breast. Lift the skin to form a pocket, being careful to leave the skin attached to the other side.

2 Put the spinach into a sieve and press out the water with a spoon. Mix with the ricotta, half the garlic and seasoning.

3 Spoon the spinach mixture under the skin of each chicken breast then secure the edge of the skin with cocktail sticks.

4 Heat the oil in a frying pan, add the onion and fry for a minute, stirring. Add the remaining garlic and red (bell) pepper and cook for 2 minutes. Stir in the tomatoes, wine or stock, olives and seasoning. Set the sauce aside and chill the chicken if preparing in advance.

5 Bring the sauce to the boil, pour into an ovenproof dish and arrange the chicken breasts on top in a single layer.

6 Cook, uncovered in a preheated oven, 200°C/400°F/Gas Mark 6, for 35 minutes until the chicken is golden and cooked through. Test by making a slit in one of the chicken breasts with a skewer to make sure the juices run clear.

7 Spoon a little of the sauce over the chicken breasts then transfer to serving plates and garnish with parsley. Serve with pasta.

Italian Chicken Spirals

These little foil parcels retain all the natural juices of the chicken while cooking conveniently over the pasta while it boils.

NUTRITIONAL INFORMATION

Calories 367	Sugars 1g	
Protein 33g	Fat 12g	
Carbohydrate ...35g	Saturates 2g	

20 MINS   20 MINS

SERVES 4

INGREDIENTS

4 skinless, boneless chicken breasts

25 g/1 oz/1 cup fresh basil leaves

15 g/½ oz/2 tbsp hazelnuts

1 garlic clove, crushed

250 g/9 oz/2 cups wholemeal (whole wheat) pasta spirals

2 sun-dried tomatoes or fresh tomatoes

1 tbsp lemon juice

1 tbsp olive oil

1 tbsp capers

60 g/2 oz/½ cup black olives

1 Beat the chicken breasts with a rolling pin to flatten evenly.

2 Place the basil and hazelnuts in a food processor and process until finely chopped. Mix with the garlic and salt and pepper to taste.

3 Spread the basil mixture over the chicken breasts and roll up from one short end to enclose the filling. Wrap the chicken roll tightly in foil so that they hold their shape, then seal the ends well.

4 Bring a pan of lightly salted water to the boil and cook the pasta for 8–10 minutes or until tender, but still firm to the bite. Meanwhile, place the chicken parcels in a steamer or colander set over the pan, cover tightly, and steam for 10 minutes.

5 Using a sharp knife, dice the tomatoes.

6 Drain the pasta and return to the pan with the lemon juice, olive oil, tomatoes, capers and olives. Heat through.

7 Pierce the chicken with a skewer to make sure that the juices run clear and not pink (this shows that the chicken is cooked through). Slice the chicken, arrange over the pasta and serve.

COOK'S TIP

Sun-dried tomatoes have a wonderful, rich flavour but if they're unavailable, use fresh tomatoes instead.

Chicken Marengo

Napoleon's chef was ordered to cook a sumptuous meal on the eve of the battle of Marengo – this feast of flavours was the result.

NUTRITIONAL INFORMATION

Calories . . . . .521 Sugars 6g
Protein . . . . .47g Fat 19g
Carbohydrate . . .34g Saturates 8g

🥘 🕐 🕐 🕐

🍲 20 MINS 🕐 50 MINS

SERVES 4

I N G R E D I E N T S

8 chicken pieces

2 tbsp olive oil

300 g/10½ oz passata (sieved tomatoes)

200 ml/7 fl oz/¾ cup white wine

2 tsp dried mixed herbs

40 g/1½ oz butter, melted

2 garlic cloves, crushed

8 slices white bread

100 g/3½ oz mixed mushrooms
   (such as button, oyster and ceps)

40 g/1½ oz black olives, chopped

1 tsp sugar

fresh basil, to garnish

1 Using a sharp knife, remove the bone from each of the chicken pieces.

2 Heat 1 tbsp of oil in a large frying pan (skillet). Add the chicken pieces and cook for about 4–5 minutes, turning occasionally, or until browned all over.

3 Add the passata (sieved tomatoes), wine and mixed herbs to the frying pan (skillet). Bring to the boil and then leave to simmer for 30 minutes or until the chicken is tender and the juices run clear when a skewer is inserted into the thickest part of the meat.

4 Mix the melted butter and crushed garlic together. Lightly toast the slices of bread and brush with the garlic butter.

5 Add the remaining oil to a separate frying pan (skillet) and cook the mushrooms for 2–3 minutes or until just browned.

6 Add the olives and sugar to the chicken mixture and warm through.

7 Transfer the chicken and sauce to serving plates. Serve with the bruschetta (fried bread) and fried mushrooms.

Mustard-Baked Chicken

Chicken pieces are cooked in a succulent, mild mustard sauce, then coated in poppy seeds and served on a bed of fresh pasta shells.

NUTRITIONAL INFORMATION

Calories	652	Sugars 5g
Protein	........51g	Fat 31g
Carbohydrate	...46g	Saturates 12g

10 MINS   35 MINS

SERVES 4

INGREDIENTS

8 chicken pieces (about 115 g/4 oz each)

60g/2 oz/4 tbsp butter, melted

4 tbsp mild mustard (see Cook's Tip)

2 tbsp lemon juice

1 tbsp brown sugar

1 tsp paprika

3 tbsp poppy seeds

400 g/14 oz fresh pasta shells

1 tbsp olive oil

salt and pepper

1 Arrange the chicken pieces in a single layer in a large ovenproof dish.

2 Mix together the butter, mustard, lemon juice, sugar and paprika in a bowl and season with salt and pepper to taste. Brush the mixture over the upper

surfaces of the chicken pieces and bake in a preheated oven at 200°C/400°F/Gas Mark 6 for 15 minutes.

3 Remove the dish from the oven and carefully turn over the chicken pieces. Coat the upper surfaces of the chicken with the remaining mustard mixture, sprinkle the chicken pieces with poppy seeds and return to the oven for a further 15 minutes.

4 Meanwhile, bring a large saucepan of lightly salted water to the boil. Add the pasta shells and olive oil and cook for 8–10 minutes or until tender, but still firm to the bite.

5 Drain the pasta thoroughly and arrange on a warmed serving dish. Top the pasta with the chicken, pour over the sauce and serve immediately.

COOK'S TIP

Dijon is the type of mustard most often used in cooking, as it has a clean and only mildly spicy flavour. German mustard has a sweet-sour taste, with Bavarian mustard being slightly sweeter. American mustard is mild and sweet.

Pan-Cooked Chicken

Artichokes are a familiar ingredient in Italian cookery. In this dish, they are used to delicately flavour chicken.

NUTRITIONAL INFORMATION

Calories	296	Sugars	.........2g
Protein	........27g	Fat	..........15g
Carbohydrate	....7g	Saturates	.......6g

15 MINS   55 MINS

SERVES 4

INGREDIENTS

4 chicken breasts, part boned

25 g/1 oz/2 tbsp butter

2 tbsp olive oil

2 red onions, cut into wedges

2 tbsp lemon juice

150 ml/¼ pt/⅔ cup dry white wine

150 ml/¼ pt/⅔ cup chicken stock

2 tsp plain (all-purpose) flour

400 g/14 oz can artichoke halves,
   drained and halved

salt and pepper

chopped fresh parsley, to garnish

1 Season the chicken with salt and pepper to taste. Heat the oil and 15 g/ ½ oz/1 tablespoon of the butter in a large frying pan (skillet). Add the chicken and fry for 4–5 minutes on each side until lightly golden. Remove from the pan using a slotted spoon.

2 Toss the onion in the lemon juice, and add to the frying pan (skillet). Gently fry, stirring, for 3–4 minutes until just beginning to soften.

3 Return the chicken to the pan. Pour in the wine and stock, bring to the boil, cover and simmer gently for 30 minutes.

4 Remove the chicken from the pan, reserving the cooking juices, and keep warm. Bring the juices to the boil, and boil rapidly for 5 minutes.

5 Blend the remaining butter with the flour to form a paste. Reduce the juices to a simmer and spoon the paste into the frying pan (skillet), stirring until thickened.

6 Adjust the seasoning according to taste, stir in the artichoke hearts and cook for a further 2 minutes. Pour the mixture over the chicken and garnish with chopped parsley.

Boned Chicken & Parmesan

It's really very easy to bone a whole chicken, but if you prefer, you can ask your butcher to do this for you.

NUTRITIONAL INFORMATION

Calories	578	Sugars	.......0.4g
Protein	........42g	Fat	.........42g
Carbohydrate	....9g	Saturates	......15g

🕐 35 MINS   🕐 1½ HOURS

SERVES 6

INGREDIENTS

1 chicken, weighing about 2.25 kg/5 lb

8 slices Mortadella or salami

125 g/4½ oz/2 cups fresh white or
　brown breadcrumbs

125 g/4½ oz/1 cup freshly grated
　Parmesan cheese

2 garlic cloves, crushed

6 tbsp chopped fresh basil or parsley

1 egg, beaten

pepper

fresh spring vegetables, to serve

1 Bone the chicken, keeping the skin intact. Dislocate each leg by breaking it at the thigh joint. Cut down each side of the backbone, taking care not to pierce the breast skin.

2 Pull the backbone clear of the flesh and discard. Remove the ribs, severing any attached flesh with a sharp knife.

3 Scrape the flesh from each leg and cut away the bone at the joint with a knife or shears.

4 Use the bones for stock. Lay out the boned chicken on a board, skin side down. Arrange the Mortadella slices over the chicken, overlapping slightly.

5 Put the breadcrumbs, Parmesan, garlic and basil or parsley in a bowl. Season

with pepper to taste and mix together well. Stir in the beaten egg to bind the mixture together. Spoon the mixture down the middle of the boned chicken, roll the meat around it and then tie securely with string.

6 Place in a roasting dish and brush lightly with olive oil. Roast in a preheated oven, 200°C/400°F/Gas Mark 6, for 1½ hours or until the juices run clear when pierced.

7 Serve hot or cold, in slices, with fresh spring vegetables.

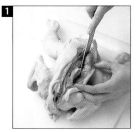

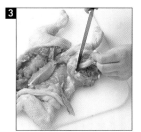

VARIATION

Replace the Mortadella with rashers of streaky bacon, if preferred.

Chicken Cacciatora

This is a popular Italian classic in which browned chicken quarters are cooked in a tomato and (bell) pepper sauce.

NUTRITIONAL INFORMATION

Calories	397	Sugars	.........4g
Protein	........37g	Fat	..........17g
Carbohydrate	...22g	Saturates	.......4g

20 MINS   1 HOUR

SERVES 4

I N G R E D I E N T S

1 roasting chicken, about 1.5 kg/ 3 lb 5 oz,
　cut into 6 or 8 serving pieces

125 g/4½ oz/1 cup plain (all-purpose) flour

3 tbsp olive oil

150 ml/¼ pint/⅔ cup dry white wine

1 green (bell) pepper, deseeded and sliced

1 red (bell) pepper, deseeded and sliced

1 carrot, chopped finely

1 celery stalk, chopped finely

1 garlic clove, crushed

200 g/7 oz can of chopped tomatoes

salt and pepper

1 Rinse and pat dry the chicken pieces with paper towels. Lightly dust them with seasoned flour.

2 Heat the oil in a large frying pan (skillet). Add the chicken and fry over a medium heat until browned all over. Remove from the pan and set aside.

3 Drain off all but 2 tablespoons of the fat in the pan. Add the wine and stir for a few minutes. Then add the (bell) peppers, carrots, celery and garlic, season with salt and pepper to taste and simmer together for about 15 minutes.

4 Add the chopped tomatoes to the pan. Cover and simmer for 30 minutes, stirring often, until the chicken is completely cooked through.

5 Check the seasoning before serving piping hot.

Chicken Lasagne

You can use your favourite mushrooms, such as chanterelles or oyster mushrooms, for this delicately flavoured dish.

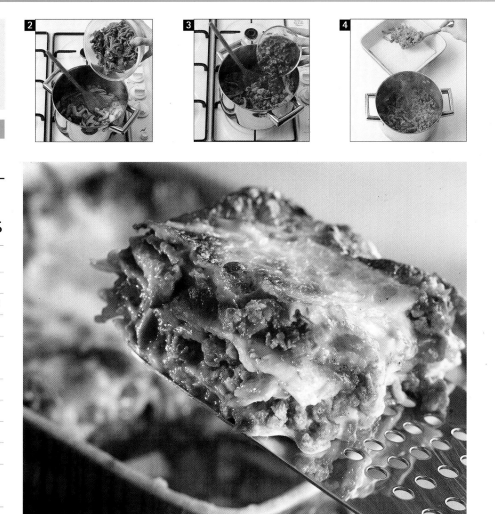

NUTRITIONAL INFORMATION

Calories 708	Sugars 17g
Protein 35g	Fat 35g
Carbohydrate . . .57g	Saturates 14g

40 MINS   1¾ HOURS

SERVES 4

I N G R E D I E N T S

butter, for greasing

14 sheets pre-cooked lasagne

850 ml/1½ pints/3¾ cups Béchamel Sauce

75 g/3 oz/1 cup grated Parmesan cheese

WILD MUSHROOM SAUCE

2 tbsp olive oil

2 garlic cloves, crushed

1 large onion, finely chopped

225 g/8 oz wild mushrooms, sliced

300 g/10½ oz/2½ cups minced
  (ground) chicken

80 g/3 oz chicken livers, finely chopped

115 g/4 oz Parma ham (prosciutto), diced

150 ml/¼ pint/⅔ cup Marsala

285g/10 oz can chopped tomatoes

1 tbsp chopped fresh basil leaves

2 tbsp tomato purée (paste)

salt and pepper

1 To make the chicken and wild mushroom sauce, heat the olive oil in a large saucepan. Add the garlic, onion and mushrooms and cook, stirring frequently, for 6 minutes.

2 Add the minced (ground) chicken, chicken livers and Parma ham (prosciutto) and cook over a low heat for 12 minutes, or until the meat has browned.

3 Stir the Marsala, tomatoes, basil and tomato purée (paste) into the mixture in the pan and cook for 4 minutes. Season with salt and pepper to taste, cover and leave to simmer for 30 minutes. Uncover the pan, stir and leave to simmer for a further 15 minutes.

4 Lightly grease an ovenproof dish with butter. Arrange sheets of lasagne over the base of the dish, spoon over a layer of wild mushroom sauce, then spoon over a layer of Béchamel Sauce. Place another layer of lasagne on top and repeat the process twice, finishing with a layer of Béchamel Sauce. Sprinkle over the grated cheese and bake in a preheated oven at 190°C/375°F/Gas Mark 5 for 35 minutes until golden brown and bubbling. Serve immediately.

Barbecued Chicken

You need a bit of brute force to prepare the chicken, but once marinated it's an easy and tasty candidate for the barbecue (grill).

NUTRITIONAL INFORMATION

Calories 129   Sugars 0g
Protein . . . . .22g   Fat 5g
Carbohydrate . . . .0g   Saturates 1g

2¹/₂ HOURS   30 MINS

SERVES 4

INGREDIENTS

1.5 kg/3 lb 5 oz chicken

grated rind of 1 lemon

4 tbsp lemon juice

2 sprigs rosemary

1 small red chilli, chopped finely

150 ml/¼ pint/⅔ cup olive oil

1 Split the chicken down the breast bone and open it out. Trim off excess fat, and remove the parson's nose, wing and leg tips. Break the leg and wing joints to enable you to pound it flat. This ensures that it cooks evenly. Cover the split chicken with clingfilm (plastic wrap) and pound it as flat as possible with a rolling pin.

2 Mix the lemon rind and juice, rosemary sprigs, chilli and olive oil together in a small bowl. Place the chicken in a large dish and pour over the marinade, turning the chicken to coat it evenly. Cover the dish and leave the chicken to marinate for at least 2 hours.

3 Cook the chicken over a hot barbecue (the coals should be white, and red when fanned) for about 30 minutes, turning it regularly until the skin is golden and crisp. To test if it is cooked, pierce one of the chicken thighs; the juices will run clear, not pink, when it is ready. Serve.

Grilled Chicken

This Italian-style dish is richly flavoured with pesto, which is a mixture of basil, olive oil, pine nuts and Parmesan cheese.

NUTRITIONAL INFORMATION

Calories 787   Sugars 6g
Protein . . . . .45g   Fat 38g
Carbohydrate . . .70g   Saturates 9g

10 MINS   25 MINS

SERVES 4

INGREDIENTS

8 part-boned chicken thighs

olive oil, for brushing

400 ml/14 fl oz/1⅔ cups passata
    (sieved tomatoes)

125 ml/4 fl oz/½ cup green or
    red pesto sauce

12 slices French bread

90 g/3 oz/1 cup freshly grated
    Parmesan cheese

60 g/2 oz/½ cup pine nuts or flaked
    (slivered) almonds

salad leaves, to serve

1 Arrange the chicken in a single layer in a wide flameproof dish and brush lightly with oil. Place under a preheated grill (broiler) for about 15 minutes, turning occasionally, until golden brown.

COOK'S TIP

Although leaving the skin on the chicken means that it will have a higher fat content, many people like the rich taste and crispy skin especially when it is blackened by the barbecue (grill). The skin also keeps in the cooking juices.

2 Pierce the chicken with a skewer to test if it is cooked through – the juices will run clear, not pink, when it is ready.

3 Pour off any excess fat. Warm the passata (sieved tomatoes) and half the pesto sauce in a small pan and pour over the chicken. Grill (broil) for a few more minutes, turning until coated.

4 Meanwhile, spread the remaining pesto on to the slices of bread. Arrange the bread over the chicken and sprinkle with the Parmesan cheese. Scatter the pine nuts over the cheese. Grill (broil) for 2–3 minutes, or until browned and bubbling. Serve with salad leaves.

Chicken with Green Olives

Olives are a popular flavouring for poultry and game in the Apulia region of Italy, where this recipe originates.

NUTRITIONAL INFORMATION

Calories 614   Sugars 6g
Protein . . . . .34g   Fat 30g
Carbohydrate . . .49g   Saturates 11g

15 MINS   1½ HOURS

SERVES 4

INGREDIENTS

3 tbsp olive oil

25 g/1 oz/2 tbsp butter

4 chicken breasts, part boned

1 large onion, finely chopped

2 garlic cloves, crushed

2 red, yellow or green (bell) peppers, cored,
 seeded and cut into large pieces

250 g/9 oz button mushrooms, sliced
 or quartered

175 g/6 oz tomatoes, skinned and halved

150 ml/¼ pint/⅔ cup dry white wine

175 g/6 oz/1½ cups stoned (pitted)
 green olives

4–6 tbsp double (heavy) cream

400 g/14 oz dried pasta

salt and pepper

chopped flat leaf parsley, to garnish

1 Heat 2 tbsp of the oil and the butter in a frying pan (skillet). Add the chicken breasts and fry until golden brown all over. Remove the chicken from the pan.

2 Add the onion and garlic to the pan and fry over a medium heat until beginning to soften. Add the (bell) peppers and mushrooms and cook for 2–3 minutes.

3 Add the tomatoes and season to taste with salt and pepper. Transfer the vegetables to a casserole and arrange the chicken on top.

4 Add the wine to the pan and bring to the boil. Pour the wine over the chicken. Cover and cook in a preheated oven at 180°C/350°F/Gas Mark 4 for 50 minutes.

5 Add the olives to the casserole and mix in. Pour in the cream, cover and return to the oven for 10–20 minutes.

6 Meanwhile, bring a large pan of lightly salted water to the boil. Add the pasta and the remaining oil and cook for 8–10 minutes or until tender, but still firm to the bite. Drain the pasta well and transfer to a serving dish.

7 Arrange the chicken on top of the pasta, spoon over the sauce, garnish with the parsley and serve immediately. Alternatively, place the pasta in a large serving bowl and serve separately.

Chicken & Balsamic Vinegar

A rich caramelized sauce, flavoured with balsamic vinegar and wine, adds a piquant flavour. The chicken needs to be marinated overnight.

NUTRITIONAL INFORMATION

Calories 148	Sugars 0.2g
Protein 11g	Fat 8g
Carbohydrate ...0.2g	Saturates 3g

10 MINS   35 MINS

SERVES 4

INGREDIENTS

4 chicken thighs, boned

2 garlic cloves, crushed

200 ml/7 fl oz/¾ cup red wine

3 tbsp white wine vinegar

1 tbsp oil

15 g/½ oz/1 tbsp butter

6 shallots

3 tbsp balsamic vinegar

2 tbsp fresh thyme

salt and pepper

cooked polenta or rice, to serve

1 Using a sharp knife, make a few slashes in the skin of the chicken. Brush the chicken with the crushed garlic and place in a non-metallic dish.

2 Pour the wine and white wine vinegar over the chicken and season with salt and pepper to taste. Cover and leave to marinate in the refrigerator overnight.

3 Remove the chicken pieces with a perforated spoon, draining well, and reserve the marinade.

4 Heat the oil and butter in a frying pan (skillet). Add the shallots and cook for 2–3 minutes or until they begin to soften.

5 Add the chicken pieces to the pan and cook for 3-4 minutes, turning, until browned all over. Reduce the heat and add half of the reserved marinade. Cover and cook for 15–20 minutes, adding more marinade when necessary.

6 Once the chicken is tender, add the balsamic vinegar and thyme and cook for a further 4 minutes.

7 Transfer the chicken and marinade to serving plates and serve with polenta or rice.

COOK'S TIP

To make the chicken pieces look a little neater, use wooden skewers to hold them togetheror secure them with a length of string.

Chicken Scallops

Served in scallop shells, this delicately flavoured dish makes a stylish presentation for a starter or a light lunch.

NUTRITIONAL INFORMATION

Calories 532	Sugars 3g	
Protein 25g	Fat 34g	
Carbohydrate ...33g	Saturates 14g	

20 MINS   25 MINS

SERVES 4

INGREDIENTS

175 g/6 oz short-cut macaroni, or other
    short pasta shapes

3 tbsp vegetable oil, plus extra for brushing

1 onion, chopped finely

3 rashers unsmoked collar or back bacon,
    rind removed, chopped

125 g/4½ oz button mushrooms, sliced
    thinly or chopped

175 g/6 oz/¾ cup cooked chicken, diced

175 ml/6 fl oz/¾ cup crème fraîche

4 tbsp dry breadcrumbs

60 g/2 oz/½ cup mature (sharp) Cheddar,
    grated

salt and pepper

flat-leaf parsley sprigs, to garnish

1 Cook the pasta in a large pan of boiling salted water, to which you have added 1 tablespoon of the oil, for 8–10 minutes or until tender. Drain the pasta, return to the pan and cover.

2 Heat the grill (broiler) to medium. Heat the remaining oil in a pan over medium heat and fry the onion until it is translucent. Add the chopped bacon and mushrooms and cook for 3–4 minutes, stirring once or twice.

3 Stir in the pasta, chicken and crème fraîche and season to taste with salt and pepper.

4 Brush four large scallop shells with oil. Spoon in the chicken mixture and smooth to make neat mounds.

5 Mix together the breadcrumbs and cheese, and sprinkle over the top of the shells. Press the topping lightly into the chicken mixture, and grill (broil) for 4–5 minutes, until golden brown and bubbling. Garnish with sprigs of flat-leaf parsley, and serve hot.

Chicken & Lobster on Penne

While this is certainly a treat to get the taste buds tingling, it is not as extravagantly expensive as it sounds.

NUTRITIONAL INFORMATION

Calories	696	Sugars	.........4g
Protein	........59g	Fat	..........32g
Carbohydrate	...45g	Saturates	.......9g

20 MINS   30 MINS

SERVES 6

I N G R E D I E N T S

butter, for greasing

6 chicken suprêmes

450 g/1 lb dried penne rigate

6 tbsp extra virgin olive oil

90 g/3 oz/1 cup freshly grated
   Parmesan cheese

salt

F I L L I N G

115 g/4 oz lobster meat, chopped

2 shallots, very finely chopped

2 figs, chopped

1 tbsp Marsala

2 tbsp breadcrumbs

1 large egg, beaten

salt and pepper

COOK'S TIP

The cut of chicken known as suprême consists of the breast and wing. It is always skinned.

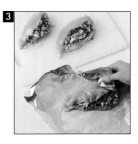

1 Grease 6 pieces of foil large enough to enclose each chicken suprême and lightly grease a baking tray (cookie sheet).

2 Place all of the filling ingredients into a mixing bowl and blend together thoroughly with a spoon.

3 Cut a pocket in each chicken suprême with a sharp knife and fill with the lobster mixture. Wrap each chicken suprême in foil, place the parcels on the greased baking tray (cookie sheet) and bake in a preheated oven at 200°C/400°F/Gas Mark 6 for 30 minutes.

4 Meanwhile, bring a large pan of lightly salted water to the boil. Add the pasta and 1 tablespoon of the olive oil and cook for about 10 minutes, or until tender but still firm to the bite. Drain the pasta thoroughly and transfer to a large serving plate. Sprinkle over the remaining olive oil and the grated Parmesan cheese, set aside and keep warm.

5 Carefully remove the foil from around the chicken suprêmes. Slice the suprêmes very thinly, arrange over the pasta and serve immediately.

Skewered Chicken Spirals

These unusual chicken kebabs (kabobs) have a wonderful Italian flavour, and the bacon helps keep them moist during cooking.

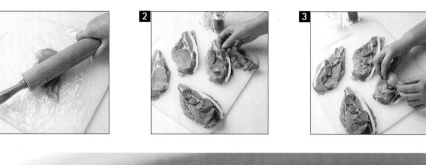

NUTRITIONAL INFORMATION

Calories 231	Sugars 1g	
Protein 29g	Fat 13g	
Carbohydrate 1g	Saturates 5g	

15 MINS   10 MINS

SERVES 4

I N G R E D I E N T S

4 skinless, boneless chicken breasts

1 garlic clove, crushed

2 tbsp tomato purée (paste)

4 slices smoked back bacon

large handful of fresh basil leaves

oil for brushing

salt and pepper

1 Spread out a piece of chicken between two sheets of cling film (plastic wrap) and beat firmly with a rolling pin to flatten the chicken to an even thickness. Repeat with the remaining chicken breasts.

2 Mix the garlic and tomato purée (paste) and spread over the chicken. Lay a bacon slice over each, then scatter with the basil. Season with salt and pepper.

3 Roll up each piece of chicken firmly, then cut into thick slices.

4 Thread the slices on to 4 skewers, making sure the skewer holds the chicken in a spiral shape.

5 Brush lightly with oil and cook on a preheated hot barbecue (grill) or grill (broiler) for about 10 minutes, turning once. Serve hot with a green salad.

Chicken with Orange Sauce

The refreshing combination of chicken and orange sauce makes this a perfect dish for a warm summer evening.

NUTRITIONAL INFORMATION

Calories 797	Sugars 28g	
Protein 59g	Fat 25g	
Carbohydrate ...77g	Saturates 6g	

🍴 🍴 🍴

15 MINS   🕐 25 MINS

SERVES 4

INGREDIENTS

30 ml/1 fl oz/⅛ cup rapeseed oil

3 tbsp olive oil

4 x 225 g/8 oz chicken suprêmes

150 ml/¼ pint/⅔ cup orange brandy

15 g/½ oz/2 tbsp plain (all-purpose) flour

150 ml/¼ pint/⅔ cup freshly squeezed orange juice

25 g/1 oz courgette (zucchini), cut into matchstick strips

25 g/1 oz red (bell) pepper, cut into matchstick strips

25 g/1 oz leek, finely shredded

400 g/14 oz dried wholemeal (whole-wheat) spaghetti

3 large oranges, peeled and cut into segments

rind of 1 orange, cut into very fine strips

2 tbsp chopped fresh tarragon

150 ml/¼ pint/⅔ cup fromage frais or ricotta cheese

salt and pepper

fresh tarragon leaves, to garnish

1 Heat the rapeseed oil and 1 tablespoon of the olive oil in a frying pan (skillet). Add the chicken and cook quickly until golden brown. Add the orange brandy and cook for 3 minutes. Sprinkle over the flour and cook for 2 minutes.

2 Lower the heat and add the orange juice, courgette (zucchini), (bell) pepper and leek and season. Simmer for 5 minutes until the sauce has thickened.

3 Meanwhile, bring a pan of salted water to the boil. Add the spaghetti and 1 tablespoon of the olive oil and cook for 10 minutes. Drain the spaghetti, transfer to a serving dish and drizzle over the remaining oil.

4 Add half of the orange segments, half of the orange rind, the tarragon and fromage frais or ricotta cheese to the sauce in the pan and cook for 3 minutes.

5 Place the chicken on top of the pasta, pour over a little sauce, garnish with orange segments, rind and tarragon. Serve immediately.

Chicken Pepperonata

All the sunshine colours and flavours of Italy are combined in this satisfying dish, which is surprisingly easy to make.

NUTRITIONAL INFORMATION

Calories ....328 Sugars 7g
Protein ....35g Fat 15g
Carbohydrate ...13g Saturates 4g

15 MINS   40 MINS

SERVES 4

INGREDIENTS

8 skinless chicken thighs

2 tbsp wholemeal (whole wheat) flour

2 tbsp olive oil

1 small onion, sliced thinly

1 garlic clove, crushed

1 each large red, yellow and green (bell)
    peppers, sliced thinly

400 g/14 oz can chopped tomatoes

1 tbsp chopped oregano

salt and pepper

fresh oregano, to garnish

crusty wholemeal (whole wheat) bread,
    to serve

1 Remove the skin from the chicken thighs and toss in the flour.

2 Heat the oil in a wide frying pan (skillet) and fry the chicken quickly until sealed and lightly browned, then remove from the pan.

3 Add the onion to the pan and gently fry until soft. Add the garlic, (bell) peppers, tomatoes and oregano, then bring to the boil, stirring.

4 Arrange the chicken over the vegetables, season well with salt and pepper, then cover the pan tightly and simmer for 20–25 minutes or until the chicken is completely cooked and tender.

5 Season with salt and pepper to taste, garnish with oregano and serve with crusty wholemeal (whole wheat) bread.

COOK'S TIP

For extra flavour, halve the (bell) peppers and grill (broil) under a preheated grill (broiler) until the skins are charred. Leave to cool then remove the skins and seeds. Slice the (bell) peppers thinly and use in the recipe.

Roman Chicken

This classic Roman dish makes an ideal light meal. It is equally good cold and could be taken on a picnic – serve with bread to mop up the juices.

NUTRITIONAL INFORMATION

Calories	317	Sugars	8g
Protein	22g	Fat	22g
Carbohydrate	9g	Saturates	4g

35 MINS   1 HOUR

SERVES 4

I N G R E D I E N T S

4 tbsp olive oil

6 chicken pieces

2 garlic cloves, crushed with 1 tsp salt

1 large red onion, sliced

4 large mixed red, green and yellow
   (bell) peppers, cored, deseeded and
   cut into strips

125 g/4½ oz/⅔ cup pitted green olives

½ quantity tomato sauce (see page 142)

300 ml/½ pint/1¼ cups hot chicken stock

2 sprigs fresh marjoram

salt and pepper

1 Heat half of the oil in a flameproof casserole and brown the chicken pieces on all sides. Remove the chicken and set aside.

2 Add the remaining oil to the casserole and fry the garlic and onion until softened. Stir in the (bell) peppers, olives and tomato sauce.

3 Return the chicken to the casserole with the stock and marjoram. Cover the casserole and simmer for about 45 minutes or until the chicken is tender. Season with salt and pepper to taste and serve with crusty bread.

Pasta with Chicken Sauce

Spinach ribbon noodles, topped with a rich tomato sauce and creamy chicken, make a very appetizing dish.

NUTRITIONAL INFORMATION

Calories 995	Sugars 8g	
Protein 36g	Fat 74g	
Carbohydrate . . .50g	Saturates 34g	

15 MINS   45 MINS

SERVES 4

INGREDIENTS

250 g/9 oz fresh green tagliatelle

1 tbsp olive oil

salt

fresh basil leaves, to garnish

TOMATO SAUCE

2 tbsp olive oil

1 small onion, chopped

1 garlic clove, chopped

400 g/14 oz can chopped tomatoes

2 tbsp chopped fresh parsley

1 tsp dried oregano

2 bay leaves

2 tbsp tomato purée (paste)

1 tsp sugar

salt and pepper

CHICKEN SAUCE

60 g/2 oz/4 tbsp unsalted butter

400 g/14 oz boned chicken breasts,
    skinned and cut into thin strips

90 g/3 oz/¾ cup blanched almonds

300 ml/½ pint/1¼ cups double
    (heavy) cream

salt and pepper

1 To make the tomato sauce, heat the oil in a pan over a medium heat. Add the onion and fry until translucent. Add the garlic and fry for 1 minute. Stir in the tomatoes, parsley, oregano, bay leaves, tomato purée (paste), sugar and salt and pepper to taste, bring to the boil and simmer, uncovered, for 15–20 minutes, until reduced by half. Remove the pan from the heat and discard the bay leaves.

2 To make the chicken sauce, melt the butter in a frying pan (skillet) over a medium heat. Add the chicken and almonds and stir-fry for 5–6 minutes, or until the chicken is cooked through.

3 Meanwhile, bring the cream to the boil in a small pan over a low heat and boil for about 10 minutes, until reduced by almost half. Pour the cream over the chicken and almonds, stir and season to taste with salt and pepper. Set aside and keep warm.

4 Bring a large pan of lightly salted water to the boil. Add the tagliatelle and olive oil and cook for 8–10 minutes until tender, but still firm to the bite. Drain and transfer to a warm serving dish. Spoon over the tomato sauce and arrange the chicken sauce down the centre. Garnish with the basil leaves and serve immediately.

Italian Chicken Parcels

This cooking method makes the chicken aromatic and succulent, and reduces the oil needed as the chicken and vegetables cook in their own juices.

NUTRITIONAL INFORMATION

Calories 234   Sugars 5g
Protein . . . . .28g   Fat 12g
Carbohydrate . . . .5g   Saturates 5g

25 MINS   30 MINS

SERVES 6

INGREDIENTS

1 tbsp olive oil

6 skinless chicken breast fillets

250 g/9 oz/2 cups Mozzarella cheese

500 g/1 lb 2 oz/3½ cups courgettes
   (zucchini), sliced

6 large tomatoes, sliced

1 small bunch fresh basil or oregano

pepper

rice or pasta, to serve

1 Cut 6 pieces of foil, each measuring about 25 cm/10 inches square. Brush the foil squares lightly with oil and set aside until required.

2 With a sharp knife, slash each chicken breast at regular intervals. Slice the Mozzarella cheese and place between the cuts in the chicken.

COOK'S TIP

To aid cooking, place the vegetables and chicken on the shiny side of the foil so that once the parcel is wrapped up the dull surface of the foil is facing outwards. This ensures that the heat is absorbed into the parcel and not reflected away from it.

3 Divide the courgettes (zucchini) and tomatoes between the pieces of foil and sprinkle with pepper to taste. Tear or roughly chop the basil or oregano and scatter over the vegetables in each parcel.

4 Place the chicken on top of each pile of vegetables then wrap in the foil to enclose the chicken and vegetables, tucking in the ends.

5 Place on a baking tray (cookie sheet) and bake in a preheated oven, 200°C/400°C/Gas Mark 6, for about 30 minutes.

6 To serve, unwrap each foil parcel and serve with rice or pasta.

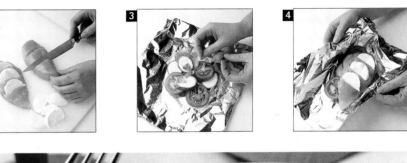

Pasta & Chicken Medley

Strips of cooked chicken are tossed with coloured pasta, grapes and carrot sticks in a pesto-flavoured dressing.

NUTRITIONAL INFORMATION

Calories	609	Sugars	........11g
Protein	........26g	Fat	.........38g
Carbohydrate	...45g	Saturates	.......6g

30 MINS   10 MINS

SERVES 2

INGREDIENTS

125–150 g/4½–5½ oz dried pasta shapes, such as twists or bows

1 tbsp oil

2 tbsp mayonnaise

2 tsp bottled pesto sauce

1 tbsp soured cream or natural fromage frais

175 g/6 oz cooked skinless, boneless chicken meat

1–2 celery stalks

125 g/4½ oz/1 cup black grapes (preferably seedless)

1 large carrot, trimmed

salt and pepper

celery leaves, to garnish

FRENCH DRESSING

1 tbsp wine vinegar

3 tbsp extra-virgin olive oil

salt and pepper

1 To make the French dressing, whisk all the ingredients together until smooth.

2 Cook the pasta with the oil for 8–10 minutes in plenty of boiling salted water until just tender. Drain thoroughly, rinse and drain again. Transfer to a bowl and mix in 1 tablespoon of the French dressing while hot; set aside until cold.

3 Combine the mayonnaise, pesto sauce and soured cream or fromage frais in a bowl, and season to taste.

4 Cut the chicken into narrow strips. Cut the celery diagonally into narrow slices. Reserve a few grapes for garnish, halve the rest and remove any pips (seeds). Cut the carrot into narrow julienne strips.

5 Add the chicken, the celery, the halved grapes, the carrot and the mayonnaise mixture to the pasta, and toss thoroughly. Check the seasoning, adding more salt and pepper if necessary.

6 Arrange the pasta mixture on two plates and garnish with the reserved black grapes and the celery leaves.

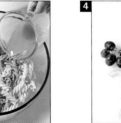

Parma-Wrapped Chicken

Stuffed with ricotta, nutmeg and spinach, then wrapped with wafer thin slices of Parma ham (prosciutto) and gently cooked in white wine.

NUTRITIONAL INFORMATION

Calories 426   Sugars 4g
Protein ....44g   Fat 21g
Carbohydrate ....9g   Saturates 8g

30 MINS   45 MINS

SERVES 4

INGREDIENTS

125 g/4½ oz/½ cup frozen spinach, defrosted

125 g/4½ oz/½ cup ricotta cheese

pinch of grated nutmeg

4 skinless, boneless chicken breasts, each weighing 175 g/6 oz

4 Parma ham (prosciutto) slices

25 g/1 oz/2 tbsp butter

1 tbsp olive oil

12 small onions or shallots

125 g/4½ oz/1½ cups button mushrooms, sliced

1 tbsp plain (all-purpose) flour

150 ml/¼ pint/⅔ cup dry white or red wine

300 ml/½ pint/1¼ cups chicken stock

salt and pepper

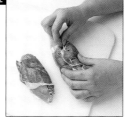

1 Put the spinach into a sieve (strainer) and press out the water with a spoon. Mix with the ricotta and nutmeg and season with salt and pepper to taste.

2 Using a sharp knife, slit each chicken breast through the side and enlarge each cut to form a pocket. Fill with the spinach mixture, reshape the chicken breasts, wrap each breast tightly in a slice of ham and secure with cocktail sticks. Cover and chill in the refrigerator.

3 Heat the butter and oil in a frying pan (skillet) and brown the chicken breasts for 2 minutes on each side. Transfer the chicken to a large, shallow ovenproof dish and keep warm until required.

4 Fry the onions and mushrooms for 2–3 minutes until lightly browned. Stir in the plain (all-purpose) flour, then gradually add the wine and stock. Bring to the boil, stirring constantly. Season with salt and pepper and spoon the mixture around the chicken.

5 Cook the chicken uncovered in a preheated oven, 200°C/400°F/Gas Mark 6, for 20 minutes. Turn the breasts over and cook for a further 10 minutes. Remove the cocktail sticks and serve with the sauce, together with carrot purée and green beans, if wished.

Chicken Tortellini

Tortellini were said to have been created in the image of the goddess Venus's navel. Whatever the story, they are a delicious blend of Italian flavours.

NUTRITIONAL INFORMATION

Calories 635	Sugars 4g	
Protein 31g	Fat 36g	
Carbohydrate . . .50g	Saturates 16g	

🕐 1 HOUR   ⏱ 35 MINS

SERVES 4

I N G R E D I E N T S

115 g/4 oz boned chicken breast, skinned

60 g/2 oz Parma ham (prosciutto)

40 g/1½ oz cooked spinach, well drained

1 tbsp finely chopped onion

2 tbsp freshly grated Parmesan cheese

pinch of ground allspice

1 egg, beaten

450 g/1 lb pasta dough

salt and pepper

2 tbsp chopped fresh parsley, to garnish

S A U C E

300 ml/½ pint/1¼ cups single (light) cream

2 garlic cloves, crushed

115 g/4 oz button mushrooms, thinly sliced

4 tbsp freshly grated Parmesan cheese

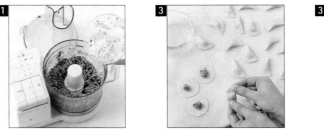
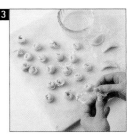

1 Bring a saucepan of seasoned water to the boil. Add the chicken and poach for about 10 minutes. Leave to cool slightly, then put in a food processor with the Parma ham (prosciutto), spinach and onion and process until finely chopped. Stir in the Parmesan cheese, allspice and egg and season with salt and pepper to taste.

2 Thinly roll out the pasta dough and cut into 4–5 cm/1½–2 inch rounds.

3 Place ½ tsp of the filling in the centre of each round. Fold the pieces in half and press the edges to seal. Then wrap each piece around your index finger, cross over the ends and curl the rest of the dough backwards to make a navel shape. Re-roll the trimmings and repeat until all of the dough is used up.

4 Bring a saucepan of salted water to the boil. Add the tortellini, in batches, bring back to the boil and cook for

5 minutes. Drain well and transfer to a serving dish.

5 To make the sauce, bring the cream and garlic to the boil in a small pan, then simmer for 3 minutes. Add the mushrooms and half of the cheese, season with salt and pepper to taste and simmer for 2–3 minutes. Pour the sauce over the chicken tortellini. Sprinkle over the remaining Parmesan cheese, garnish with the parsley and serve.

Rich Chicken Casserole

This casserole is packed with the sunshine flavours of Italy.
Sun-dried tomatoes add a wonderful richness.

NUTRITIONAL INFORMATION

Calories	320	Sugars	.........8g
Protein	........34g	Fat	..........17g
Carbohydrate	....8g	Saturates	.......4g

15 MINS   1¼ HOURS

SERVES 4

INGREDIENTS

8 chicken thighs

2 tbsp olive oil

1 medium red onion, sliced

2 garlic cloves, crushed

1 large red (bell) pepper, sliced thickly

thinly pared rind and juice of 1 small orange

125 ml/4 fl oz/½ cup chicken stock

400 g/14 oz can chopped tomatoes

25 g/1 oz/½ cup sun-dried tomatoes,
    thinly sliced

1 tbsp chopped fresh thyme

50 g/1¾ oz/½ cup pitted black olives

salt and pepper

orange rind and thyme sprigs, to garnish

crusty fresh bread, to serve

1 In a heavy or non-stick large frying pan (skillet), fry the chicken without fat over a fairly high heat, turning occasionally until golden brown. Using a slotted spoon, drain off any excess fat from the chicken and transfer to a flameproof casserole.

2 Add the oil to the pan and fry the onion, garlic and (bell) pepper over a moderate heat for 3–4 minutes. Transfer the vegetables to the casserole.

3 Add the orange rind and juice, chicken stock, canned tomatoes and sun-dried tomatoes to the casserole and stir to combine.

4 Bring to the boil then cover the casserole with a lid and simmer very gently over a low heat for about 1 hour, stirring occasionally. Add the chopped fresh thyme and pitted black olives, then adjust the seasoning with salt and pepper to taste.

5 Scatter orange rind and thyme over the casserole to garnish, and serve with crusty bread.

COOK'S TIP

Sun-dried tomatoes
have a dense texture and
concentrated taste, and these
elements add intense flavour to
slow-cooking casseroles.

Chicken with Vegetables

This dish combines succulent chicken with tasty vegetables, flavoured with wine and olives.

NUTRITIONAL INFORMATION

Calories 470	Sugars 7g	
Protein 29g	Fat 34g	
Carbohydrate 7g	Saturates 16g	

20 MINS   1¹/₂ HOURS

SERVES 4

I N G R E D I E N T S

4 chicken breasts, part boned

25 g/1 oz/2 tbsp butter

2 tbsp olive oil

1 large onion, chopped finely

2 garlic cloves, crushed

2 (bell) peppers, red, yellow or green, cored,
    deseeded and cut into large pieces

225 g/8 oz large closed cup mushrooms,
    sliced or quartered

175 g/6 oz tomatoes, peeled and halved

150 ml/¹/₄ pint/²/₃ cup dry white wine

125–175 g/4–6 oz green olives, pitted

4–6 tbsp double (heavy) cream

salt and pepper

chopped flat-leaf parsley, to garnish

1 Season the chicken with salt and pepper to taste. Heat the oil and butter in a frying pan (skillet), add the chicken and fry until browned all over. Remove the chicken from the pan.

2 Add the onion and garlic to the frying pan (skillet) and fry gently until just beginning to soften. Add the (bell) peppers to the pan with the mushrooms and continue to cook for a few minutes longer, stirring occasionally.

3 Add the tomatoes and plenty of seasoning to the pan and then transfer the vegetable mixture to an ovenproof casserole. Place the chicken on the bed of vegetables.

4 Add the wine to the frying pan (skillet) and bring to the boil. Pour the wine over the chicken and cover the casserole tightly. Cook in a preheated oven, 180°C/350°F/Gas Mark 4, for 50 minutes.

5 Add the olives to the chicken, mix lightly then pour on the cream. Re-cover the casserole and return to the oven for 10–20 minutes or until the chicken is very tender.

6 Adjust the seasoning and serve the pieces of chicken, surrounded by the vegetables and sauce, with pasta or tiny new potatoes. Sprinkle with chopped parsley to garnish.

Chicken & Seafood Parcels

These mouth-watering mini-parcels of chicken and prawns (shrimp) on a bed of pasta will delight your guests.

NUTRITIONAL INFORMATION

Calories	799	Sugars	.........5g
Protein	........50g	Fat	..........45g
Carbohydrate	...51g	Saturates	......13g

🐟 🐟 🐟 🐟

45 MINS   25 MINS

SERVES 4

I N G R E D I E N T S

60 g/2 oz/4 tbsp butter, plus extra
   for greasing

4 x 200 g/7 oz chicken suprêmes, trimmed

115 g/4 oz large spinach leaves, trimmed
   and blanched in hot salted water

4 slices of Parma ham (prosciutto)

12–16 raw tiger prawns (shrimp), shelled
   and deveined

450 g/1 lb dried tagliatelle

1 tbsp olive oil

3 leeks, shredded

1 large carrot, grated

150 ml/¼ pint/⅔ cup thick mayonnaise

2 large cooked beetroot (beet)

salt

1 Grease 4 large pieces of foil and set aside. Place each suprême between 2 pieces of baking parchment and pound with a rolling pin to flatten.

2 Divide half of the spinach between the suprêmes, add a slice of ham to each and top with more spinach. Place 3-4 prawns (shrimp) on top of the spinach. Fold the pointed end of the suprême over the prawns (shrimp), then fold over again to form a parcel. Wrap in

foil, place on a baking tray (cookie sheet) and bake in a preheated oven at 200°C/400°F/Gas Mark 6 for 20 minutes.

3 Meanwhile, bring a saucepan of salted water to the boil. Add the pasta and oil and cook for 8–10 minutes or until tender. Drain and transfer to a serving dish.

4 Melt the butter in a frying pan (skillet). Fry the leeks and carrots for 3 minutes. Transfer the vegetables to the centre of the pasta.

5 Work the mayonnaise and 1 beetroot (beet) in a food processor or blender until smooth. Rub through a strainer and pour around the pasta and vegetables.

6 Cut the remaining beetroot (beet) into diamond shapes and place them neatly around the mayonnaise. Remove the foil from the chicken and, using a sharp knife, cut the suprêmes into thin slices. Arrange the chicken and prawn (shrimp) slices on top of the vegetables and pasta, and serve.

Chicken Pasta Bake

Tender lean chicken is baked with pasta in a creamy low-fat sauce which contrasts well with the fennel and the sweetness of the raisins.

NUTRITIONAL INFORMATION

Calories ....380 Sugars 15g
Protein ....39g Fat 14g
Carbohydrate ...27g Saturates 6g

15 MINS   45 MINS

SERVES 4

I N G R E D I E N T S

2 bulbs fennel

2 medium red onions, finely shredded

1 tbsp lemon juice

125 g/4½ oz button mushrooms

1 tbsp olive oil

225 g/8 oz penne (quills)

60 g/2 oz/⅓ cup raisins

225 g/8 oz lean, boneless cooked chicken,
skinned and shredded

375 g/13 oz low-fat soft cheese with garlic
and herbs

125 g/4½ oz low-fat Mozzarella cheese,
thinly sliced

2 tbsp Parmesan cheese, grated

salt and pepper

chopped fennel fronds, to garnish

1 Preheat the oven to 200°C/400°F/Gas Mark 6. Trim the fennel, reserving the green fronds, and slice the bulbs thinly.

2 Generously coat the onions in the lemon juice. Quarter the mushrooms.

3 Heat the oil in a large frying pan (skillet) and fry the fennel, onion and mushrooms for 4–5 minutes, stirring, until just softened. Season well, transfer the mixture to a large bowl and set aside.

4 Bring a pan of lightly salted water to the boil and cook the penne (quills) according to the instructions on the packet until just cooked. Drain and mix the pasta with the vegetables.

5 Stir the raisins and chicken into the pasta mixture. Soften the soft cheese by beating it, then mix into the pasta and chicken – the heat from the pasta should make the cheese melt slightly.

6 Put the mixture into an ovenproof baking dish and transfer to a baking tray (cookie sheet). Arrange slices of Mozzarella cheese over the top and sprinkle with the grated Parmesan.

7 Bake in the oven for 20–25 minutes until golden-brown.

8 Garnish with chopped fennel fronds and serve hot.

Chicken & Tomato Lasagne

This variation of the traditional beef dish has layers of pasta and chicken or turkey baked in red wine, tomatoes and a delicious cheese sauce.

NUTRITIONAL INFORMATION

Calories 550	Sugars 11g
Protein 35g	Fat 29g
Carbohydrate . . .34g	Saturates 12g

🕑 20 MINS   🕐 1¼ HOURS

SERVES 4

I N G R E D I E N T S

350 g/12 oz fresh lasagne (about 9 sheets)
  or 150 g/5½ oz dried lasagne
  (about 9 sheets)

1 tbsp olive oil

1 red onion, finely chopped

1 garlic clove, crushed

100 g/3½ oz mushrooms, wiped and sliced

350 g/12 oz chicken or turkey breast, cut
  into chunks

150 ml/¼ pint/⅔ cup red wine, diluted with
  100 ml/3½ fl oz/scant ⅓ cup water

250 g/9 oz passata (sieved tomatoes)

1 tsp sugar

B E C H A M E L   S A U C E

75 g/2¾ oz/5 tbsp butter

50 g/1¾ oz plain (all-purpose) flour

600 ml/1 pint/2½ cups milk

1 egg, beaten

75 g/2¾ oz Parmesan cheese, grated

salt and pepper

1 Cook the lasagne in a pan of boiling water according to the instructions on the packet. Lightly grease a deep ovenproof dish.

2 Heat the oil in a pan. Add the onion and garlic and cook for 3–4 minutes. Add the mushrooms and chicken and stir-fry for 4 minutes or until the meat browns.

3 Add the wine, bring to the boil, then simmer for 5 minutes. Stir in the passata (sieved tomatoes) and sugar and cook for 3–5 minutes until the meat is tender and cooked through. The sauce should have thickened, but still be quite runny.

4 To make the Béchamel Sauce, melt the butter in a pan, stir in the flour and cook for 2 minutes. Remove the pan from the heat and gradually add the milk, mixing to form a smooth sauce. Return the pan to the heat and bring to the boil, stirring until thickened. Leave to cool slightly, then beat in the egg and half of the cheese. Season to taste.

5 Place 3 sheets of lasagne in the base of the dish and spread with half of the chicken mixture. Repeat the layers. Top with the last 3 sheets of lasagne, pour over the Béchamel Sauce and sprinkle with the Parmesan. Bake in a preheated oven, at 190°C/375°F/Gas Mark 5, for 30 minutes until golden and the pasta is cooked.

Tagliatelle & Chicken Sauce

Spinach ribbon noodles covered with a rich tomato sauce and topped with creamy chicken makes a very appetizing dish.

NUTRITIONAL INFORMATION

Calories 853	Sugars 6g
Protein 32g	Fat 71g
Carbohydrate ...23g	Saturates 34g

30 MINS   25 MINS

SERVES 4

INGREDIENTS

Tomato sauce (see page 142)

225 g/8 oz fresh green ribbon noodles

1 tbsp olive oil

salt

basil leaves, to garnish

CHICKEN SAUCE

60 g/2 oz/¼ cup unsalted butter

400 g/14 oz boned, skinned chicken
   breast, thinly sliced

90 g/3 oz/¾ cup blanched almonds

300 ml/½ pint/1¼ cups double
   (heavy) cream

salt and pepper

basil leaves, to garnish

1 Make the tomato sauce, and keep warm.

2 To make the chicken sauce, melt the butter in a pan over a medium heat and fry the chicken strips and almonds for 5–6 minutes, stirring frequently, until the chicken is cooked through.

3 Meanwhile, pour the cream into a small pan over a low heat, bring it to the boil and boil for about 10 minutes, until reduced by almost half. Pour the cream over the chicken and almonds, stir well, and season with salt and pepper to taste. Set aside and keep warm.

4 Cook the pasta in a pan of boiling salted water, to which you have added the oil, for 8–10 minutes or until tender. Drain, then return to the pan, cover and keep warm.

5 Turn the pasta into a warmed serving dish and spoon the tomato sauce over it. Spoon the chicken and cream over the centre, scatter over the basil leaves and serve at once.

Chicken & Spinach Lasagne

A delicious pasta bake with all the colours of the Italian flag – red tomatoes, green spinach and pasta, and white chicken and sauce.

NUTRITIONAL INFORMATION

Calories 358   Sugars 12g
Protein . . . . .42g   Fat 9g
Carbohydrate . . .22g   Saturates 4g

25 MINS   50 MINS

SERVES 4

INGREDIENTS

350 g/12 oz frozen chopped spinach, thawed and drained

½ tsp ground nutmeg

450 g/1 lb lean, cooked chicken meat, skinned and diced

4 sheets no-pre-cook lasagne verde

1½ tbsp cornflour (cornstarch)

425 ml/15 fl oz/1¾ cups skimmed milk

4 tbsp Parmesan cheese, freshly grated

salt and pepper

TOMATO SAUCE

400 g/14 oz can chopped tomatoes

1 medium onion, finely chopped

1 garlic clove, crushed (minced)

150 ml/5 fl oz/⅔ cup white wine

3 tbsp tomato purée (paste)

1 tsp dried oregano

green salad, to serve

1 Preheat the oven to 200°C/400°F/Gas Mark 6. For the tomato sauce, place the tomatoes in a saucepan and stir in the onion, garlic, wine, tomato purée (paste) and oregano. Bring to the boil and simmer for 20 minutes until thick. Season well.

2 Drain the spinach again and spread it out on kitchen paper (paper towels) to make sure that as much water as possible is removed. Layer the spinach in the base of an ovenproof baking dish. Sprinkle with nutmeg and season.

3 Arrange the diced chicken over the spinach and spoon over the tomato sauce. Arrange the sheets of lasagne over the tomato sauce.

4 Blend the cornflour (cornstarch) with a little of the milk to make a paste.

Pour the remaining milk into a saucepan and stir in the cornflour (cornstarch) paste. Heat for 2–3 minutes, stirring, until the sauce thickens. Season well.

5 Spoon the sauce over the lasagne and transfer the dish to a baking tray (cookie sheet). Sprinkle the grated cheese over the sauce and bake in the oven for 25 minutes until golden-brown. Serve with a fresh green salad.

Garlic & Herb Chicken

There is a delicious surprise of creamy herb and garlic soft cheese hidden inside these chicken parcels!

NUTRITIONAL INFORMATION

Calories 272	Sugars 4g	
Protein 29g	Fat 13g	
Carbohydrate 4g	Saturates 6g	

20 MINS   25 MINS

SERVES 4

I N G R E D I E N T S

4 chicken breasts, skin removed

100 g/3½ oz full fat soft cheese, flavoured
    with herbs and garlic

8 slices Parma ham (prosciutto)

150 ml/¼ pint/⅔ cup red wine

150 ml/¼ pint/⅔ cup chicken stock

1 tbsp brown sugar

1 Using a sharp knife, make a horizontal slit along the length of each chicken breast to form a pocket.

2 Beat the cheese with a wooden spoon to soften it. Spoon the cheese into the pocket of the chicken breasts.

3 Wrap 2 slices of Parma ham (prosciutto) around each chicken breast and secure firmly in place with a length of string.

4 Pour the wine and chicken stock into a large frying pan (skillet) and bring to the boil. When the mixture is just starting to boil, add the sugar and stir well to dissolve.

5 Add the chicken breasts to the mixture in the frying pan (skillet). Leave to simmer for 12–15 minutes or until the chicken is tender and the juices run clear when a skewer is inserted into the thickest part of the meat.

6 Remove the chicken from the pan, set aside and keep warm.

7 Reheat the sauce and boil until reduced and thickened. Remove the string from the chicken and cut into slices. Pour the sauce over the chicken to serve.

VARIATION

Try adding 2 finely chopped sun-dried tomatoes to the soft cheese in step 2, if you prefer.

Italian-Style Sunday Roast

A mixture of cheese, rosemary and sun-dried tomatoes is stuffed under the chicken skin, then roasted with garlic, potatoes and vegetables.

NUTRITIONAL INFORMATION

Calories . . . . .488 Sugars 6g
Protein . . . . .37g Fat 23g
Carbohydrate . . .34g Saturates 11g

35 MINS 1¹/₂ HOURS

SERVES 6

I N G R E D I E N T S

2.5 kg/5 lb 8 oz chicken

sprigs of fresh rosemary

175 g/6 oz/¾ cup feta cheese,
   coarsely grated

2 tbsp sun-dried tomato paste

60 g/2 oz/4 tbsp butter, softened

1 bulb garlic

1 kg/2 lb 4 oz new potatoes, halved if large

1 each red, green and yellow (bell) pepper,
   cut into chunks

3 courgettes (zucchini), sliced thinly

2 tbsp olive oil

2 tbsp plain (all-purpose) flour

600 ml/1 pint/2½ cups chicken stock

salt and pepper

1 Rinse the chicken inside and out with cold water and drain well. Carefully cut between the skin and the top of the breast meat using a small pointed knife. Slide a finger into the slit and carefully enlarge it to form a pocket. Continue until the skin is completely lifted away from both breasts and the top of the legs.

2 Chop the leaves from 3 rosemary stems. Mix with the feta cheese, sun-dried tomato paste, butter and pepper to taste, then spoon under the skin. Put the chicken in a large roasting tin (pan), cover with foil and cook in a preheated oven, 190°C/375°F/Gas Mark 5, for 20 minutes per 500 g/1 lb 2 oz, plus 20 minutes.

3 Break the garlic bulb into cloves but do not peel. Add the vegetables to the chicken after 40 minutes.

4 Drizzle with oil, tuck in a few stems of rosemary and season with salt and pepper. Cook for the remaining calculated time, removing the foil for the last 40 minutes to brown the chicken.

5 Transfer the chicken to a serving platter. Place some of the vegetables around the chicken and transfer the remainder to a warmed serving dish. Pour the fat out of the roasting tin (pan) and stir the flour into the remaining pan juices. Cook for 2 minutes then gradually stir in the stock. Bring to the boil, stirring until thickened. Strain into a sauce boat and serve with the chicken.

Slices of Duckling with Pasta

A raspberry and honey sauce superbly counterbalances the richness of the duckling.

NUTRITIONAL INFORMATION

Calories ....686 Sugars 15g
Protein ....62g Fat 20g
Carbohydrate ...70g Saturates 7g

15 MINS   25 MINS

SERVES 4

INGREDIENTS

4 x 275 g/9 oz boned breasts of duckling

25 g/1 oz/2 tbsp butter

50 g/1¾ oz/⅜ cup finely chopped carrots

50 g/1¾ oz/4 tbsp finely chopped shallots

1 tbsp lemon juice

150 ml/¼ pint/⅔ cup meat stock

4 tbsp clear honey

115 g/4 oz/¾ cup fresh or thawed frozen
   raspberries

25 g/1 oz/¼ cup plain (all-purpose) flour

1 tbsp Worcestershire sauce

400 g/14 oz fresh linguine

1 tbsp olive oil

salt and pepper

TO GARNISH

fresh raspberries

fresh sprig of flat-leaf parsley

1 Trim and score the duck breasts with a sharp knife and season well all over. Melt the butter in a frying pan (skillet), add the duck breasts and fry all over until lightly coloured.

2 Add the carrots, shallots, lemon juice and half the meat stock and simmer over a low heat for 1 minute. Stir in half of the honey and half of the raspberries.

Sprinkle over half of the flour and cook, stirring constantly for 3 minutes. Season with pepper to taste and add the Worcestershire sauce.

3 Stir in the remaining stock and cook for 1 minute. Stir in the remaining honey and remaining raspberries and sprinkle over the remaining flour. Cook for a further 3 minutes.

4 Remove the duck breasts from the pan, but leave the sauce to continue simmering over a very low heat.

5 Meanwhile, bring a large saucepan of lightly salted water to the boil. Add the linguine and olive oil and cook for 8–10 minutes or until tender, but still firm to the bite. Drain and divide between 4 individual plates.

6 Slice the duck breast lengthways into 5 mm/¼ inch thick pieces. Pour a little sauce over the pasta and arrange the sliced duck in a fan shape on top of it. Garnish with raspberries and flat-leaf parsley and serve immediately.

Pesto Baked Partridge

Partridge has a more delicate flavour than many game birds and this subtle sauce perfectly complements it.

NUTRITIONAL INFORMATION

Calories 895   Sugars 5g
Protein . . . . .79g   Fat 45g
Carbohydrate . . .45g   Saturates 18g

15 MINS   40 MINS

SERVES 4

INGREDIENTS

8 partridge pieces (about 115 g/4 oz each)

60 g/2 oz/4 tbsp butter, melted

4 tbsp Dijon mustard

2 tbsp lime juice

1 tbsp brown sugar

6 tbsp pesto sauce (shop bought)

450 g/1 lb dried rigatoni

1 tbsp olive oil

115 g/4 oz/1⅓ cups freshly grated
    Parmesan cheese

salt and pepper

1 Arrange the partridge pieces, smooth side down, in a single layer in a large, ovenproof dish.

2 Mix together the butter, Dijon mustard, lime juice and brown sugar in a bowl. Season to taste. Brush this mixture over the partridge pieces and bake in a preheated oven at 200°C/400°F/Gas Mark 6 for 15 minutes.

3 Remove the dish from the oven and coat the partridge pieces with 3 tbsp of the Pesto Sauce. Return to the oven and bake for a further 12 minutes.

4 Remove the dish from the oven and carefully turn over the partridge pieces. Coat the top of the partridges with the remaining mustard mixture and return to the oven for a further 10 minutes.

5 Meanwhile, bring a large pan of lightly salted water to the boil. Add the rigatoni and olive oil and cook for 8–10 minutes until tender, but still firm to the bite. Drain and transfer to a serving dish. Toss the pasta with the remaining Pesto Sauce and the Parmesan cheese.

6 Serve the partridge with the pasta, pouring over the cooking juices.

VARIATION
You could also prepare young pheasant in the same way.

Chinese Dishes

Second to pork, poultry is one of the most popular foods throughout China. It also plays an important symbolic role in Chinese cooking. The cockerel symbolizes the male, positiveness and aggression while the duck represents

happiness and fidelity. Being uniformly tender, poultry is ideal for Chinese cooking methods, which rely on the rapid cooking of small, even-sized pieces of meat. Poultry can be cut into wafer-thin slices, thin matchstick strips or cubes, and can be quickly cooked without any loss of moisture or tenderness. This chapter contains dishes which are stir-fried, braised, steamed and roasted.

Chicken Chop Suey

Chop suey is a well known and popular dish based on bean sprouts and soy sauce with a meat or vegetable flavouring.

NUTRITIONAL INFORMATION

Calories 337	Sugars 7g
Protein 32g	Fat 18g
Carbohydrate ...14g	Saturates 3g

25 MINS   15 MINS

SERVES 4

INGREDIENTS

4 tbsp light soy sauce

2 tsp light brown sugar

500 g/1 lb 2 oz skinless, boneless chicken breasts

3 tbsp vegetable oil

2 onions, quartered

2 garlic cloves, crushed

350 g/12 oz bean sprouts

3 tsp sesame oil

1 tbsp cornflour (cornstarch)

3 tbsp water

425 ml/¾ pint/2 cups chicken stock

shredded leek, to garnish

VARIATION

This recipe may be made with strips of lean steak, pork or with mixed vegetables. Change the type of stock accordingly.

1 Mix the soy sauce and sugar together, stirring until the sugar has dissolved.

2 Trim any fat from the chicken and cut into thin strips. Place the meat in a shallow dish and spoon the soy mixture over them, turning to coat. Marinate in the refrigerator for 20 minutes.

3 Heat the oil in a wok and stir-fry the chicken for 2–3 minutes, until golden brown. Add the onions and garlic and cook for a further 2 minutes. Add the bean sprouts, cook for 4–5 minutes, then add the sesame oil.

4 Mix the cornflour (cornstarch) and water to form a smooth paste. Pour the stock into the wok, add the cornflour (cornstarch) paste and bring to the boil, stirring until the sauce is thickened and clear. Serve, garnished with shredded leek.

Cashew Chicken

Yellow bean sauce is available from large supermarkets. Try to buy a chunky sauce rather than a smooth sauce for texture.

NUTRITIONAL INFORMATION

Calories 398	Sugars 2g	
Protein 31g	Fat 27g	
Carbohydrate 8g	Saturates 4g	

10 MINS   15 MINS

SERVES 4

INGREDIENTS

450 g/1 lb boneless chicken breasts

2 tbsp vegetable oil

1 red onion, sliced

175 g/6 oz/1½ cups flat mushrooms, sliced

100 g/3½ oz/⅓ cup cashew nuts

75 g/2¾ oz jar yellow bean sauce

fresh coriander (cilantro), to garnish

egg fried rice or plain boiled rice, to serve

1 Using a sharp knife, remove the excess skin from the chicken breasts, if desired. Cut the chicken into small, bite-sized chunks.

2 Heat the vegetable oil in a preheated wok or frying pan (skillet).

3 Add the chicken to the wok and stir-fry for 5 minutes.

4 Add the red onion and mushrooms to the wok and continue to stir-fry for a further 5 minutes.

5 Place the cashew nuts on a baking tray (cookie sheet) and toast under a preheated medium grill (broiler) until just browning – toasting nuts brings out their flavour.

6 Toss the toasted cashew nuts into the wok together with the yellow bean sauce and heat through.

7 Allow the sauce to bubble for 2–3 minutes.

8 Transfer the chop suey to warm serving bowls and garnish with fresh coriander (cilantro). Serve hot with egg fried rice or plain boiled rice.

VARIATION

Chicken thighs could be used instead of the chicken breasts for a more economical dish.

Lemon Chicken

This is on everyone's list of favourite Chinese dishes, and it is so simple to make. Serve with stir-fried vegetables for a truly delicious meal.

NUTRITIONAL INFORMATION

Calories ....272 Sugars 1g
Protein ....36g Fat 11g
Carbohydrate ....5g Saturates 2g

5 MINS   15 MINS

SERVES 4

INGREDIENTS

vegetable oil, for deep-frying

650 g/1 lb 7 oz skinless, boneless
    chicken, cut into strips

lemon slices and shredded spring onion
    (scallion), to garnish

SAUCE

1 tbsp cornflour (cornstarch)

6 tbsp cold water

3 tbsp fresh lemon juice

2 tbsp sweet sherry

½ tsp caster (superfine) sugar

1 Heat the oil for deep-frying in a preheated wok or frying pan (skillet) to 180°C/350°F or until a cube of bread browns in 30 seconds.

2 Reduce the heat and stir-fry the chicken strips for 3–4 minutes, until cooked through.

3 Remove the chicken with a slotted spoon, set aside and keep warm. Drain the oil from the wok.

4 To make the sauce, mix the cornflour (cornstarch) with 2 tablespoons of the water to form a paste.

5 Pour the lemon juice and remaining water into the mixture in the wok.

6 Add the sweet sherry and caster (superfine) sugar and bring to the boil, stirring until the sugar has completely dissolved.

7 Stir in the cornflour (cornstarch) mixture and return to the boil. Reduce the heat and simmer, stirring constantly, for 2-3 minutes, until the sauce is thickened and clear.

8 Transfer the chicken to a warm serving plate and pour the sauce over the top.

9 Garnish the chicken with the lemon slices and shredded spring onion (scallion) and serve immediately.

COOK'S TIP

If you would prefer to use chicken portions rather than strips, cook them in the oil, covered, over a low heat for about 30 minutes, or until cooked through.

Celery & Cashew Chicken

Stir-fry yellow bean sauce gives this quick and easy Chinese dish a really authentic taste. Pecan nuts can be used in place of the cashews.

NUTRITIONAL INFORMATION

Calories ....549 Sugars 24g
Protein ....41g Fat 31g
Carbohydrate ...28g Saturates 5g

5 MINS   10 MINS

SERVES 4

INGREDIENTS

3-4 boneless, skinned chicken breasts, about 625g/1 lb 6 oz

2 tbsp sunflower or vegetable oil

125 g/4½ oz/1 cup cashew nuts (unsalted)

4-6 spring onions (scallions), thinly sliced diagonally

5-6 celery sticks, thinly sliced diagonally

1 x 175 g/6 oz jar stir-fry yellow bean sauce

salt and pepper

celery leaves, to garnish (optional)

plain boiled rice, to serve

1 Using a sharp knife or metal cleaver, cut the chicken into thin slices across the grain.

2 Heat the oil in a preheated wok or large frying pan (skillet), swirling it around until it is really hot.

3 Add the cashew nuts and stir-fry until they begin to brown but do not allow them to burn.

4 Add the chicken and stir-fry until well sealed and almost cooked through.

5 Add the spring onions (scallions) and celery and continue to stir-fry for 2–3 minutes, stirring the food well around the wok.

6 Add the stir-fry yellow bean sauce to the wok or frying pan (skillet) and season lightly with salt and pepper.

7 Toss the mixture in the wok until the chicken and vegetables are thoroughly coated with the sauce and piping hot.

8 Serve at once with plain boiled rice, garnished with celery leaves, if liked.

VARIATION

This recipe can be adapted to use turkey fillets or steaks, or pork fillet or boneless steaks. Cut the turkey or pork lengthwise first, then slice thinly across the grain. Alternatively, cut into 2 cm/½ inch cubes.

Stir-Fried Ginger Chicken

The oranges add colour and piquancy to this refreshing dish, which complements the delicate flavour of the chicken well.

NUTRITIONAL INFORMATION

Calories ....289 Sugars 15g
Protein ....20g Fat 9g
Carbohydrate ...17g Saturates 2g

5 MINS   20 MINS

SERVES 4

INGREDIENTS

2 tbsp sunflower oil

1 onion, sliced

175 g/6 oz carrots, cut into thin sticks

1 clove garlic, crushed

350 g/12 oz boneless skinless chicken breasts

2 tbsp fresh ginger, peeled and grated

1 tsp ground ginger

4 tbsp sweet sherry

1 tbsp tomato purée (tomato paste)

1 tbsp demerara sugar

100 ml/3½ fl oz/⅓ cup orange juice

1 tsp cornflour (cornstarch)

1 orange, peeled and segmented

fresh snipped chives, to garnish

1 Heat the oil in a large preheated wok. Add the onion, carrots and garlic and stir-fry over a high heat for 3 minutes or until the vegetables begin to soften.

2 Slice the chicken into thin strips. Add to the wok with the fresh and ground ginger. Stir-fry for a further 10 minutes, or until the chicken is well cooked through and golden in colour.

3 Mix together the sherry, tomato purée (tomato paste), sugar, orange juice and cornflour (cornstarch) in a bowl. Stir the mixture into the wok and heat through until the mixture bubbles and the juices start to thicken.

4 Add the orange segments and carefully toss to mix.

5 Transfer the stir-fried chicken to warm serving bowls and garnish with freshly snipped chives. Serve immediately.

COOK'S TIP

Make sure that you do not continue cooking the dish once the orange segments have been added in step 4, otherwise they will break up.

Barbecued Chicken Legs

Just the thing to put on the barbecue – chicken legs, coated with a spicy, curry-like butter, then grilled until crispy and golden.

NUTRITIONAL INFORMATION

Calories	660	Sugars	.........4g
Protein	........34g	Fat	..........57g
Carbohydrate	....4g	Saturates	......30g

5 MINS   20 MINS

SERVES 4

INGREDIENTS

12 chicken drumsticks

SPICED BUTTER

175 g/6 oz/¾ cup butter

2 garlic cloves, crushed

1 tsp grated ginger root

2 tsp ground turmeric

4 tsp cayenne pepper

2 tbsp lime juice

3 tbsp mango chutney

TO SERVE

crisp green seasonal salad

boiled rice

VARIATION

This spicy butter mixture would be equally effective on grilled chicken or turkey breast fillets. Skin before coating with the mixture.

1 To make the Spiced Butter mixture, beat the butter with the garlic, ginger, turmeric, cayenne pepper, lime juice and chutney until well blended.

2 Using a sharp knife, slash each chicken leg to the bone 3-4 times.

3 Cook the drumsticks over a moderate barbecue (grill) for about 12-15 minutes or until almost cooked.

Alternatively, grill (broil) the chicken for about 10-12 minutes until almost cooked, turning halfway through.

4 Spread the chicken legs liberally with the butter mixture and continue to cook for a further 5-6 minutes, turning and basting frequently with the butter until golden and crisp. Serve the chicken legs hot or cold with a crisp green salad and rice.

Braised Chicken

This is a delicious way to cook a whole chicken. It has a wonderful glaze, which is served as a sauce.

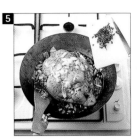

NUTRITIONAL INFORMATION

Calories 294   Sugars 9g
Protein ....31g   Fat 15g
Carbohydrate ...10g   Saturates 3g

5 MINS   1¹/₄ HOURS

SERVES 4

INGREDIENTS

1.5 kg/3 lb 5 oz chicken

3 tbsp vegetable oil

1 tbsp peanut oil

2 tbsp dark brown sugar

5 tbsp dark soy sauce

150 ml/¼ pint/⅔ cup water

2 garlic cloves, crushed

1 small onion, chopped

1 fresh red chilli, chopped

celery leaves and chives,
  to garnish

1 Preheat a large wok or large frying pan (skillet).

2 Clean the chicken inside and out with damp kitchen paper (paper towels).

3 Put the vegetable oil and peanut oil in the wok, add the dark brown sugar and heat gently until the sugar caramelizes.

4 Stir the soy sauce into the wok. Add the chicken and turn it in the mixture to coat thoroughly on all sides.

5 Add the water, garlic, onion and chilli. Cover and simmer, turning the chicken occasionally, for about 1 hour, or

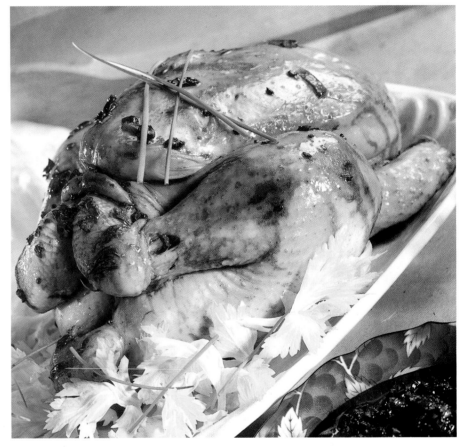

until cooked through. Test by piercing a thigh with the point of a knife or a skewer – the juices will run clear when the chicken is cooked.

6 Remove the chicken from the wok and set aside. Increase the heat and reduce the sauce in the wok until thickened. Transfer the chicken to a serving plate, garnish with celery leaves and chives and serve with the sauce.

COOK'S TIP

For a spicier sauce, add 1 tbsp finely chopped fresh root ginger and 1 tbsp ground Szechuan peppercorns with the chilli in step 5.

Yellow Bean Chicken

Ready-made yellow bean sauce is available from large supermarkets and Chinese food stores. It is made from yellow soya beans and is quite salty.

NUTRITIONAL INFORMATION

Calories	234	Sugars	.........1g
Protein	........26g	Fat	..........12g
Carbohydrate	....6g	Saturates	.......2g

25 MINS   10 MINS

SERVES 4

I N G R E D I E N T S

450 g/1 lb skinless, boneless chicken breasts

1 egg white, beaten

1 tbsp cornflour (cornstarch)

1 tbsp rice wine vinegar

1 tbsp light soy sauce

1 tsp caster (superfine) sugar

3 tbsp vegetable oil

1 garlic clove, crushed

1-cm/½-inch piece fresh root ginger, grated

1 green (bell) pepper, seeded and diced

2 large mushrooms, sliced

3 tbsp yellow bean sauce

yellow or green (bell) pepper strips, to garnish

VARIATION

Black bean sauce would work equally well with this recipe. Although this would affect the appearance of the dish, as it is much darker in colour, the flavours would be compatible.

1   Trim any fat from the chicken and cut the meat into 2.5-cm/1-inch cubes.

2   Mix the egg white and cornflour (cornstarch) in a shallow bowl. Add the chicken and turn in the mixture to coat. Set aside for 20 minutes.

3   Mix the rice wine vinegar, soy sauce and caster (superfine) sugar in a bowl.

4   Remove the chicken from the egg white mixture.

5   Heat the oil in a preheated wok, add the chicken and stir-fry for 3–4 minutes, until golden brown. Remove the chicken from the wok with a slotted spoon, set aside and keep warm.

6   Add the garlic, ginger, (bell) pepper and mushrooms to the wok and stir-fry for 1–2 minutes.

7   Add the yellow bean sauce and cook for 1 minute. Stir in the vinegar mixture and return the chicken to the wok. Cook for 1–2 minutes and serve hot, garnished with (bell) pepper strips.

Kung Po Chicken

In this recipe, cashew nuts are used but peanuts, walnuts or almonds can be substituted, if preferred.

NUTRITIONAL INFORMATION

Calories	294	Sugars	.........3g
Protein	........21g	Fat	..........18g
Carbohydrate	...10g	Saturates	.......4g

10 MINS   5 MINS

SERVES 4

INGREDIENTS

250-300 g/9-10½ oz chicken meat, boned and skinned

¼ tsp salt

⅓ egg white

1 tsp cornflour (cornstarch) paste (see page 15)

1 medium green (bell) pepper, cored and seeded

4 tbsp vegetable oil

1 spring onion (scallion), cut into short sections

a few small slices of ginger root

4-5 small dried red chillies, soaked, seeded and shredded

2 tbsp crushed yellow bean sauce

1 tsp rice wine or dry sherry

125 g/4½ oz roasted cashew nuts

a few drops of sesame oil

boiled rice, to serve

1 Cut the chicken into small cubes about the size of sugar lumps. Place the chicken in a small bowl and mix with a pinch of salt, the egg white and the cornflour (cornstarch) paste, in that order.

2 Cut the green (bell) pepper into cubes or triangles about the same size as the chicken pieces.

3 Heat the oil in a wok, add the chicken and stir-fry for 1 minute. Remove with a slotted spoon and keep warm.

4 Add the spring onion (scallion), ginger, chillies and green (bell) pepper. Stir-fry for 1 minute, then add the chicken with the yellow bean sauce and wine. Blend well and stir-fry for another minute. Finally stir in the cashew nuts and sesame oil. Serve hot with boiled rice.

VARIATION

Any nuts can be used in place of the cashew nuts, if preferred. The important point is the crunchy texture, which is very much a feature of Szechuan cooking.

Green Chicken Stir-Fry

Tender chicken is mixed with a selection of spring greens and flavoured with yellow bean sauce in this crunchy stir-fry.

NUTRITIONAL INFORMATION

Calories 297   Sugars 5g
Protein . . . . .30g   Fat 16g
Carbohydrate . . . .8g   Saturates 3g

5 MINS   15 MINS

SERVES 4

I N G R E D I E N T S

2 tbsp sunflower oil

450 g/1 lb skinless, boneless chicken
breasts

2 cloves garlic, crushed

1 green (bell) pepper

100 g/3½ oz/1½ cups mangetout (snow
peas)

6 spring onions (scallions), sliced, plus
extra to garnish

225 g/8 oz spring greens or cabbage,
shredded

160 g/5¾ oz jar yellow bean sauce

50 g/1¾ oz/3 tbsp roasted cashew nuts

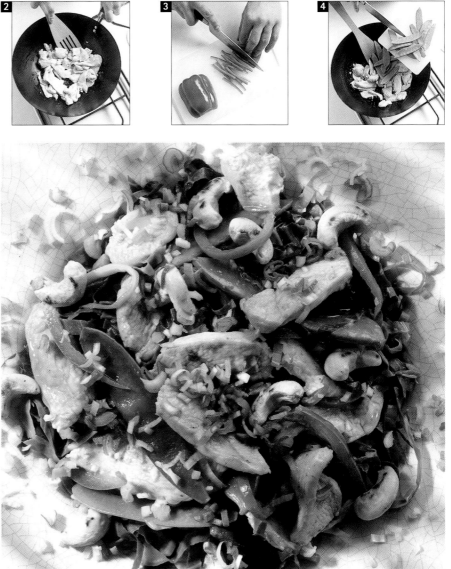

1 Heat the sunflower oil in a large
preheated wok.

2 Slice the chicken into thin strips and
add to the wok together with the
garlic. Stir-fry for about 5 minutes or until
the chicken is sealed on all sides and
beginning to turn golden.

3 Using a sharp knife, deseed the green
(bell) pepper and cut into thin strips.

4 Add the mangetout (snow peas),
spring onions (scallions), green (bell)
pepper strips and spring greens or cabbage
to the wok. Stir-fry for a further 5 minutes
or until the vegetables are just tender.

5 Stir in the yellow bean sauce and
heat through for about 2 minutes or
until the mixture starts to bubble.

6 Scatter the roasted cashew nuts into
the wok.

7 Transfer the stir-fry to warm serving
plates and garnish with extra spring
onions (scallions), if desired. Serve the
stir-fry immediately.

COOK'S TIP

Do not add salted
cashew nuts to this dish
otherwise the dish will
be too salty.

Chicken with Bean Sprouts

This is the basic Chicken Chop Suey to be found in almost every Chinese restaurant and takeaway all over the world.

NUTRITIONAL INFORMATION

Calories 153   Sugars 4g
Protein ....9g   Fat 10g
Carbohydrate ....8g   Saturates 1g

3¹/₂ HOURS   10 MINS

SERVES 4

INGREDIENTS

125 g/4½ oz chicken breast fillet, skinned

1 tsp salt

¼ egg white, lightly beaten

2 tsp cornflour (cornstarch) paste
  (see page 15)

about 300 ml/½ pint/1¼ cups vegetable oil

1 small onion, thinly shredded

1 small green (bell) pepper, cored, seeded
  and thinly shredded

1 small carrot, thinly shredded

125 g/4½ oz fresh beansprouts

½ tsp sugar

1 tbsp light soy sauce

1 tsp rice wine or dry sherry

2-3 tbsp Chinese Stock (see page 14)

a few drops of sesame oil

chilli sauce, to serve

COOK'S TIP

Chop Suey actually originated in San Francisco at the turn of the century when Chinese immigrants were first settling there, and was first devised as a handy dish for using up leftovers.

1 Using a sharp knife or meat cleaver, cut the chicken into thin shreds and place in a bowl.

2 Add a pinch of the salt, the egg white and cornflour (cornstarch) paste to the chicken and mix well.

3 Heat the vegetable oil in a preheated wok or large frying pan (skillet).

4 Add the chicken and stir-fry for about 1 minute, stirring to separate the shreds. Remove with a slotted spoon and drain on kitchen paper (paper towels).

5 Pour off the oil, leaving about 2 tablespoons in the wok. Add the onion, green (bell) pepper and carrot and stir-fry for about 2 minutes.

6 Add the bean sprouts and stir-fry for a few seconds.

7 Add the chicken with the remaining salt, sugar, soy sauce and rice wine or dry sherry, blend well and add the Chinese stock or water.

8 Sprinkle the stir-fry with the sesame oil and serve with the chilli sauce.

Chilli Coconut Chicken

This tasty dish combines the flavours of lime, peanut, coconut and chilli. You'll find coconut cream in most supermarkets or delicatessens.

NUTRITIONAL INFORMATION

Calories	348	Sugars	........2g
Protein	........36g	Fat	.........21g
Carbohydrate	....3g	Saturates	.......8g

5 MINS   15 MINS

SERVES 4

INGREDIENTS

150 ml/¼ pint/⅔ cup hot chicken stock

25 g/1 oz/⅓ cup coconut cream

1 tbsp sunflower oil

8 skinless, boneless chicken thighs, cut into long, thin strips

1 small red chilli, sliced thinly

4 spring onions (scallions), sliced thinly

4 tbsp smooth or crunchy peanut butter

finely grated rind and juice of 1 lime

1 fresh red chilli and spring onion (scallion) tassel, to garnish

boiled rice, to serve

1 Pour the chicken stock into a measuring jug or small bowl. Crumble the coconut cream into the chicken stock and stir the mixture until the coconut cream dissolves.

2 Heat the oil in a preheated wok or large heavy pan.

3 Add the chicken strips and cook, stirring, until the chicken turns a golden colour.

4 Stir in the chopped red chilli and spring onions (scallions) and cook gently for a few minutes.

5 Add the peanut butter, coconut cream and chicken stock mixture, lime rind, lime juice and simmer, uncovered, for about 5 minutes, stirring frequently to prevent the mixture sticking to the base of the wok or pan.

6 Transfer the chilli coconut chicken to a warm serving dish, garnish with the red chilli and spring onion (scallion) tassel and serve with boiled rice.

COOK'S TIP

Serve jasmine rice with this spicy dish. It has a fragrant aroma that is well-suited to the flavours in this dish.

Chicken with Black Bean Sauce

This tasty chicken stir-fry is quick and easy to make and is full of fresh flavours and crunchy vegetables.

NUTRITIONAL INFORMATION

Calories	205	Sugars	.........4g
Protein	........25g	Fat	...........9g
Carbohydrate	....6g	Saturates	.......2g

40 MINS   10 MINS

SERVES 4

I N G R E D I E N T S

425 g/15 oz chicken breasts, sliced thinly

pinch of salt

pinch of cornflour (cornstarch)

2 tbsp oil

1 garlic clove, crushed

1 tbsp black bean sauce

1 each small red and green (bell) pepper, cut into strips

1 red chilli, chopped finely

75 g/2¾ oz/1 cup mushrooms, sliced

1 onion, chopped

6 spring onions (scallions), chopped

salt and pepper

S E A S O N I N G

½ tsp salt

½ tsp sugar

3 tbsp chicken stock

1 tbsp dark soy sauce

2 tbsp beef stock

2 tbsp rice wine

1 tsp cornflour (cornstarch), blended with a little rice wine

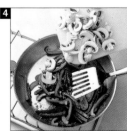

1 Put the chicken strips in a bowl. Add a pinch of salt and a pinch of cornflour (cornstarch) and cover with water. Leave to stand for 30 minutes.

2 Heat 1 tablespoon of the oil in a wok or deep-sided frying pan (skillet) and stir-fry the chicken for 4 minutes.

3 Remove the chicken to a warm serving dish and clean the wok.

4 Add the remaining oil to the wok and add the garlic, black bean sauce, green and red (bell) peppers, chilli, mushrooms, onion and spring onions (scallions). Stir-fry for 2 minutes then return the chicken to the wok.

5 Add the seasoning ingredients, fry for 3 minutes and thicken with a little of the cornflour (cornstarch) blend. Serve with fresh noodles.

Garlic & Lime Chicken

Garlic and coriander (cilantro) flavour the chicken breasts which are served with a caramelised sauce, sharpened with lime juice.

NUTRITIONAL INFORMATION

Calories	280	Sugars	........7g
Protein	........26g	Fat	..........17g
Carbohydrate	....7g	Saturates	.......8g

🕐 10 MINS   ⏱ 25 MINS

SERVES 4

I N G R E D I E N T S

4 large skinless, boneless
  chicken breasts

50 g/1¾ oz/3 tbsp garlic butter,
  softened

3 tbsp chopped fresh coriander
  (cilantro)

1 tbsp sunflower oil

finely grated zest and juice of 2 limes,
  plus extra zest, to garnish

25 g/1 oz/4 tbsp palm sugar or
  demerara (brown crystal) sugar

TO SERVE

boiled rice

lemon wedges

1 Place each chicken breast between 2 sheets of cling film (plastic wrap) and pound with a rolling pin until flattened to about 1 cm/½ inch thick.

2 Mix together the garlic butter and coriander (cilantro) and spread over each flattened chicken breast. Roll up like a Swiss roll and secure with a cocktail stick (toothpick).

3 Heat the sunflower oil in a preheated wok or heavy-based frying pan (skillet).

4 Add the chicken rolls to the wok or pan and cook, turning, for 15–20 minutes or until cooked through.

5 Remove the chicken from the wok and transfer to a board. Cut each chicken roll into slices.

6 Add the lime zest, juice and sugar to the wok and heat gently, stirring, until the sugar has dissolved. Raise the heat and allow to bubble for 2 minutes.

7 Arrange the chicken on warmed serving plates and spoon the pan juices over to serve.

8 Garnish the garlic and lime chicken with extra lime zest, if desired.

COOK'S TIP

Be sure to check that the chicken is cooked through before slicing and serving. Cook over a gentle heat so as not to overcook the outside, while the inside remains raw.

Orange Chicken Stir-Fry

Chicken thighs are inexpensive, meaty portions which are readily available. Although not as tender as breast, it is perfect for stir-frying.

NUTRITIONAL INFORMATION

Calories 267   Sugars 11g
Protein . . . . .23g   Fat 11g
Carbohydrate . . .15g   Saturates 2g

10 MINS   15 MINS

SERVES 4

INGREDIENTS

3 tbsp sunflower oil

350 g/12 oz boneless chicken thighs,
   skinned and cut into thin strips

1 onion, sliced

1 clove garlic, crushed

1 red (bell) pepper, deseeded and sliced

75 g/2¾ oz/1¼ cups mangetout (snow peas)

4 tbsp light soy sauce

4 tbsp sherry

1 tbsp tomato purée (tomato paste)

finely grated rind and juice of 1 orange

1 tsp cornflour (cornstarch)

2 oranges

100 g/3½ oz/1 cup bean sprouts

cooked rice or noodles, to serve

1 Heat the oil in a large preheated wok. Add the chicken and stir-fry for 2–3 minutes or until sealed on all sides.

2 Add the onion, garlic, (bell) pepper and mangetout (snow peas) to the wok. Stir-fry for a further 5 minutes, or until the vegetables are just tender and the chicken is completely cooked through.

3 Mix together the soy sauce, sherry, tomato purée (tomato paste), orange rind and juice and the cornflour (cornstarch). Add to the wok and cook, stirring, until the juices start to thicken.

4 Using a sharp knife, peel and segment the oranges. Add the segments to the mixture in the wok with the bean sprouts and heat through for a further 2 minutes.

5 Transfer the stir-fry to serving plates and serve at once with cooked rice or noodles.

COOK'S TIP

Bean sprouts are sprouting mung beans and are a regular ingredient in Chinese cooking. They require very little cooking and may even be eaten raw, if wished.

Sweet Mango Chicken

The heavily scented flavour of mango gives this dish its characteristic sweetness and piquancy.

NUTRITIONAL INFORMATION

Calories 244   Sugars 18g
Protein . . . . .27g   Fat 7g
Carbohydrate . . .2.1g   Saturates 2g

10 MINS   15 MINS

SERVES 4

INGREDIENTS

1 tbsp sunflower oil

6 skinless, boneless chicken thighs

1 ripe mango

2 cloves garlic, crushed

225 g/8 oz leeks, shredded

100 g/3½ oz/1 cup bean sprouts

150 ml/¼ pint/⅔ cup mango juice

1 tbsp white wine vinegar

2 tbsp clear honey

2 tbsp tomato ketchup

1 tsp cornflour (cornstarch)

COOK'S TIP

Mango juice is avaialable in jars from most supermarkets and is quite thick and sweet. If it is unavailable, purée and sieve a ripe mango and add a little water to make up the required quantity.

1 Heat the sunflower oil in a large preheated wok.

2 Cut the chicken into bite-sized cubes, add to the wok and stir-fry over a high heat for 10 minutes, tossing frequently until the chicken is cooked through and golden in colour.

3 Peel and slice the mango and add to the wok with the garlic, leeks and bean sprouts. Stir-fry for a further 2–3 minutes, or until softened.

4 Mix together the mango juice, white wine vinegar, honey, tomato ketchup and cornflour (cornstarch). Pour into the wok and stir-fry for a further 2 minutes, or until the juices start to thicken.

5 Transfer to a warmed serving dish and serve immediately.

Szechuan Chilli Chicken

In China, the chicken pieces are chopped through the bone for this dish, but if you do not possess a cleaver, use filleted chicken meat.

NUTRITIONAL INFORMATION

Calories 218   Sugars 4g
Protein . . . . .23g   Fat 9g
Carbohydrate . . . .8g   Saturates 2g

4 HOURS   15 MINS

SERVES 4

INGREDIENTS

500 g/1 lb 2 oz chicken thighs

¼ tsp pepper

1 tbsp sugar

2 tsp light soy sauce

1 tsp dark soy sauce

1 tbsp rice wine or dry sherry

2 tsp cornflour (cornstarch)

2-3 tbsp vegetable oil

1-2 garlic cloves, crushed

2 spring onions (scallions), cut into
   short sections, with the green
   and white parts separated

4-6 small dried red chillies, soaked and
   seeded

2 tbsp crushed yellow bean sauce

about 150 ml/¼ pint/⅔ cup Chinese Stock
   (see page 14) or water

1 Cut or chop the chicken thighs into bite-sized pieces and marinate with the pepper, sugar, soy sauce, wine and cornflour (cornstarch) for 25-30 minutes.

2 Heat the oil in a pre-heated wok and stir-fry the chicken for about 1–2 minutes until lightly brown. Remove with a slotted spoon, transfer to a warm dish and reserve. Add the garlic, the white parts of the spring onions (scallions), the chillies and yellow bean sauce to the wok and stir-fry for about 30 seconds.

3 Return the chicken to the wok, stirring constantly for about 1-2 minutes, then add the stock or water, bring to the boil and cover. Braise over a medium heat for 5-6 minutes, stirring once or twice. Garnish with the green parts of the spring onions (scallions) and serve immediately.

COOK'S TIP

One of the striking features of Szechuan cooking is the quantity of chillies used. Food generally in this region is much hotter than elsewhere in China – people tend to keep a string of dry chillies hanging from the eaves of their houses.

Chicken with Mushrooms

Dried Chinese mushrooms (Shiitake) should be used for this dish – otherwise use black rather than white fresh mushrooms.

NUTRITIONAL INFORMATION

Calories . . . . . . .125 Sugars 0.3g
Protein . . . . .20g Fat 3g
Carbohydrates . . . .3g Saturates 1g

1¼ HOURS   20 MINS

SERVES 4

I N G R E D I E N T S

300-350 g/10½-12 oz chicken, boned and skinned

½ tsp sugar

1 tbsp light soy sauce

1 tsp rice wine or dry sherry

2 tsp cornflour (cornstarch)

4-6 dried Chinese mushrooms, soaked in warm water

1 tbsp finely shredded ginger root

salt and pepper

a few drops of sesame oil

coriander (cilantro) leaves, to garnish

1 Using a sharp knife or meat cleaver, cut the chicken into small bite-sized pieces and place in a bowl.

2 Add the sugar, light soy sauce, wine or sherry and cornflour (cornstarch) to the chicken, toss to coat and leave to marinate for 25-30 minutes.

3 Drain the mushrooms and dry on absorbent kitchen paper (paper towels). Slice the mushrooms into thin shreds, discarding any hard pieces of stem.

4 Place the chicken pieces on a heat-proof dish that will fit inside a bamboo steamer. Arrange the mushroom slices and ginger shreds on top of the chicken and sprinkle with salt, pepper and sesame oil.

5 Place the dish on the rack inside a hot steamer or on a rack in a wok filled with hot water and steam over a high heat for 20 minutes.

6 Serve hot, garnished with coriander (cilantro) leaves.

COOK'S TIP

Do not throw away the soaking water from the dried Chinese mushrooms. It is very useful, as it can be added to soups and stocks to give extra flavour.

Chicken with Vegetables

Coconut adds a creamy texture and delicious flavour to this stir-fry, which is spiked with green chilli.

NUTRITIONAL INFORMATION

Calories 330	Sugars 4g
Protein 23g	Fat 24g
Carbohydrate 6g	Saturates 10g

10 MINS   10 MINS

SERVES 4

INGREDIENTS

3 tbsp sesame oil

350 g/12 oz chicken breast, sliced thinly

8 shallots, sliced

2 garlic cloves, finely chopped

2.5 cm/1 inch piece fresh root ginger, grated

1 green chilli, finely chopped

1 each red and green (bell) pepper, sliced thinly

3 courgettes (zucchini), thinly sliced

2 tbsp ground almonds

1 tsp ground cinnamon

1 tbsp oyster sauce

50 g/1¾ oz/¼ cup creamed coconut, grated

salt and pepper

1 Heat the sesame oil in a preheated wok or large frying pan (skillet).

2 Add the chicken slices to the wok or frying pan (skillet), season with salt and pepper and stir fry for about 4 minutes.

3 Add the shallots, garlic, ginger and chilli and stir-fry for 2 minutes.

4 Add the red and green (bell) peppers and courgettes (zucchini) and cook for about 1 minute.

5 Finally, add the ground almonds, cinnamon, oyster sauce and coconut. Stir fry for 1 minute.

6 Transfer to a warm serving dish and serve immediately.

VARIATION

You can vary the vegetables in this dish according to seasonal availability or whatever you have at hand. Try broccoli florets or baby sweetcorn cobs.

Cumin-Spiced Chicken

Cumin seeds are more frequently associated with Indian cooking, but they are used in this Chinese recipe for their earthy flavour.

NUTRITIONAL INFORMATION

Calories 245   Sugars 9g
Protein ....28g   Fat 10g
Carbohydrate ....11g   Saturates 2g

5 MINS   15 MINS

SERVES 4

INGREDIENTS

450 g/1 lb boneless, skinless chicken breasts

2 tbsp sunflower oil

1 clove garlic, crushed

1 tbsp cumin seeds

1 tbsp grated fresh ginger root

1 red chilli, deseeded and sliced

1 red (bell) pepper, deseeded and sliced

1 green (bell) pepper, deseeded and sliced

1 yellow (bell) pepper, deseeded and sliced

100 g/3½ oz/1 cup bean sprouts

350 g/12 oz pak choi or other green leaves

2 tbsp sweet chilli sauce

3 tbsp light soy sauce

deep-fried crispy ginger, to garnish (see Cook's Tip)

COOK'S TIP

To make the deep-fried ginger garnish, peel and thinly slice a large piece of root ginger. Carefully lower the slices of ginger into a wok or small pan of hot oil and cook for about 30 seconds. Transfer to kitchen paper and leave to drain thoroughly.

1 Using a sharp knife, slice the chicken breasts into thin strips.

2 Heat the oil in a large preheated wok.

3 Add the chicken to the wok and stir-fry for 5 minutes.

4 Add the garlic, cumin seeds, ginger and chilli to the wok, stirring to mix.

5 Add all the (bell) peppers to the wok and stir-fry for a further 5 minutes.

6 Toss in the bean sprouts and pak choi together with the sweet chilli sauce and soy sauce and continue to cook until the pak choi leaves start to wilt.

7 Transfer to warm serving bowls and garnish with deep-fried ginger (see Cook's Tip).

Spicy Peanut Chicken

This quick dish has many variations, but this version includes the classic combination of peanuts, chicken and chillies.

NUTRITIONAL INFORMATION

Calories .... .342   Sugars 3g
Protein .... .25g   Fat .... .24g
Carbohydrate ....6g   Saturates 5g

5 MINS   10 MINS

SERVES 4

INGREDIENTS

300 g/10½ oz skinless, boneless
   chicken breast

2 tbsp peanut oil

125 g/4½ oz/1 cup shelled peanuts

1 fresh red chilli, sliced

1 green (bell) pepper, seeded and
   cut into strips

fried rice, to serve

SAUCE

150 ml/¼ pint/⅔ cup chicken stock

1 tbsp Chinese rice wine or
   dry sherry

1 tbsp light soy sauce

1½ tsp light brown sugar

2 garlic cloves, crushed

1 tsp grated fresh root ginger

1 tsp rice wine vinegar

1 tsp sesame oil

1 Trim any fat from the chicken and cut the meat into 2.5-cm/1-inch cubes. Set aside until required.

2 Heat the peanut oil in a preheated wok or frying pan (skillet).

3 Add the peanuts to the wok and stir-fry for 1 minute. Remove the peanuts with a slotted spoon and set aside.

4 Add the chicken to the wok and cook for 1–2 minutes.

5 Stir in the chilli and green (bell) pepper and cook for 1 minute. Remove from the wok with a slotted spoon and set aside.

6 Put half of the peanuts in a food processor and process until almost smooth. If necessary, add a little stock to form a softer paste. Alternatively, place them in a plastic bag and crush them with a rolling pin.

7 To make the sauce, add the chicken stock, Chinese rice wine or dry sherry, light soy sauce, light brown sugar, crushed garlic cloves, grated fresh root ginger and rice wine vinegar to the wok.

8 Heat the sauce without boiling and stir in the peanut purée, remaining peanuts, chicken, sliced red chilli and green (bell) pepper strips. Mix well until all the ingredients are thoroughly combined.

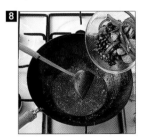

9 Sprinkle the sesame oil into the wok, stir and cook for 1 minute. Transfer the spicy peanut chicken to a warm serving dish and serve hot with fried rice.

Peppered Chicken

Crushed mixed peppercorns coat tender, thin strips of chicken which are cooked with green and red (bell) peppers for a really colourful dish.

NUTRITIONAL INFORMATION

Calories 219	Sugars 6g	
Protein 22g	Fat 10g	
Carbohydrate 11g	Saturates 2g	

5 MINS   15 MINS

SERVES 4

INGREDIENTS

2 tbsp tomato ketchup

2 tbsp soy sauce

450 g/1 lb boneless, skinless chicken breasts

2 tbsp crushed mixed peppercorns

2 tbsp sunflower oil

1 red (bell) pepper

1 green (bell) pepper

175 g/6 oz/2½ cups sugar snap peas

2 tbsp oyster sauce

1 Mix the tomato ketchup with the soy sauce in a bowl.

2 Using a sharp knife, slice the chicken into thin strips.

3 Toss the chicken in the tomato ketchup and soy sauce mixture until the chicken is well coated.

4 Sprinkle the crushed peppercorns on to a plate. Dip the coated chicken in the peppercorns until evenly coated.

5 Heat the sunflower oil in a preheated wok or large frying pan (skillet), until the oil is smoking.

6 Add the chicken to the wok and stir-fry for 5 minutes.

7 Using a sharp knife, deseed and slice the (bell) peppers.

8 Add the (bell) peppers to the wok together with the sugar snap peas and stir-fry for a further 5 minutes.

9 Add the oyster sauce and allow to bubble for 2 minutes. Transfer the peppered chicken to serving bowls and serve immediately.

VARIATION

Use mangetout (snow peas) instead of the sugar snap peas, if you prefer.

Chicken & Corn Sauté

This quick and healthy dish is stir-fried, which means you need use only the minimum of fat.

NUTRITIONAL INFORMATION

Calories 280   Sugars 7g
Protein ....31g   Fat 11g
Carbohydrate ....9g   Saturates 2g

5 MINS   10 MINS

SERVES 4

INGREDIENTS

4 skinless, boneless chicken breasts

250 g/9 oz/1⅓ cups baby sweetcorn (corn-on-the-cob)

250 g/9 oz mangetout (snow peas)

2 tbsp sunflower oil

1 tbsp sherry vinegar

1 tbsp honey

1 tbsp light soy sauce

1 tbsp sunflower seeds

pepper

rice or Chinese egg noodles, to serve

1 Using a sharp knife, slice the chicken breasts into long, thin strips.

2 Cut the baby sweetcorn in half lengthways and top and tail the mangetout (snow peas).

3 Heat the sunflower oil in a preheated wok or a wide frying pan (skillet).

4 Add the chicken and fry over a fairly high heat, stirring, for 1 minute.

5 Add the baby sweetcorn and mangetout (snow peas) and stir-fry over a moderate heat for 5–8 minutes, until evenly cooked. The vegetables should still be slightly crunchy.

6 Mix together the sherry vinegar, honey and soy sauce in a small bowl.

7 Stir the vinegar mixture into the pan with the sunflower seeds.

8 Season well with pepper. Cook, stirring, for 1 minute.

9 Serve the chicken & corn sauté hot with rice or Chinese egg noodles.

VARIATION

Rice vinegar or balsamic vinegar makes a good substitute for the sherry vinegar.

Chicken with Peppers

Red (bell) pepper or celery can also be used in this recipe, the method is the same.

NUTRITIONAL INFORMATION

Calories 113   Sugars 1g
Protein . . . . .17g   Fat 3g
Carbohydrate . . . .4g   Saturates 1g

5 MINS   5 MINS

SERVES 4

I N G R E D I E N T S

300 g/10½ oz boned, skinned chicken breast

1 tsp salt

½ egg white

2 tsp cornflour (cornstarch) paste (see page 15)

1 medium green (bell) pepper, cored and seeded

300 ml/½ pint/1¼ cups vegetable oil

1 spring onion (scallion), finely shredded

a few strips of ginger root, thinly shredded

1-2 red chillies, seeded and thinly shredded

½ tsp sugar

1 tbsp rice wine or dry sherry

a few drops of sesame oil

1 Cut the chicken breast into strips. Mix the chicken with a pinch of the salt, the egg white and cornflour (cornstarch).

2 Cut the green (bell) pepper into fairly thin shreds.

3 Heat the oil in a preheated wok, and deep-fry the chicken strips in batches for about 1 minute, or until the chicken changes colour. Remove the chicken strips with a slotted spoon, pat dry on kitchen paper (paper towels) and keep warm.

4 Pour off the excess oil from the wok, leaving about 1 tablespoon. Add the spring onion (scallion), ginger, chillies and green (bell) pepper and stir-fry for 1 minute.

5 Return the chicken to the wok with the remaining salt, the sugar and wine or sherry. Stir-fry for another minute, sprinkle with sesame oil and serve immediately.

COOK'S TIP

Rice wine is used everywhere in China for both cooking and drinking. Made from glutinous rice, it is known as 'yellow wine' because of its rich amber colour. Sherry is the best substitute as a cooking ingredient.

Honey & Soy Chicken

Clear honey is often added to Chinese recipes for sweetness. It combines well with the saltiness of the soy sauce.

NUTRITIONAL INFORMATION

Calories	279	Sugars	........10g
Protein	........38g	Fat	...........8g
Carbohydrate	...12g	Saturates	.......2g

35 MINS   25 MINS

SERVES 4

INGREDIENTS

2 tbsp clear honey

3 tbsp light soy sauce

1 tsp Chinese five-spice powder

1 tbsp sweet sherry

1 clove garlic, crushed

8 chicken thighs

1 tbsp sunflower oil

1 red chilli

100 g/3½ oz/1¼ cups baby corn cobs, halved

8 spring onions (scallions), sliced

150 g/5½ oz/1½ cups bean sprouts

1 Mix together the honey, soy sauce, Chinese five-spice powder, sherry and garlic in a large bowl.

2 Using a sharp knife, make 3 slashes in the skin of each chicken thigh. Brush the honey and soy marinade over the chicken thighs, cover and leave to stand for at least 30 minutes.

3 Heat the oil in a large preheated wok. Add the chicken and cook over a fairly high heat for 12–15 minutes, or until the chicken browns and the skin begins to crispen. Remove the chicken with a slotted spoon and keep warm until required.

4 Using a sharp knife, deseed and very finely chop the chilli.

5 Add the chilli, corn cobs, spring onions (scallions) and bean sprouts to the wok and stir-fry for 5 minutes.

6 Return the chicken to the wok and mix all of the ingredients together until completely heated through. Transfer to serving plates and serve immediately.

COOK'S TIP

Chinese five-spice powder is found in most large supermarkets and is a blend of star anise, fennel seeds, cloves, cinnamon bark and Szechuan pepper.

Roast Baby Chickens

Poussins are stuffed with lemon grass and lime leaves, coated with a spicy marinade, then roasted until crisp and golden.

NUTRITIONAL INFORMATION

Calories 183	Sugars 1g
Protein 30g	Fat 7g
Carbohydrate 1g	Saturates 2g

🄶 🄶 🄶

10 MINS   55 MINS

SERVES 4

INGREDIENTS

4 small poussins, weighing about 350-500 g/12 oz-1 lb 2 oz each

coriander (cilantro) leaves and lime wedges, to garnish

a mixture of wild rice and Basmati rice, to serve

MARINADE

4 garlic cloves, peeled

2 fresh coriander roots

1 tbsp light soy sauce

salt and pepper

STUFFING

4 blades lemon grass

4 kaffir lime leaves

4 slices ginger root

about 6 tbsp coconut milk, to brush

1 Wash the chickens and dry on kitchen paper (paper towels).

2 Place all the ingredients for the marinade in a small blender and purée until smooth. Alternatively, grind to a paste in a pestle and mortar. Season to taste with salt and pepper.

3 Rub this marinade mixture into the skin of the chickens, using the back of a spoon to spread it evenly over the skins.

4 Place a blade of lemon grass, a lime leaf and a piece of ginger in the cavity of each chicken.

5 Place the chickens in a roasting pan and brush lightly with the coconut milk. Roast for about 30 minutes in a preheated oven.

6 Remove from the oven, brush again with coconut milk, return to the oven and cook for a further 15-25 minutes, until golden and cooked through, depending upon the size of the chickens. The chickens are cooked when the juices from the thigh run clear and are not tinged at all with pink.

7 Serve the baby chickens with the pan juices poured over. Garnish with coriander (cilantro) leaves and lime wedges and serve with rice.

Chicken & Vegetables

This is a popular dish in Chinese restaurants in the West, although nothing beats making it yourself.

NUTRITIONAL INFORMATION

Calories . . . . . . .298 Sugars 4g
Protein . . . . .22g Fat 19g
Carbohydrate . . . .11g Saturates 4g

30 MINS · 15 MINS

SERVES 4

INGREDIENTS

300 g/10½ oz boneless, skinless chicken breasts

1 tbsp cornflour (cornstarch)

1 tsp sesame oil

1 tbsp hoisin sauce

1 tsp light soy sauce

3 garlic cloves, crushed

2 tbsp vegetable oil

75 g/2¾ oz/¾ cup unsalted cashew nuts

25 g/1 oz mangetout (snow peas)

1 celery stick, sliced

1 onion, cut into 8 pieces

60 g/2 oz bean sprouts

1 red (bell) pepper, seeded and diced

SAUCE

2 tsp cornflour (cornstarch)

2 tbsp hoisin sauce

200 ml/7 fl oz/⅞ cup chicken stock

1 Trim any fat from the chicken breasts and cut the meat into thin strips. Place the chicken in a mixing bowl. Sprinkle with the cornflour (cornstarch) and toss to coat the chicken, shaking off any excess. Mix together the sesame oil, hoisin sauce, soy sauce and 1 garlic clove. Pour this mixture over the chicken, turning to coat. Leave to marinate for 20 minutes.

2 Heat half of the vegetable oil in a preheated wok. Add the cashew nuts and stir-fry for 1 minute, until browned.

3 Add the mangetout (snow peas), celery, the remaining garlic, the onion, bean sprouts and red (bell) pepper and cook, stirring occasionally, for 2–3 minutes. Remove the vegetables from the wok with a slotted spoon, set aside and keep warm.

4 Heat the remaining oil in the wok. Remove the chicken from the marinade and stir-fry for 3–4 minutes. Return the vegetables to the wok.

5 To make the sauce, mix the cornflour (cornstarch), hoisin sauce and chicken stock together and pour into the wok. Bring to the boil, stirring until thickened and clear. Tranfer the stir-fry to a warm serving dish and serve.

Peanut Sesame Chicken

Sesame seeds and peanuts give extra crunch and flavour to this stir-fry and the fruit juice glaze gives a lovely shiny coating to the sauce.

NUTRITIONAL INFORMATION

Calories	435	Sugars	........10g
Protein	........38g	Fat	..........26g
Carbohydrate	...14g	Saturates	.......4g

10 MINS   15 MINS

SERVES 4

INGREDIENTS

2 tbsp vegetable oil

2 tbsp sesame oil

500 g/1 lb 2 oz boneless, skinned chicken breasts, sliced into strips

250 g/9 oz broccoli, divided into small florets

250 g/9 oz baby or dwarf corn, halved if large

1 small red (bell) pepper, cored, seeded and sliced

2 tbsp soy sauce

250 ml/9 fl oz/1 cup orange juice

2 tsp cornflour (cornstarch)

2 tbsp toasted sesame seeds

60 g/2 oz/⅓ cup roasted, shelled, unsalted peanuts

rice or noodles, to serve

1 Heat the vegetable oil and sesame oil in a large, heavy-based frying pan (skillet) or wok until smoking. Add the chicken strips and stir-fry until browned, about 4-5 minutes.

2 Add the broccoli, corn and red (bell) pepper and stir-fry for a further 1-2 minutes.

3 Meanwhile, mix the soy sauce with the orange juice and cornflour (cornstarch). Stir into the chicken and vegetable mixture, stirring constantly until the sauce has slightly thickened and a glaze develops.

4 Stir in the sesame seeds and peanuts, mixing well. Heat the stir-fry for a further 3-4 minutes.

5 Transfer the stir-fry to a warm serving dish and serve with rice or noodles.

COOK'S TIP

Make sure you use the unsalted variety of peanuts or the dish will be too salty, as the soy sauce adds saltiness.

Chicken Fu-Yung

Although commonly described as an omelette, a foo-yung ('white lotus petals') should use egg whites only to create a very delicate texture.

NUTRITIONAL INFORMATION

Calories 220	Sugars 1g
Protein 16g	Fat 14g
Carbohydrate 7g	Saturates 3g

5 MINS   5 MINS

SERVES 4

I N G R E D I E N T S

175 g/6 oz chicken breast fillet, skinned

½ tsp salt

pepper

1 tsp rice wine or dry sherry

1 tbsp cornflour (cornstarch)

3 eggs

½ tsp finely chopped spring onions (scallions)

3 tbsp vegetable oil

125 g/4½ oz green peas

1 tsp light soy sauce

salt

few drops of sesame oil

1 Cut the chicken across the grain into very small, paper-thin slices, using a cleaver. Place the chicken slices in a shallow dish.

2 In a small bowl, mix together ½ teaspoon salt, pepper, rice wine or dry sherry and cornflour (cornstarch).

3 Pour the mixture over the chicken slices in the dish, turning the chicken until well coated.

4 Beat the eggs in a small bowl with a pinch of salt and the spring onions (scallions).

5 Heat the vegetable oil in a preheated wok, add the chicken slices and stir-fry for about 1 minute, making sure that the slices are kept separated.

6 Pour the beaten eggs over the chicken, and lightly scramble until set. Do not stir too vigorously, or the mixture will break up in the oil. Stir the oil from the bottom of the wok so that the foo-yung rises to the surface.

7 Add the peas, light soy sauce and salt to taste and blend well. Transfer to warm serving dishes, sprinkle with sesame oil and serve.

COOK'S TIP

If available, chicken *goujons* can be used for this dish: these are small, delicate strips of chicken which require no further cutting and are very tender.

Coconut Chicken Curry

Okra is often called ladies' fingers and has a slightly bitter taste. The pineapple and coconut in this recipe offsets okra in colour and flavour.

NUTRITIONAL INFORMATION

Calories 456   Sugars 21g
Protein ....29g   Fat 29g
Carbohydrate ...22g   Saturates 17g

🄶 🄶 🄶

5 MINS   45 MINS

SERVES 4

I N G R E D I E N T S

2 tbsp sunflower oil

450 g/1 lb boneless, skinless chicken thighs or breasts

150 g/5½ oz/1 cup okra

1 large onion, sliced

2 cloves garlic, crushed

3 tbsp mild curry paste

300 ml/½ pint/2¼ cups chicken stock

1 tbsp fresh lemon juice

100 g/3½ oz/½ cup creamed coconut, coarsely grated

175 g/6 oz/1¼ cups fresh or canned pineapple, cubed

150 ml/¼ pint/⅔ cup thick, natural (unsweetened) yogurt

2 tbsp chopped fresh coriander (cilantro)

freshly boiled rice, to serve

TO GARNISH

lemon wedges

fresh coriander (cilantro) sprigs

1 Heat the oil in a wok. Cut the chicken into bite-sized pieces, add to the wok and stir-fry until evenly browned.

2 Using a sharp knife, trim the okra. Add the onion, garlic and okra to the wok and cook for a further 2–3 minutes, stirring constantly.

3 Mix the curry paste with the chicken stock and lemon juice and pour into the wok. Bring to the boil, cover and leave to simmer for 30 minutes.

4 Stir the grated coconut into the curry and cook for about 5 minutes.

5 Add the pineapple, yogurt and coriander (cilantro) and cook for 2 minutes, stirring. Garnish and serve.

COOK'S TIP

Score around the top of the okra with a knife before cooking to release the sticky glue-like substance which is bitter in taste.

Crispy Chicken

In this recipe, the chicken is brushed with a syrup and deep-fried until golden. It is a little time consuming, but well worth the effort.

NUTRITIONAL INFORMATION

Calories ....283 Sugars 8g
Protein ....29g Fat 15g
Carbohydrate ....8g Saturates 3g

15 HOURS   35 MINS

SERVES 4

INGREDIENTS

1.5 kg/3 lb 5 oz oven-ready chicken

2 tbsp clear honey

2 tsp Chinese five-spice powder

2 tbsp rice wine vinegar

850 ml/1½ pints/3¾ cups vegetable oil,
   for deep-frying

chilli sauce, to serve

1 Rinse the chicken inside and out under cold running water and pat dry with kitchen paper (paper towels).

2 Bring a large saucepan of water to the boil and remove from the heat. Place the chicken in the water, cover and set aside for 20 minutes.

3 Remove the chicken from the water and pat dry with absorbent kitchen

paper (paper towels). Cool and leave to chill in the refrigerator overnight.

4 To make the glaze, mix the honey, Chinese five-spice powder and rice wine vinegar.

5 Brush some of the glaze all over the chicken and return to the refrigerator for 20 minutes.

6 Repeat this process of glazing and refrigerating the chicken until all of the glaze has been used up. Return the chicken to the refrigerator for at least 2 hours after the final coating.

7 Using a cleaver or heavy kitchen knife, open the chicken out by splitting it through the centre through the breast and then cut each half into 4 pieces.

8 Heat the oil for deep-frying in a wok until almost smoking. Reduce the heat and fry each piece of chicken for 5–7 minutes, until golden and cooked through. Remove from the oil with a slotted spoon and drain on absorbent kitchen paper (paper towels).

9 Transfer to a serving dish and serve hot with a little chilli sauce.

COOK'S TIP

If it is easier, use chicken portions instead of a whole chicken. You could also use chicken legs for this recipe, if you prefer.

Red Chicken with Tomatoes

This is a really colourful dish, the red of the tomatoes perfectly complementing the orange sweet potato.

NUTRITIONAL INFORMATION

Calories	316	Sugars	5g
Protein	28g	Fat	19g
Carbohydrate	8g	Saturates	3g

5 MINS   35 MINS

SERVES 4

I N G R E D I E N T S

1 tbsp sunflower oil

450 g/1 lb boneless, skinless chicken

2 cloves garlic, crushed

2 tbsp red curry paste

2 tbsp fresh grated galangal or
　root ginger

1 tbsp tamarind paste

4 lime leaves

225 g/8 oz sweet potato

600 ml/1 pint/2½ cups coconut milk

225 g/8 oz cherry tomatoes, halved

3 tbsp chopped fresh coriander (cilantro)

cooked jasmine or fragrant rice,
　to serve

1 Heat the sunflower oil in a large preheated wok or heavy-based frying pan (skillet).

COOK'S TIP

Fresh root galangal is a spice very similar to ginger but not as pungent. It can be bought fresh from Oriental food stores but is also available dried and as a powder. The fresh root needs to be peeled before slicing to use.

2 Using a sharp knife, thinly slice the chicken. Add the chicken to the wok or frying pan (skillet) and stir-fry for 5 minutes until lightly browned.

3 Add the garlic, curry paste, galangal or root ginger, tamarind paste and lime leaves to the wok and stir-fry for 1 minute.

4 Using a sharp knife, peel and dice the sweet potato.

5 Add the coconut milk and sweet potato to the mixture in the wok and bring to the boil. Allow to bubble over a medium heat for 20 minutes, or until the juices start to thicken and reduce.

6 Add the cherry tomatoes and coriander (cilantro) to the curry and cook for a further 5 minutes, stirring occasionally. Transfer to serving plates and serve hot with cooked jasmine or fragrant rice.

Chilli Chicken

This is quite a hot dish, using fresh chillies. If you prefer a milder dish, halve the number of chillies used.

NUTRITIONAL INFORMATION

Calories . . . . . . .265 Sugars 3g
Protein . . . . .21g Fat 14g
Carbohydrate . . . .11g Saturates 2g

10 MINS   10 MINS

SERVES 4

INGREDIENTS

350 g/12 oz skinless, boneless lean chicken

½ tsp salt

1 egg white, lightly beaten

2 tbsp cornflour (cornstarch)

4 tbsp vegetable oil

2 garlic cloves, crushed

1-cm/½-inch piece fresh root ginger, grated

1 red (bell) pepper, seeded and diced

1 green (bell) pepper, seeded and diced

2 fresh red chillies, chopped

2 tbsp light soy sauce

1 tbsp dry sherry or Chinese rice wine

1 tbsp wine vinegar

1 Cut the chicken into cubes and place in a mixing bowl.

2 Mix together the salt, egg white, cornflour (cornstarch) and 1 tablespoon of the oil and pour over the chicken. Turn the chicken in the mixture to coat thoroughly.

3 Heat the remaining oil in a preheated wok or large frying pan (skillet).

4 Add the garlic and ginger and stir-fry for 30 seconds.

5 Add the chicken pieces to the wok and stir-fry for 2–3 minutes, or until browned.

6 Stir in the red and green (bell) peppers, chillies, soy sauce, sherry or Chinese rice wine and wine vinegar and cook for a further 2–3 minutes, until the chicken is cooked through. Transfer the chilli chicken to a warm serving dish and serve immediately.

COOK'S TIP

When preparing chillies, wear rubber gloves to prevent the juices from burning and irritating your hands. Be careful not to touch your face, especially your lips or eyes, until you have washed your hands.

Lemon & Sesame Chicken

Sesame seeds have a strong flavour which adds nuttiness to recipes.
They are perfect for coating these thin chicken strips.

NUTRITIONAL INFORMATION

Calories 273   Sugars 5g
Protein ....29g   Fat 13g
Carbohydrate ....11g   Saturates 3g

10 MINS   10 MINS

SERVES 4

I N G R E D I E N T S

4 boneless, skinless chicken breasts

1 egg white

25 g/1 oz/2 tbsp sesame seeds

2 tbsp vegetable oil

1 onion, sliced

1 tbsp demerara (brown crystal)
   sugar

finely grated zest and juice of
   1 lemon

3 tbsp lemon curd

200 g/7 oz can water chestnuts,
   drained

lemon zest, to garnish

COOK'S TIP

Water chestnuts are
commonly added to Chinese
recipes for their crunchy
texture as they do not have a
great deal of flavour.

1 Place the chicken breasts between 2 sheets of cling film (plastic wrap) and pound with a rolling pin to flatten. Slice the chicken into thin strips.

2 Whisk the egg white until light and foamy. Dip the chicken strips into the egg white, then coat in the sesame seeds.

3 Heat the oil in a wok and stir-fry the onion for 2 minutes until softened.

4 Add the chicken to the wok and stir-fry for 5 minutes, or until the chicken turns golden.

5 Mix the sugar, lemon zest, lemon juice and lemon curd and add to the wok. Allow it to bubble slightly.

6 Slice the water chestnuts thinly, add to the wok and cook for 2 minutes. Garnish with lemon zest and serve hot.

Chicken with Peanut Sauce

A tangy stir-fry with a strong peanut flavour. Serve with freshly boiled rice or noodles.

NUTRITIONAL INFORMATION

Calories 538	Sugars 5g	
Protein 45g	Fat 36g	
Carbohydrate . . .10g	Saturates 16g	

🔥 🔥 🔥

🍳 10 MINS   🕐 10 MINS

SERVES 4

INGREDIENTS

4 boneless, skinned chicken breasts, about 625 g/1 lb 6 oz

4 tbsp soy sauce

4 tbsp sherry

3 tbsp crunchy peanut butter

350 g/12 oz courgettes (zucchini), trimmed

2 tbsp sunflower oil

4-6 spring onions (scallions), thinly sliced diagonally

1 x 250 g/9 oz can bamboo shoots, well drained and sliced

salt and pepper

4 tbsp desiccated (shredded) coconut, toasted

1 Cut the chicken into thin strips across the grain and season lightly with salt and pepper.

2 Stir the soy sauce in a bowl with the sherry and peanut butter until smooth and well blended.

3 Cut the courgettes (zucchini) into 5 cm/2 inch lengths and then cut into sticks about 5 mm/¼ inch thick.

4 Heat the oil in a preheated wok, swirling it around until it is really hot.

5 Add the spring onions (scallions) and stir-fry for 1 minute or so, then add the chicken strips and stir-fry for 3-4 minutes until well sealed and almost cooked.

6 Add the courgettes (zucchini) and bamboo shoots and continue to stir-fry for 1-2 minutes.

7 Add the peanut butter mixture and heat thoroughly, stirring all the time so everything is coated in the sauce as it thickens.

8 Adjust the seasoning to taste and serve the chicken very hot, sprinkled with toasted coconut.

VARIATION

This dish can also be made with turkey fillet or pork fillet.

For coconut lovers dissolve 25 g/1 oz creamed coconut in 2-3 tablespoons boiling water and add to the soy sauce mixture before adding to the wok.

Chicken with Chilli & Basil

Chicken drumsticks are cooked in a delicious sauce and served with deep-fried basil for colour and flavour.

NUTRITIONAL INFORMATION

Calories 196   Sugars 2g
Protein . . . . .23g   Fat 10g
Carbohydrate . . . .3g   Saturates 2g

5 MINS   30 MINS

SERVES 4

INGREDIENTS

8 chicken drumsticks

2 tbsp soy sauce

1 tbsp sunflower oil

1 red chilli

100 g/3½ oz carrots, cut into thin sticks

6 celery stalks, cut into sticks

3 tbsp sweet chilli sauce

oil, for frying

about 50 fresh basil leaves

1 Remove the skin from the chicken drumsticks if desired. Make 3 slashes in each drumstick. Brush the drumsticks with the soy sauce.

2 Heat the sunflower oil in a preheated wok and fry the drumsticks for 20 minutes, turning frequently, until they are cooked through.

3 Deseed and finely chop the chilli. Add the chilli, carrots and celery to the wok and cook for a further 5 minutes. Stir in the chilli sauce, cover and allow to bubble gently whilst preparing the basil leaves.

4 Heat a little oil in a heavy based pan. Carefully add the basil leaves – stand well away from the pan and protect

your hand with a tea towel (dish cloth) as they may spit a little. Cook the basil leaves for about 30 seconds or until they begin to curl up but not brown. Leave the leaves to drain on absorbent kitchen paper (paper towels).

5 Arrange the cooked chicken, vegetables and pan juices on to a warm serving plate, garnish with the deep-fried crispy basil leaves and serve immediately.

COOK'S TIP

Basil has a very strong flavour which is perfect with chicken and Chinese flavourings. You could use baby spinach instead of the basil, if you prefer.

Honey-Glazed Duck

The honey and soy glaze gives a wonderful sheen and flavour to the duck skin. Such a simple recipe, yet the result is unutterably delicious.

NUTRITIONAL INFORMATION

Calories 176	Sugars 8g	
Protein 22g	Fat 5g	
Carbohydrate ...10g	Saturates 1g	

2¼ HOURS   30 MINS

SERVES 4

INGREDIENTS

1 tsp dark soy sauce

2 tbsp clear honey

1 tsp garlic vinegar

2 garlic cloves, crushed

1 tsp ground star anise

2 tsp cornflour (cornstarch)

2 tsp water

2 large boneless duck breasts, about 225g/8 oz each

celery leaves, cucumber wedges and snipped chives, to garnish

1 Mix together the soy sauce, honey, garlic vinegar, garlic and star anise.

2 Blend the cornflour (cornstarch) with the water to form a smooth paste and stir it into the soy sauce mixture.

3 Place the duck breasts in a shallow ovenproof dish. Brush with the soy marinade, turning to coat them completely. Cover and leave to marinate in the refrigerator for at least 2 hours, or overnight if possible.

4 Remove the duck from the marinade and cook in a preheated oven, at 220°C/425°F/Gas Mark 7, for 20-25 minutes, basting frequently with the glaze.

5 Remove the duck from the oven and transfer to a preheated grill (broiler). Grill (broil) for about 3-4 minutes to caramelize the top.

6 Remove the duck from the grill (broiler) pan and cut into thin slices. Arrange the duck slices in a warm serving dish, garnish with celery leaves, cucumber wedges and snipped chives and serve immediately.

COOK'S TIP

If the duck begins to burn slightly while it is cooking in the oven, cover with foil. Check that the duck breasts are cooked through by inserting the point of a sharp knife into the thickest part of the flesh – the juices should run clear.

Duck with Pineapple

For best results, use ready-cooked duck meat, widely available from Chinese restaurants and takeaways.

NUTRITIONAL INFORMATION

Calories ....187 Sugars 7g
Protein ....10g Fat 12g
Carbohydrate ....11g Saturates 2g

25 MINS   10 MINS

SERVES 4

INGREDIENTS

125-175 g/4½-6 oz cooked duck meat

3 tbsp vegetable oil

1 small onion, thinly shredded

2-3 slices ginger root, thinly shredded

1 spring onion (scallion), thinly shredded

1 small carrot, thinly shredded

125 g/4½ oz canned pineapple, cut into small slices

½ tsp salt

1 tbsp red rice vinegar

2 tbsp syrup from the pineapple

1 tbsp cornflour (cornstarch) paste (see page 15)

black bean sauce, to serve (optional)

1 Using a sharp knife or metal cleaver, cut the cooked duck meat into thin even-sized strips and set aside until required.

COOK'S TIP

Red rice vinegar is made from fermented rice. It has a distinctive dark colour and depth of flavour. If unavailable, use red wine vinegar, which is similar in flavour.

2 Heat the oil in a preheated wok or large heavy-based frying pan (skillet).

3 Add the shredded onion and stir-fry until the shreds are opaque.

4 Add the slices of ginger root, spring onion (scallion) shreds and carrot shreds to the wok and stir-fry for about 1 minute.

5 Add the duck shreds and pineapple to the wok together with the salt, rice vinegar and the pineapple syrup. Stir until the mixture is well blended.

6 Add the cornflour (cornstarch) paste and stir for 1-2 minutes until the sauce has thickened.

7 Transfer to a serving dish and serve with black bean sauce, if desired.

Duck with Mangoes

Use fresh mangoes in this recipe for a terrific flavour and colour. If they are unavailable, use canned mangoes and rinse them before using.

NUTRITIONAL INFORMATION

Calories	235	Sugars	.........6g
Protein	........23g	Fat	..........14g
Carbohydrate	....6g	Saturates	.......2g

5 MINS   35 MINS

SERVES 4

INGREDIENTS

2 medium-size ripe mangoes

300 ml/½ pint/1¼ cups chicken stock

2 garlic cloves, crushed

1 tsp grated fresh root ginger

3 tbsp vegetable oil

2 large skinless duck breasts, about 225 g/8 oz each

1 tsp wine vinegar

1 tsp light soy sauce

1 leek, sliced

freshly chopped parsley, to garnish

1 Peel the mangoes and cut the flesh from each side of the stones (pits). Cut the flesh into strips.

2 Put half of the mango pieces and the chicken stock in a food processor and process until smooth. Alternatively, press half of the mangoes through a fine sieve and mix with the stock.

3 Rub the garlic and ginger over the duck. Heat the vegetable oil in a preheated wok and cook the duck breasts, turning, until sealed. Reserve the oil in the wok and remove the duck.

4 Place the duck on a rack set over a roasting tin (pan) and cook in a preheated oven, at 220°C/425°F/Gas Mark 7, for 20 minutes, until the duck is cooked through.

5 Meanwhile, place the mango and stock mixture in a saucepan and add the wine vinegar and light soy sauce.

6 Bring the mixture in the saucepan to the boil and cook over a high heat, stirring, until reduced by half.

7 Heat the oil reserved in the wok and stir-fry the sliced leek and remaining mango for 1 minute. Remove from the wok, transfer to a serving dish and keep warm until required.

8 Slice the cooked duck breasts and arrange the slices on top of the leek and mango mixture. Pour the sauce over the duck slices, garnish and serve.

Duck with Broccoli & Peppers

This is a colourful dish using different coloured (bell) peppers and broccoli to make it both tasty and appealing to the eye.

NUTRITIONAL INFORMATION

Calories 261   Sugars 3g
Protein . . . . .26g   Fat 13g
Carbohydrate . . . .11g   Saturates 2g

35 MINS   15 MINS

SERVES 4

INGREDIENTS

1 egg white

2 tbsp cornflour (cornstarch)

450 g/1 lb skinless, boneless duck meat

vegetable oil, for deep-frying

1 red (bell) pepper, seeded and diced

1 yellow (bell) pepper, seeded and diced

125 g/4½ oz small broccoli florets

1 garlic clove, crushed

2 tbsp light soy sauce

2 tsp Chinese rice wine or dry sherry

1 tsp light brown sugar

125 ml/4 fl oz/½ cup chicken stock

2 tsp sesame seeds

1 In a mixing bowl, beat together the egg white and cornflour (cornstarch).

2 Using a sharp knife, cut the duck into 2.5-cm/1-inch cubes and stir into the egg white mixture. Leave to stand for 30 minutes.

3 Heat the oil for deep-frying in a preheated wok or heavy-based frying pan (skillet) until almost smoking.

4 Remove the duck from the egg white mixture, add to the wok and fry in the oil for 4–5 minutes, until crisp. Remove the duck from the oil with a slotted spoon and drain on kitchen paper (paper towels).

5 Add the (bell) peppers and broccoli to the wok and fry for 2–3 minutes. Remove with a slotted spoon and drain on kitchen paper (paper towels).

6 Pour all but 2 tablespoons of the oil from the wok and return to the heat. Add the garlic and stir-fry for 30 seconds. Stir in the soy sauce, Chinese rice wine or sherry, sugar and chicken stock and bring to the boil.

7 Stir in the duck and reserved vegetables and cook for 1–2 minutes.

8 Carefully spoon the duck and vegetables on to a warmed serving dish and sprinkle with the sesame seeds. Serve immediately.

Duck with Leek & Cabbage

Duck is a strongly-flavoured meat which benefits from the added citrus peel to counteract this rich taste.

NUTRITIONAL INFORMATION

Calories 192	Sugars 5g
Protein 26g	Fat 7g
Carbohydrate 6g	Saturates 2g

🕐 10 MINS   🕐 40 MINS

SERVES 4

INGREDIENTS

4 duck breasts

350 g/12 oz green cabbage, thinly shredded

225 g/8 oz leeks, sliced

finely grated zest of 1 orange

6 tbsp oyster sauce

1 tsp toasted sesame seeds, to serve

1 Heat a large wok and dry-fry the duck breasts, with the skin on, for about 5 minutes on each side (you may need to do this in 2 batches).

2 Remove the duck breasts from the wok and transfer to a clean board.

3 Using a sharp knife, cut the duck breasts into thin slices.

4 Remove all but 1 tablespoon of the fat from the duck left in the wok; discard the rest.

5 Using a sharp knife, thinly shred the green cabbage.

6 Add the leeks, green cabbage and orange zest to the wok and stir-fry for about 5 minutes, or until the vegetables have softened.

7 Return the duck to the wok and heat through for 2–3 minutes.

8 Drizzle the oyster sauce over the mixture in the wok, toss well until all the ingredients are combined and then heat through.

9 Scatter the stir-fry with toasted sesame seeds, transfer to a warm serving dish and serve hot.

VARIATION

Use Chinese leaves (cabbage) for a lighter, sweeter flavour instead of the green cabbage, if you prefer.

Duck with Lime & Kiwi Fruit

Tender breasts of duck served in thin slices, with a sweet but very tangy lime and wine sauce, full of pieces of kiwi fruit.

NUTRITIONAL INFORMATION

Calories	264	Sugars	.......20g
Protein	........20g	Fat	.........10g
Carbohydrate	...21g	Saturates	.......2g

1¼ HOURS   15 MINS

SERVES 4

INGREDIENTS

4 boneless or part-boned
  duck breasts

grated rind and juice of 2 large limes

2 tbsp sunflower oil

4 spring onions (scallions), thinly
  sliced diagonally

125 g/4½ oz carrots, cut into
  matchsticks

6 tbsp dry white wine

60 g/2 oz/¼ cup white sugar

2 kiwi fruit, peeled, halved and sliced

salt and pepper

parsley sprigs and lime halves tied in knots
  (see Cook's Tip), to garnish

1 Trim any fat from the duck, then prick the skin all over with a fork and lay in a shallow dish. Add half the grated lime and half the juice to the duck breasts, rubbing in thoroughly. Leave to stand in a cool place for at least 1 hour, turning the breasts at least once.

2 Drain the duck breasts, reserving the marinade. Heat 1 tbsp of oil in a wok. Add the duck and fry quickly to seal all over then lower the heat and continue to cook for about 5 minutes, turning several times until just cooked through and well browned all over. Remove and keep warm.

3 Wipe the wok clean with kitchen paper (paper towels) and heat the remaining oil. Add the spring onions (scallions) and carrots and stir-fry for 1 minute, then add the remaining lime marinade, wine and sugar. Bring to the boil and simmer for 2-3 minutes until slightly syrupy.

4 Add the duck breasts to the sauce, season and add the kiwi fruit. Stir-fry for a minute or until really hot and both the duck and kiwi fruit are well coated in the sauce.

5 Cut each duck breast into slices, leaving a 'hinge' at one end, open out into a fan shape and arrange on plates. Spoon the sauce over the duck, sprinkle with the remaining pieces of lime peel, garnish and serve.

COOK'S TIP

To make the garnish, trim a piece off the base of each lime half so they stand upright. Pare off a thin strip of rind from the top of the lime halves, about 5 mm/¼ inch thick, but do not detach it. Tie the strip into a knot with the end bending over the cut surface of the lime.

Duck in Spicy Sauce

Chinese five-spice powder gives a lovely flavour to this sliced duck, and the chilli adds a little subtle heat.

NUTRITIONAL INFORMATION

Calories	162	Sugars	.........2g
Protein	........20g	Fat	...........7g
Carbohydrate	....3g	Saturates	.......2g

5 MINS   25 MINS

SERVES 4

INGREDIENTS

1 tbsp vegetable oil

1 tsp grated fresh root ginger

1 garlic clove, crushed

1 fresh red chilli, chopped

350 g/12 oz skinless, boneless duck meat, cut into strips

125 g/4½ oz cauliflower, cut into florets

60 g/2 oz mangetout (snow peas)

60 g/2 oz baby corn cobs, halved lengthways

300 ml/½ pint/1¼ cups chicken stock

1 tsp Chinese five-spice powder

2 tsp Chinese rice wine or dry sherry

1 tsp cornflour (cornstarch)

2 tsp water

1 tsp sesame oil

1 Heat the oil in a wok. Lower the heat slightly, add the ginger, garlic, chilli and duck and stir-fry for 2–3 minutes. Remove from the wok and set aside.

2 Add the vegetables to the wok and stir-fry for 2–3 minutes. Pour off any excess oil from the wok and push the vegetables to one side.

3 Return the duck to the wok and pour in the stock. Sprinkle the Chinese five-spice powder over the top, stir in the wine or sherry and cook over a low heat for 15 minutes, or until the duck is tender.

4 Blend the cornflour (cornstarch) with the water to form a paste and stir into the wok with the sesame oil. Bring to the boil, stirring until the sauce has thickened and cleared. Transfer the duck and spicy sauce to a warm serving dish and serve immediately.

COOK'S TIP
Omit the chilli for a milder dish, or deseed the chilli before adding it to remove some of the heat.

Turkey with Cranberry Glaze

Traditional Christmas ingredients are given a Chinese twist in this stir-fry which containing cranberries, ginger, chestnuts and soy sauce!

NUTRITIONAL INFORMATION

Calories	167	Sugars	........11g
Protein	.........8g	Fat	...........7g
Carbohydrate	...20g	Saturates	.......1g

5 MINS   15 MINS

SERVES 4

INGREDIENTS

1 turkey breast

2 tbsp sunflower oil

15 g/½oz/2 tbsp stem ginger

50 g/1¾ oz/½ cup fresh or frozen cranberries

100 g/3½ oz/¼ cup canned chestnuts

4 tbsp cranberry sauce

3 tbsp light soy sauce

salt and pepper

1 Remove any skin from the turkey breast. Using a sharp knife, thinly slice the turkey breast.

2 Heat the sunflower oil in a large preheated wok or heavy-based frying pan (skillet).

3 Add the turkey to the wok and stir-fry for 5 minutes, or until cooked through.

4 Using a sharp knife, finely chop the stem ginger.

5 Add the ginger and the cranberries to the wok or frying pan (skillet) and stir-fry for 2–3 minutes or until the cranberries have softened.

6 Add the chestnuts, cranberry sauce and soy sauce, season to taste with salt and pepper and allow to bubble for 2–3 minutes.

7 Transfer the turkey stir-fry to warm serving dishes and serve immediately.

COOK'S TIP

It is very important that the wok is very hot before you stir-fry. Test by by holding your hand flat about 7.5 cm/3 inches above the base of the interior – you should be able to feel the heat radiating from it.

Peking Duck

No Chinese cookery book would be complete without this famous recipe in which crispy skinned duck is served with pancakes and a tangy sauce.

NUTRITIONAL INFORMATION

Calories . . . . . . .357 Sugars 48g
Protein . . . . .20g Fat 10g
Carbohydrate . . .49g Saturates 2g

6¼ HOURS   1½ HOURS

SERVES 4

I N G R E D I E N T S

1.8 kg/4 lb duck

1.75 litres/3 pints/7½ cups boiling water

4 tbsp clear honey

2 tsp dark soy sauce

2 tbsp sesame oil

125 ml/4 fl oz/½ cup hoisin sauce

125 g/4½ oz/⅔ cup caster (superfine) sugar

125 ml/4 fl oz/½ cup water

carrot strips, to garnish

Chinese pancakes, cucumber matchsticks and spring onions (scallions), to serve

1 Place the duck on a rack set over a roasting tin (pan) and pour 1.2 litres/2 pints/5 cups of the boiling water over it.

2 Remove the duck and rack and discard the water. Pat dry with absorbent kitchen paper (paper towels), replace the duck and the rack and set aside for several hours.

3 In a small bowl, mix together the clear honey, remaining boiling water and dark soy sauce, until they are thoroughly combined.

4 Brush the mixture over the skin and inside the duck. Reserve the remaining glaze. Set the duck aside for 1 hour, until the glaze has dried.

5 Coat the duck with another layer of glaze. Let dry and repeat until all of the glaze is used.

6 Heat the sesame oil in a saucepan and add the hoisin sauce, caster (superfine) sugar and water. Simmer for 2–3 minutes, until thickened. Leave to cool and then refrigerate until required.

7 Cook the duck in a preheated oven, at 190°C/375°F/Gas Mark 5, for 30 minutes. Turn the duck over and cook for 20 minutes. Turn the duck again and cook for 20–30 minutes, or until cooked through and the skin is crisp.

8 Remove the duck from the oven and set aside for 10 minutes.

9 Meanwhile, heat the pancakes in a steamer for 5–7 minutes or according to the instructions on the packet. Cut the skin and duck meat into strips, garnish with the carrot strips and serve with the pancakes, sauce, cucumber and spring onions (scallions).

Red Chicken Curry

The chicken is cooked with a curry paste using red chillies. It is a fiery hot sauce – for a milder version, reduce the number of chillies used.

NUTRITIONAL INFORMATION

Calories 331	Sugars 5g	
Protein 36g	Fat 17g	
Carbohydrate 7g	Saturates 3g	

10 MINS   10 MINS

SERVES 4

INGREDIENTS

4 tbsp vegetable oil

2 garlic cloves, crushed

400 ml/14 fl oz/1¾ cups coconut milk

6 chicken breast fillets, skinned and
   cut into bite-sized pieces

125 ml/4 fl oz/½ cup chicken stock

2 tbsp fish sauce

sliced red and green chillies,
   to garnish

boiled rice, to serve

RED CURRY PASTE

8 dried red chillies, seeded
   and chopped

2.5 cm/1 inch galangal or ginger root,
   peeled and sliced

3 stalks lemon grass, chopped

1 garlic clove, peeled

2 tsp shrimp paste

1 kaffir lime leaf, chopped

1 tsp ground coriander

¾ tsp ground cumin

1 tbsp chopped fresh coriander
   (cilantro)

1 tsp salt and black pepper

1 To make the red curry paste, place all the ingredients in a food processor or blender and process until smooth.

2 Heat the vegetable oil in a large, heavy-based pan or wok. Add the garlic and cook for 1 minute or until it turns golden.

3 Stir in the red curry paste and cook for 10-15 seconds.

4 Gradually add the coconut milk, stirring constantly (don't worry if the mixture starts to look curdled at this stage).

5 Add the chicken pieces and turn in the sauce mixture to coat. Cook gently for about 3-5 minutes or until almost tender.

6 Stir in the chicken stock and fish sauce, mixing well, then cook for a further 2 minutes.

7 Transfer the chicken curry to a warmed serving dish and garnish with sliced red and green chillies. Serve with rice.

Barbecued Duckling

The sweet, spicy marinade used in this recipe gives the duckling a subtle flavour of the Orient.

NUTRITIONAL INFORMATION

Calories 249	Sugars 20g
Protein 27g	Fat 6g
Carbohydrate . . .23g	Saturates 2g

6¼ HOURS   30 MINS

SERVES 4

INGREDIENTS

3 cloves garlic, crushed

150 ml/5 fl oz/⅔ cup light soy sauce

5 tbsp light muscovado sugar

2.5 cm/1 inch piece root ginger, grated

1 tbsp chopped, fresh coriander (cilantro)

1 tsp five-spice powder

4 duckling breasts

sprig of fresh coriander (cilantro),
    to garnish (optional)

1 To make the marinade, mix together the garlic, soy sauce, sugar, grated ginger, chopped coriander (cilantro) and five-spice powder in a small bowl until well combined.

2 Place the duckling breasts in a shallow, non-metallic dish and pour over the marinade. Carefully turn over the duckling so that it is fully coated with the marinade on both sides.

3 Cover the bowl with cling film (plastic wrap) and leave to marinate for 1-6 hours, turning the duckling once or twice so that the marinade is fully absorbed.

4 Remove the duckling from the marinade, reserving the marinade for basting.

5 Barbecue (grill) the duckling breasts over hot coals for about 20–30 minutes, turning and basting frequently with the reserved marinade, using a pastry brush.

6 Cut the duckling into slices and transfer to warm serving plates. Serve the barbecued (grilled) duckling garnished with a sprig of fresh coriander (cilantro), if using.

COOK'S TIP

Duckling is quite a fatty meat so there is no need to add oil to the marinade. However, you must remember to oil the barbecue (grill) rack to prevent the duckling from sticking. Oil the barbecue (grill) rack well away from the barbecue (grill) to avoid any danger of a flare-up.

Indian Charred Chicken

An Indian-influenced dish that is delicious served with naan bread and a cucumber raita.

NUTRITIONAL INFORMATION

Calories 228	Sugars 12g	
Protein 28g	Fat 8g	
Carbohydrate ...12g	Saturates 2g	

20 MINS   10 MINS

SERVES 4

INGREDIENTS

4 chicken breasts, skinned and boned

2 tbsp curry paste

1 tbsp sunflower oil

1 tbsp light muscovado sugar

1 tsp ground ginger

½ tsp ground cumin

TO SERVE

naan bread

green salad leaves

CUCUMBER RAITA

¼ cucumber

salt

150 ml/5 fl oz/⅔ cup low-fat natural yogurt

¼ tsp chilli powder

1 Place the chicken breasts between 2 sheets of baking parchment or cling film (plastic wrap). Pound them with the flat side of a meat mallet or rolling pin to flatten them.

2 Mix together the curry paste, oil, sugar, ginger and cumin in a small bowl. Spread the mixture over both sides of the chicken and set aside until required.

3 To make the raita, peel the cucumber and scoop out the seeds with a spoon. Grate the cucumber flesh, sprinkle with salt, place in a sieve and leave to stand for 10 minutes. Rinse off the salt and squeeze out any moisture by pressing the cucumber with the base of a glass or back of a spoon.

4 Mix the cucumber with the yogurt and stir in the chilli powder. Leave to chill until required.

5 Transfer the chicken to an oiled rack and barbecue (grill) over hot coals for 10 minutes, turning once.

6 Warm the naan bread at the side of the barbecue.

7 Serve the chicken with the naan bread and raita and accompanied with fresh green salad leaves.

Fruity Duck Stir-Fry

The pineapple and plum sauce add a sweetness and fruity flavour to this colourful recipe which blends well with the duck.

NUTRITIONAL INFORMATION

Calories . . . . .241 Sugars 7g
Protein . . . . .26g Fat 8g
Carbohydrate . . .16g Saturates 2g

5 MINS   25 MINS

SERVES 4

I N G R E D I E N T S

4 duck breasts

1 tsp Chinese five-spice powder

1 tbsp cornflour (cornstarch)

1 tbsp chilli oil

225 g/8 oz baby onions, peeled

2 cloves garlic, crushed

100 g/3½ oz/1 cup baby corn cobs

175 g/6 oz/1¼ cups canned pineapple chunks

6 spring onions (scallions), sliced

100 g/3½ oz/1 cup bean sprouts

2 tbsp plum sauce

1 Remove any skin from the duck breasts. Cut the duck into thin slices.

2 Mix the five-spice powder and the cornflour (cornstarch). Toss the duck in the mixture until well coated.

3 Heat the oil in a preheated wok. Stir-fry the duck for 10 minutes, or until just begining to crispen around the edges. Remove from the wok and set aside.

4 Add the onions and garlic to the wok and stir-fry for 5 minutes, or until softened. Add the baby corn cobs and stir-fry for a further 5 minutes. Add the pineapple, spring onions (scallions) and bean sprouts and stir-fry for 3–4 minutes. Stir in the plum sauce.

5 Return the cooked duck to the wok and toss until well mixed. Transfer to warm serving dishes and serve hot.

COOK'S TIP

Buy pineapple chunks in natural juice rather than syrup for a fresher flavour. If you can only obtain pineapple in syrup, rinse it in cold water and drain thoroughly before using.

Aromatic & Crispy Duck

As it is very time-consuming to make the pancakes, buy ready-made ones from Oriental stores, or use crisp lettuce leaves as the wrapper.

NUTRITIONAL INFORMATION

Calories ....169 Sugars 1g
Protein ....7g Fat 11g
Carbohydrate ....7g Saturates 3g

🕒 9¼ HOURS   ⏱ 3¼ HOURS

SERVES 4

I N G R E D I E N T S

2 large duckling quarters

1 tsp salt

3-4 pieces star anise

1 tsp Szechuan red peppercorns

1 tsp cloves

2 cinnamon sticks, broken into pieces

2-3 spring onions (scallions), cut into short sections

4-5 small slices ginger root

3-4 tbsp rice wine or dry sherry

vegetable oil, for deep-frying

TO SERVE

12 ready-made pancakes or 12 crisp lettuce leaves

hoisin or plum sauce

¼ cucumber, thinly shredded

3-4 spring onions (scallions), thinly shredded

1 Rub the duck with the salt and arrange the star anise, peppercorns, cloves and cinnamon on top. Sprinkle with the spring onions (scallions), ginger and wine and marinate for at least 3-4 hours.

2 Arrange the duck pieces on a plate that will fit inside a bamboo steamer. Pour some hot water into a wok, place the bamboo steamer on top, sitting on a trivet. Add the duck and cover with the bamboo lid. Steam the duck over a high heat for 2-3 hours, until tender and cooked through. Top up the hot water from time to time as required. Remove the duck and leave to cool for at least 4-5 hours so the duck becomes crispy.

3 Pour off the water and wipe the wok dry. Pour in the oil and heat until smoking. Deep-fry the duck pieces, skin-side down, for 4-5 minutes or until crisp and brown. Remove and drain.

4 To serve, scrape the meat off the bone, place about 1 teaspoon of hoisin or plum sauce on the centre of a pancake (or lettuce leaf), add a few pieces of cucumber and spring onion (scallion) with a portion of the duck meat. Wrap up to form a small parcel and eat with your fingers.

Duck with Ginger & Lime

Just the thing for a lazy summer day – roasted duck sliced and served with a dressing made of ginger, lime juice, sesame oil and fish sauce.

NUTRITIONAL INFORMATION

Calories	529	Sugars	........3g
Protein	........38g	Fat	..........41g
Carbohydrate	....3g	Saturates	.......6g

20 MINS   25 MINS

SERVES 4

INGREDIENTS

3 boneless Barbary duck breasts, about 250 g/9 oz each

salt

DRESSING

125 ml/4 fl oz/½ cup olive oil

2 tsp sesame oil

2 tbsp lime juice

grated rind and juice of 1 orange

2 tsp fish sauce

1 tbsp grated ginger root

1 garlic clove, crushed

2 tsp light soy sauce

3 spring onions (scallions), finely chopped

1 tsp sugar

about 250 g/9 oz assorted salad leaves

orange slices, to garnish (optional)

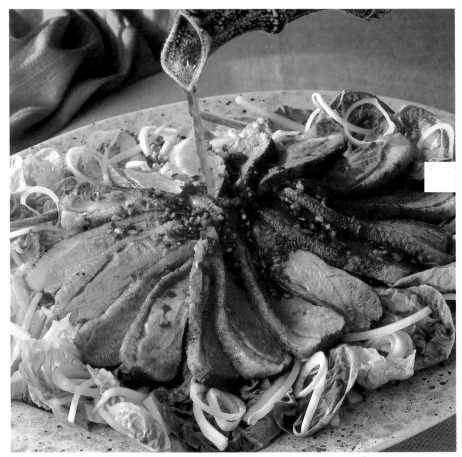

1 Wash the duck breasts, dry on kitchen paper (paper towels), then cut in half. Prick the skin all over with a fork and season well with salt. Place the duck pieces, skin-side down, on a wire rack or trivet over a roasting tin (pan).

2 Cook the duck in a preheated oven for 10 minutes, then turn over and cook for a further 12-15 minutes, or until the duck is cooked, but still pink in the centre, and the skin is crisp.

3 To make the dressing, beat the olive oil and sesame oil with the lime juice, orange rind and juice, fish sauce, grated ginger root, garlic, light soy sauce, spring onions (scallions) and sugar until well blended.

4 Remove the duck from the oven, and allow to cool. Using a sharp knife, cut the duck into thick slices.

5 Add a little of the dressing to moisten and coat the duck.

6 To serve, arrange assorted salad leaves on a serving dish. Top with the sliced duck breasts and drizzle with the remaining salad dressing.

7 Garnish with orange slices, if using, then serve at once.

Noodles in Soup

Noodles in soup are far more popular than fried noodles in China. You can use different ingredients for the dressing according to taste.

NUTRITIONAL INFORMATION

Calories 231	Sugars 1g
Protein 18g	Fat 11g
Carbohydrate . . .16g	Saturates 2g

4 HOURS   15 MINS

SERVES 4

I N G R E D I E N T S

250 g/9 oz chicken fillet, pork fillet, or any other ready-cooked meat

3-4 Chinese dried mushrooms, soaked

125 g/4½ oz canned sliced bamboo shoots, rinsed and drained

125 g/4½ oz spinach leaves, lettuce hearts, or Chinese leaves (cabbage), shredded

2 spring onions (scallions), finely shredded

250 g/9 oz egg noodles

about 600 ml/1 pint/2½ cups Chinese Stock (see page 14)

2 tbsp light soy sauce

2 tbsp vegetable oil

1 tsp salt

½ tsp sugar

2 tsp Chinese rice wine or dry sherry

a few drops sesame oil

1 tsp red chilli oil (optional)

1 Using a sharp knife or meat cleaver, cut the meat into thin shreds.

2 Squeeze dry the soaked Chinese mushrooms and discard the hard stalk.

3 Thinly shred the mushrooms, bamboo shoots, spinach leaves and spring onions (scallions).

4 Cook the noodles in boiling water according to the instructions on the packet, then drain and rinse under cold water. Place the noodles in a bowl.

5 Bring the Chinese stock to the boil, add about 1 tablespoon soy sauce and pour over the noodles. Keep warm.

6 Heat the vegetable oil in a preheated wok, add about half of the spring onions (scallions), the meat and the vegetables (mushrooms, bamboo shoots and greens). Stir-fry for about 2-3 minutes. Add all the seasonings and stir until well combined.

7 Pour the mixture in the wok over the noodles, garnish with the remaining spring onions (scallions) and serve immediately.

COOK'S TIP

Noodle soup is wonderfully satisfying and is ideal to serve on cold winter days.

Pulses, Grains  & Noodles

Pulses are a valuable source of protein, vitamins and minerals, so stock up on soya beans, haricot beans, red kidney beans, cannellini beans and chickpeas as well as 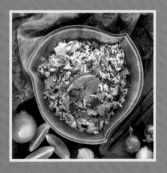 lentils, split peas and butter beans. It is also useful to store a variety of grains, such as barley, bulgur, polenta, oats and tapioca. Rice is an integral part of anyone's store cupboard; choose long-grain, basmati, arborio and short-grain rice. Noodles can be made from wheat, buckwheat or rice flours; stock a  range for quick, easy and tasty meals.

Sage Chicken & Rice

Cooking in a single pot means that all of the flavours are retained. This is a substantial meal that needs only a salad and some crusty bread.

NUTRITIONAL INFORMATION

Calories 247   Sugars 5g
Protein ....26g   Fat 5g
Carbohydrate ...25g   Saturates 2g

10 MINS   50 MINS

SERVES 4

INGREDIENTS

1 large onion, chopped

1 garlic clove, crushed

2 sticks celery, sliced

2 carrots, diced

2 sprigs fresh sage

300 ml/½ pint/1¼ cups chicken stock

350 g/12 oz boneless, skinless chicken breasts

225 g/8 oz/1⅓ cups mixed brown and wild rice

400 g/14 oz can chopped tomatoes

dash of Tabasco sauce

2 medium courgettes (zucchini), trimmed and thinly sliced

100 g/3½ oz lean ham, diced

salt and pepper

fresh sage, to garnish

TO SERVE

salad leaves

crusty bread

1 Place the pieces of onion, garlic, celery, carrots and sprigs of fresh sage in a large saucepan and pour in the chicken stock.

2 Bring to the boil, cover the pan and simmer for 5 minutes.

3 Cut the chicken into 2.5 cm/1 inch cubes and stir into the pan with the vegetables. Cover the pan and continue to cook for a further 5 minutes.

4 Stir in the mixed brown and wild rice and chopped tomatoes.

5 Add a dash of Tabasco sauce to taste and season well. Bring to the boil, cover and simmer for 25 minutes.

6 Stir in the sliced courgettes (zucchini) and diced ham and continue to cook, uncovered, for a further 10 minutes, stirring occasionally, until the rice is just tender.

7 Remove and discard the sprigs of sage.

8 Garnish with sage leaves and serve with a salad and fresh crusty bread.

Garlic Chicken Cassoulet

This is a cassoulet with a twist – it is made with chicken instead of duck and lamb. If you use canned beans, the result will be just as tasty.

NUTRITIONAL INFORMATION

Calories	550	Sugars	.........2g
Protein	........60g	Fat	..........19g
Carbohydrate	...26g	Saturates	......4g

5 MINS   2¹/₄ HOURS

SERVES 4

I N G R E D I E N T S

4 tbsp sunflower oil

900 g/2 lb chicken meat, chopped

225 g/8 oz/3 cups mushrooms, sliced

16 shallots

6 garlic cloves, crushed

1 tbsp plain (all-purpose) flour

225 ml/8 fl oz/1 cup white wine

225 ml/8 fl oz/1 cup chicken stock

1 bouquet garni (1 bay leaf, sprig thyme, celery, parsley & sage tied with string)

400 g/14 oz can borlotti beans

salt and pepper

1 Heat the sunflower oil in an ovenproof casserole and fry the chicken until browned all over. Remove from the casserole with a slotted spoon.

2 Add the mushrooms, shallots and garlic to the oil in the casserole and cook for 4 minutes.

3 Return the chicken to the casserole and sprinkle with the flour then cook for a further 2 minutes.

4 Add the wine and stock, stir until boiling then add the bouquet garni. Season well with salt and pepper.

5 Stir in the borlotti beans.

6 Cover and place in the centre of a preheated oven, 150°C/300°F/Gas Mark 2, for 2 hours.

7 Remove the bouquet garni and serve piping hot.

COOK'S TIP

Add chunks of potatoes and other vegetables, such as carrots and celery, for a delicious one-pot meal.

Orange Turkey with Rice

This is a good way to use up left-over rice. Use fresh or canned sweet pink grapefruit for an interesting alternative to the orange.

NUTRITIONAL INFORMATION

Calories 337	Sugars 12g
Protein 32g	Fat 7g
Carbohydrate ...40g	Saturates 1g

30 MINS   40 MINS

SERVES 4

INGREDIENTS

1 tbsp olive oil

1 medium onion, chopped

450 g/1 lb skinless lean turkey (such as fillet), cut into thin strips

300 ml/½ pint/1¼ cups unsweetened orange juice

1 bay leaf

225 g/8 oz small broccoli florets

1 large courgette (zucchini), diced

1 large orange

350 g/12 oz/6 cups cooked brown rice

salt and pepper

tomato and onion salad, to serve

TO GARNISH

25 g/1 oz pitted black olives in brine, drained and quartered

shredded basil leaves

1 Heat the oil in a large frying pan (skillet) and fry the onion and turkey, stirring, for 4–5 minutes until lightly browned.

2 Pour in the orange juice and add the bay leaf and seasoning. Bring to the boil and simmer for 10 minutes.

3 Meanwhile, bring a large saucepan of water to the boil and cook the broccoli florets, covered, for 2 minutes. Add the diced courgette (zucchini), bring back to the boil, cover and cook for a further 3 minutes (do not overcook). Drain and set aside.

4 Using a sharp knife, peel off the skin and white pith from the orange.

5 Thinly slice down the orange to make round slices, then halve each slice.

6 Stir the broccoli, courgette (zucchini), rice and orange slices into the turkey mixture. Gently mix together and season, then heat through for a further 3–4 minutes until piping hot.

7 Transfer the turkey rice to warm serving plates and garnish with black olives and shredded basil leaves. Serve the turkey with a fresh tomato and onion salad.

Chicken & Beans

Pulses are a valuable source of nourishment. You could use any variety of pulses in this recipe, but adjust the cooking times accordingly.

NUTRITIONAL INFORMATION

Calories . . . . .291 Sugars 3g
Protein . . . . .33g Fat 10g
Carbohydrate . . .18g Saturates 2g

12 HOURS   1HOUR

SERVES 4

INGREDIENTS

225 g/8 oz/1 generous cup dried
   black-eye beans (peas), soaked
   overnight and drained

1 tsp salt

2 onions, chopped

2 garlic cloves, crushed

1 tsp ground turmeric

1 tsp ground cumin

1.25 kg/2 lb 12 oz chicken, jointed into 8
   pieces

1 green (bell) pepper, chopped

2 tbsp oil

2.5 cm/1 inch piece ginger root, grated

2 tsp coriander seeds

½ tsp fennel seeds

2 tsp Garam Masala

1 tbsp chopped fresh coriander (cilantro),
   to garnish

1 Put the dried black-eye beans (peas) into a Balti pan or wok with the salt, onions, garlic, turmeric and cumin. Cover the beans with water, bring to the boil and cook for 15 minutes.

2 Add the chicken and green (bell) pepper to the pan and bring to the boil. Lower the heat and simmer gently for 30 minutes until the beans are tender and the chicken juices run clear when the thickest parts of the pieces are pierced with a sharp knife or skewer.

3 Heat the oil in a Balti pan or wok and fry the ginger, coriander seeds and fennel seeds for 30 seconds.

4 Stir the spices into the chicken and add the garam masala. Simmer for a further 5 minutes, garnish and serve.

COOK'S TIP

For convenience, use a 425 g/15 oz can of black-eye beans (peas) instead of dried beans (peas). Add at step 2.

Fragrant Spiced Chicken

The combination of chicken and chickpeas (garbanzo beans) is particlarly good. Use the canned variety for a quick meal.

NUTRITIONAL INFORMATION

Calories	343	Sugars	.........5g
Protein	........28g	Fat	..........16g
Carbohydrate	...24g	Saturates	......3g

🥗 5 MINS   🕐 30 MINS

SERVES 4

INGREDIENTS

3 tbsp ghee or vegetable oil

8 small chicken portions, such as thighs or drumsticks

1 large onion, peeled and chopped

2 garlic cloves, peeled and crushed

1-2 fresh green chillies, seeded and chopped, or use 1-2 tsp minced chilli (from a jar)

2 tsp ground cumin

2 tsp ground coriander

1 tsp garam masala

1 tsp ground turmeric

1 x 400 g/14 oz can chopped tomatoes

150 ml/¼ pint/⅔ cup water

1 tbsp chopped fresh mint

1 x 400 g/14 oz can chickpeas (garbanzo beans), drained

salt

1 tbsp chopped fresh coriander (cilantro)

low-fat natural yogurt, to serve (optional)

1 Heat the ghee or oil in a large saucepan and fry the chicken until sealed all over and lightly golden.

2 Remove from the pan. Add the onion, garlic, chilli and spices and cook very gently for 2 minutes, stirring frequently.

3 Stir in the tomatoes, water, mint and chickpeas (garbanzo beans). Mix well, return the chicken portions to the pan, season with salt, then cover and simmer gently for about 20 minutes or until the chicken is tender.

4 Taste and adjust the seasoning, then sprinkle with the coriander (cilantro) and serve hot with yogurt (if using)

VARIATION

Canned black-eyed beans and red kidney beans also make delicious additions to this spicy chicken dish. Be sure to drain and rinse canned beans before adding to the pan.

Chicken with Rice & Peas

The secret of this dish is that it must be brown in colour, which is achieved by caramelizing the chicken first.

NUTRITIONAL INFORMATION

Calories 335	Sugars 11g
Protein 20g	Fat 12g
Carbohydrate ...38g	Saturates 6g

10 MINS   1 HOUR

SERVES 6

INGREDIENTS

1 onion, chopped

2 garlic cloves

1 tbsp chopped fresh chives

1 tbsp chopped fresh thyme

2 celery stalks with leaves, chopped

350 ml/12 fl oz/1½ cups water

½ fresh coconut, chopped

liquid from 1 fresh coconut

500 g/1 lb 2 oz can pigeon peas or kidney
    beans, drained

1 red chilli, deseeded and sliced thinly

2 tbsp groundnut oil

2 tbsp caster (superfine) sugar

1.5 kg/3 lb 5 oz chicken pieces

250 g/9 oz/1¼ cups white long-grain rice,
    rinsed and drained

salt and pepper

celery leaves, to garnish

1 Put the onion, garlic, chives, thyme, celery and 4 tablespoons of the water into a food processor. Blend until smooth.

2 Alternatively, chop the onion and celery very finely, then grind with the garlic and herbs in a pestle and mortar, gradually mixing in the water. Pour into a saucepan and set aside.

3 Put the chopped coconut and liquid into the food processor and mix to a thick milk, adding water if necessary. Alternatively, finely grate the coconut and mix with the liquid. Add to the onion and celery mixture. Stir in the drained pigeon peas or kidney beans and chilli. Cook over a low heat for 15 minutes, then season.

4 Put the oil and sugar in a heavy-based casserole and cook over a moderate heat until the sugar begins to caramelize. Add the chicken and cook for 15–20 minutes, turning frequently, until browned all over.

5 Stir in the coconut mixture, the rice and remaining water. Bring to the boil, then reduce the heat, cover and simmer for 20 minutes until the chicken and rice are tender and the liquid has been absorbed. Garnish with celery leaves.

Cajun Chicken Gumbo

This complete main course is cooked in one saucepan. If you're cooking for one, halve the ingredients – the cooking time should stay the same.

NUTRITIONAL INFORMATION

Calories 425	Sugars 8g
Protein 34g	Fat 12g
Carbohydrate ...48g	Saturates 3g

5 MINS   25 MINS

SERVES 2

INGREDIENTS

1 tbsp sunflower oil

4 chicken thighs

1 small onion, diced

2 sticks (stalks) celery, diced

1 small green (bell) pepper, diced

90 g/3 oz/½ cup long grain rice

300 ml/½ pint/1¼ cups chicken stock

1 small red chilli

225 g/8 oz okra

15 ml/1 tbsp tomato purée (paste)

salt and pepper

1 Heat the oil in a wide pan and fry the chicken until golden. Remove the chicken from the pan.

2 Stir in the onion, celery and pepper and fry for 1 minute. Pour off any excess oil.

3 Add the rice and fry, stirring for a further minute. Add the stock and heat until boiling. Thinly slice the chilli and trim the okra. Add to the pan with the tomato purée (paste). Season to taste.

4 Return the chicken to the pan and stir. Cover tightly and simmer gently for 15 minutes, or until the rice is tender, the chicken is thoroughly cooked and the liquid absorbed. Stir occasionally and if it becomes too dry, add a little extra stock.

COOK'S TIP

The whole chilli makes the dish hot and spicy – if you prefer a milder flavour, discard the seeds of the chilli.

Chicken & Chilli Bean Pot

This aromatic chicken dish has a spicy Mexican kick. Chicken thighs have a wonderful flavour when cooked in this way.

NUTRITIONAL INFORMATION

Calories	333	Sugars	........10g
Protein	........25g	Fat	..........13g
Carbohydrate	...32g	Saturates	......2g

10 MINS   40 MINS

SERVES 4

INGREDIENTS

2 tbsp plain (all-purpose) flour

1 tsp chilli powder

8 chicken thighs or 4 chicken legs

3 tbsp vegetable oil

2 garlic cloves, crushed

1 large onion, chopped

1 green or red (bell) pepper, deseeded and chopped

300 ml/½ pint/1¼ cups chicken stock

350 g/12 oz tomatoes, chopped

400 g/14 oz can red kidney beans, rinsed and drained

2 tbsp tomato purée (paste)

salt and pepper

1 Mix together the flour, chilli powder and seasoning in a shallow dish. Rinse the chicken, but do not dry. Dip the chicken into the seasoned flour, turning to coat it on all sides.

2 Heat the oil in a large, deep frying pan (skillet) or saucepan and add the chicken. Cook over a high heat for 3–4 minutes, turning the pieces to brown them all over.

3 Lift the chicken out of the pan with a perforated spoon and drain on kitchen paper (paper towels).

4 Add the garlic, onion and (bell) pepper to the pan and cook for 2–3 minutes until softened.

5 Add the stock, tomatoes, kidney beans and tomato purée (paste), stirring well. Bring to the boil, then return the chicken to the pan. Reduce the heat and simmer, covered, for about 30 minutes, until the chicken is tender. Season to taste and serve at once.

COOK'S TIP

For extra intensity of flavour, use sun-dried tomato paste instead of ordinary tomato purée (paste).

Golden Chicken Risotto

Long-grain rice can be used instead of risotto rice, but it won't give you the traditional, creamy texture that is typical of Italian risottos.

NUTRITIONAL INFORMATION

Calories 701	Sugars 7g
Protein 35g	Fat 26g
Carbohydrate . . .88g	Saturates 8g

10 MINS   30 MINS

SERVES 4

I N G R E D I E N T S

2 tbsp sunflower oil

15 g/ ½ oz/1 tbsp butter or margarine

1 medium leek, thinly sliced

1 large yellow (bell) pepper, diced

3 skinless, boneless chicken breasts, diced

350 g/12 oz arborio (risotto) rice

a few strands of saffron

1.5 litres/2 ¾ pints/6 ¼ cups chicken stock

200 g/7 oz can sweetcorn
   (corn-on-the-cob)

60 g/2 oz/ ½ cup toasted unsalted peanuts

60 g/2 oz/ ½ cup grated Parmesan cheese

salt and pepper

1 Heat the sunflower oil and butter or margarine in a large saucepan. Fry the leek and (bell) pepper for 1 minute, then stir in the chicken and cook, stirring until golden brown.

2 Stir in the arborio (risotto) rice and cook for 2–3 minutes.

3 Stir in the saffron strands and salt and pepper to taste. Add the chicken stock, a little at a time, cover and cook over a low heat, stirring occasionally, for about 20 minutes, or until the rice is tender and most of the liquid has been absorbed. Do not let the risotto dry out – add more stock if necessary.

4 Stir in the sweetcorn (corn-on-the-cob), peanuts and Parmesan cheese, then season with salt and pepper to taste. Serve hot.

COOK'S TIP

Risottos can be frozen, before adding the Parmesan cheese, for up to 1 month, but remember to reheat this risotto thoroughly as it contains chicken.

Chicken Risotto Milanese

This famous dish is known throughout the world, and it is perhaps the best known of all Italian risottos, although there are many variations.

NUTRITIONAL INFORMATION

Calories 857   Sugars 1g
Protein . . . . .57g   Fat 38g
Carbohydrate . . .72g   Saturates 21g

5 MINS   55 MINS

SERVES 4

INGREDIENTS

125 g/4½ oz/½ cup butter

900 g/2 lb chicken meat, sliced thinly

1 large onion, chopped

500 g/1 lb 2 oz/2½ cups risotto rice

600 ml/1 pint/2½ cups chicken stock

150 ml/¼ pint/⅔ cup white wine

1 tsp crumbled saffron

salt and pepper

60 g/2 oz/½ cup grated Parmesan cheese,
   to serve

1 Heat 60 g/2 oz/4 tbsp of butter in a deep frying pan (skillet), and fry the chicken and onion until golden brown.

2 Add the rice, stir well, and cook for 15 minutes.

3 Heat the stock until boiling and gradually add to the rice. Add the white wine, saffron, salt and pepper to taste and mix well. Simmer gently for 20 minutes, stirring occasionally, and adding more stock if the risotto becomes too dry.

4 Leave to stand for 2–3 minutes and just before serving, add a little more stock and simmer for 10 minutes. Serve the risotto, sprinkled with the grated Parmesan cheese and the remaining butter.

Rice with Five-Spice Chicken

This dish has a wonderful colour obtained from the turmeric, and a great spicy flavour, making it very appealing all round.

NUTRITIONAL INFORMATION

Calories 412   Sugars 1g
Protein ....23g   Fat 13g
Carbohydrate ...53g   Saturates 2g

5 MINS   20 MINS

SERVES 4

INGREDIENTS

1 tbsp Chinese five-spice powder

2 tbsp cornflour (cornstarch)

350 g/12 oz boneless, skinless chicken breasts, cubed

3 tbsp groundnut oil

1 onion, diced

225 g/8 oz/1 cup long-grain white rice

½ tsp turmeric

600 ml/1 pint/2½ cups chicken stock

2 tbsp snipped fresh chives

1 Place the Chinese five-spice powder and cornflour (cornstarch) in a large bowl. Add the chicken pieces and toss to coat all over.

2 Heat 2 tablespoons of the groundnut oil in a large preheated wok. Add the chicken pieces to the wok and stir-fry for 5 minutes. Using a slotted spoon, remove the chicken and set aside.

3 Add the remaining groundnut oil to the wok.

4 Add the onion to the wok and stir-fry for 1 minute.

5 Add the rice, turmeric and chicken stock to the wok and gently bring to the boil.

6 Return the chicken pieces to the wok, reduce the heat and leave to simmer for 10 minutes, or until the liquid has been absorbed and the rice is tender.

7 Add the snipped fresh chives, stir to mix and serve hot.

COOK'S TIP

Be careful when using turmeric as it can stain the hands and clothes a distinctive shade of yellow.

Hot & Spicy Chicken Rice

Chicken is cooked with rice and vegetables and flavoured with red curry paste, ginger, coriander and lime for a deliciously spicy dish.

NUTRITIONAL INFORMATION

Calories 350	Sugars 2g	
Protein 26g	Fat 16g	
Carbohydrate . . .27g	Saturates 3g	

🌶 🌶 🌶

🍲 10 MINS   🕐 30 MINS

SERVES 4

I N G R E D I E N T S

250 g/9 oz/generous 1 cup white
   long-grain rice

4 tbsp vegetable oil

2 garlic cloves, chopped finely

6 shallots, sliced finely

1 red (bell) pepper, deseeded and diced

125 g/4½ oz French (green) beans,
   cut into 2.5 cm/1 inch lengths

1 tbsp red curry paste

350 g/12 oz cooked skinless, boneless
   chicken, chopped

½ tsp ground coriander seeds

1 tsp finely grated fresh ginger root

2 tbsp fish sauce

finely grated rind of 1 lime

3 tbsp lime juice

1 tbsp chopped fresh coriander
   (cilantro)

salt and pepper

TO GARNISH

lime wedges

sprigs of fresh coriander (cilantro)

1 Cook the rice in plenty of boiling, lightly salted water for 12–15 minutes until tender. Drain, rinse in cold water and drain thoroughly.

2 Heat the vegetable oil in a large preheated wok or frying pan (skillet).

3 Add the garlic and shallots to the wok or frying pan (skillet) and fry gently for 2–3 minutes until golden.

4 Add the (bell) pepper and French (green) beans and stir-fry for 2 minutes. Add the red curry paste and stir-fry for 1 minute.

5 Add the cooked rice to the wok or frying pan (skillet), then add the cooked chicken, ground coriander seeds, ginger, fish sauce, lime rind and juice, and fresh coriander (cilantro).

6 Stir-fry the mixture in the wok over a medium-high heat for about 4–5 minutes, until the rice and chicken are thoroughly reheated. Season to taste.

7 Transfer the chicken and rice mixture to a warm serving dish, garnish with lime wedges and fresh coriander (cilantro) and serve immediately.

Chinese Chicken Rice

This is a really colourful main meal or side dish which tastes just as good as it looks.

NUTRITIONAL INFORMATION

Calories	324	Sugars	.........4g
Protein	........24g	Fat	..........10g
Carbohydrate	...37g	Saturates	.......2g

5 MINS   25 MINS

SERVES 4

INGREDIENTS

350 g/12 oz/1¾ cups long-grain white rice

1 tsp turmeric

2 tbsp sunflower oil

350 g/12 oz skinless, boneless chicken breasts or thighs, sliced

1 red (bell) pepper, deseeded and sliced

1 green (bell) pepper, deseeded and sliced

1 green chilli, deseeded and finely chopped

1 medium carrot, coarsely grated

150 g/5½ oz/1½ cups bean sprouts

6 spring onions (scallions), sliced, plus extra to garnish

2 tbsp soy sauce

salt

1 Place the rice and turmeric in a large saucepan of lightly salted water and cook until the grains of rice are just tender, about 10 minutes. Drain the rice thoroughly and press out any excess water with kitchen paper (paper towels)

2 Heat the sunflower oil in a large preheated wok or frying pan (skillet).

3 Add the strips of chicken to the wok or frying pan (skillet) and stir-fry over a high heat until the chicken is just beginning to turn a golden colour.

4 Add the sliced (bell) peppers and green chilli to the wok and stir-fry for 2–3 minutes.

5 Add the cooked rice to the wok, a little at a time, tossing well after each addition until well combined and the grains of rice are separated.

6 Add the carrot, bean sprouts and spring onions (scallions) to the wok and stir-fry for a further 2 minutes.

7 Drizzle with the soy sauce and toss to combine.

8 Transfer the Chinese chicken rice to a warm serving dish, garnish with extra spring onions (scallions), if wished and serve at once.

Chicken & Rice Casserole

This is a quick-cooking, spicy casserole of rice, chicken, vegetables and chilli in a soy and ginger flavoured liquor.

NUTRITIONAL INFORMATION

Calories 502   Sugars 2g
Protein ....55g   Fat 9g
Carbohydrate ...52g   Saturates 3g

35 MINS   50 MINS

SERVES 4

I N G R E D I E N T S

150 g/5½ oz/⅔ cup long-grain rice

1 tbsp dry sherry

2 tbsp light soy sauce

2 tbsp dark soy sauce

2 tsp dark brown sugar

1 tsp salt

1 tsp sesame oil

900 g/2 lb skinless, boneless chicken meat, diced

850 ml/1½ pints/3¾ cups chicken stock

2 open-cap mushrooms, sliced

60 g/2 oz water chestnuts, halved

75 g/2¾ oz broccoli florets

1 yellow (bell) pepper, sliced

4 tsp grated fresh root ginger

whole chives, to garnish

VARIATION

This dish would work equally well with beef or pork. Chinese dried mushrooms may be used instead of the open-cap mushrooms, if rehydrated before adding to the dish.

1 Cook the rice in a saucepan of boiling water for about 15 minutes. Drain well, rinse under cold water and drain again thoroughly.

2 Mix together the sherry, soy sauces, sugar, salt and sesame oil.

3 Stir the chicken into the soy mixture, turning to coat the chicken well. Leave to marinate for about 30 minutes.

4 Bring the stock to the boil in a saucepan or preheated wok. Add the chicken with the marinade, mushrooms, water chestnuts, broccoli, (bell) pepper and ginger.

5 Stir in the rice, reduce the heat, cover and cook for 25-30 minutes, until the chicken and vegetables are cooked through. Transfer to serving plates, garnish with chives and serve.

Chicken & Noodle One-Pot

Flavoursome chicken and vegetables cooked with Chinese egg noodles in a coconut sauce. Serve in deep soup bowls.

NUTRITIONAL INFORMATION

Calories 256   Sugars 7g
Protein ....30g   Fat 8g
Carbohydrate ...18g   Saturates 2g

5 MINS   20 MINS

SERVES 4

INGREDIENTS

1 tbsp sunflower oil

1 onion, sliced

1 garlic clove, crushed

2.5 cm/1 inch root ginger, peeled and grated

1 bunch spring onions (scallions), sliced diagonally

500 g/1 lb 2 oz chicken breast fillet, skinned and cut into bite-sized pieces

2 tbsp mild curry paste

450 ml/16 fl oz/2 cups coconut milk

300 ml/½ pint/1¼ cups chicken stock

250 g/9 oz Chinese egg noodles

2 tsp lime juice

salt and pepper

basil sprigs, to garnish

1 Heat the sunflower oil in a wok or large, heavy-based frying pan (skillet).

2 Add the onion, garlic, ginger and spring onions (scallions) to the wok and stir-fry for 2 minutes until softened.

3 Add the chicken and curry paste and stir-fry for 4 minutes, or until the vegetables and chicken are golden brown. Stir in the coconut milk, stock and salt and pepper to taste, and mix well.

4 Bring to the boil, break the noodles into large pieces, if necessary, add to the pan, cover and simmer for about 6-8 minutes until the noodles are just tender, stirring occasionally.

5 Add the lime juice and adjust the seasoning, if necessary.

6 Serve the chicken and noodle one-pot at once in deep soup bowls, garnished with basil sprigs.

COOK'S TIP

If you enjoy hot flavours, substitute the mild curry paste in the above recipe with hot curry paste (found in most supermarkets) but reduce the quantity to 1 tablespoon.

Quick Chicken Chow Mein

A quick stir-fry of chicken and vegetables which are mixed with Chinese egg noodles and a dash of sesame oil.

NUTRITIONAL INFORMATION

Calories	300	Sugars	.........5g
Protein	........23g	Fat	..........15g
Carbohydrate	...18g	Saturates	.......2g

20 MINS   15 MINS

SERVES 4

INGREDIENTS

2 tbsp sesame seeds

250 g/9 oz thread egg noodles

175 g/6 oz broccoli florets

3 tbsp sunflower oil

1 garlic clove, sliced

2.5 cm/1 inch piece ginger root, peeled and chopped

250 g/9 oz chicken fillet, sliced thinly

1 onion, sliced

125 g/4½ oz shiitake mushrooms, sliced

1 red (bell) pepper, deseeded and cut into thin strips

1 tsp cornflour (cornstarch)

2 tbsp water

425 g/15 oz can baby sweetcorn, drained and halved

2 tbsp dry sherry

2 tbsp soy sauce

1 tsp sesame oil

COOK'S TIP

As well as adding protein, vitamins and useful fats to the diet, nuts and seeds add important flavour and texture.

1 Put the sesame seeds in a heavy-based frying pan (skillet) and cook for 2–3 minutes until they turn brown and begin to pop. Cover the pan so the seeds do not jump out and shake them constantly to prevent them burning. Remove from the pan and set aside until required.

2 Put the noodles in a bowl, cover with boiling water and leave to stand for 4 minutes. Drain thoroughly.

3 Meanwhile, blanch the broccoli in boiling salted water for 2 minutes, then drain.

4 Heat the sunflower oil in a wok or large frying pan (skillet), add the garlic, ginger, chicken and onion and stir-fry for 2 minutes until the chicken is golden and the onion softened.

5 Add the broccoli, mushrooms and red (bell) pepper and stir-fry for a further 2 minutes.

6 Mix the cornflour (cornstarch) with the water then stir into the pan with the baby sweetcorn, sherry, soy sauce, drained noodles and sesame oil and cook, stirring, until the sauce is thickened and the noodles warmed through. Sprinkle with the sesame seeds and serve.

Chicken Chow Mein

This classic dish requires no introduction as it is already a favourite amongst most Chinese food-eaters.

NUTRITIONAL INFORMATION

Calories	230	Sugars	.........2g
Protein	........19g	Fat	...........11g
Carbohydrate	...14g	Saturates	.......2g

5 MINS   20 MINS

SERVES 4

INGREDIENTS

250 g/9 oz packet medium egg noodles

2 tbsp sunflower oil

275 g/9½ oz cooked chicken breasts, shredded

1 clove garlic, finely chopped

1 red (bell) pepper, deseeded and thinly sliced

100 g/3½ oz shiitake mushrooms, sliced

6 spring onions (scallions), sliced

100 g/3½ oz/1 cup bean sprouts

3 tbsp soy sauce

1 tbsp sesame oil

1 Place the egg noodles in a large bowl or dish and break them up slightly. Pour over enough boiling water to cover the noodles and leave to stand.

2 Heat the sunflower oil in a large preheated wok. Add the shredded chicken, finely chopped garlic, (bell) pepper slices, mushrooms, spring onions (scallions) and bean sprouts to the wok and stir-fry for about 5 minutes.

3 Drain the noodles thoroughly. Add the noodles to the wok, toss well and stir-fry for a further 5 minutes.

4 Drizzle the soy sauce and sesame oil over the chow mein and toss until well combined.

5 Transfer the chicken chow mein to warm serving bowls and serve immediately.

VARIATION

You can make the chow mein with a selection of vegetables for a vegetarian dish, if you prefer.

Chicken Noodles

Rice noodles are used in this recipe. They are available in large supermarkets or specialist Chinese supermarkets.

NUTRITIONAL INFORMATION

Calories . . . . . . .169 Sugars 2g
Protein . . . . .14g Fat 7g
Carbohydrate . . .12g Saturates 2g

🍴 🍴 🍴

🍚 5 MINS   🕐 15 MINS

SERVES 4

INGREDIENTS

225 g/8 oz rice noodles

2 tbsp peanut oil

225 g/8 oz skinless, boneless chicken breast, sliced

2 garlic cloves, crushed

1 tsp grated fresh root ginger

1 tsp Chinese curry powder

1 red (bell) pepper, seeded and thinly sliced

75 g/2¾ oz mangetout (snow peas), shredded

1 tbsp light soy sauce

2 tsp Chinese rice wine

2 tbsp chicken stock

1 tsp sesame oil

1 tbsp chopped fresh coriander (cilantro)

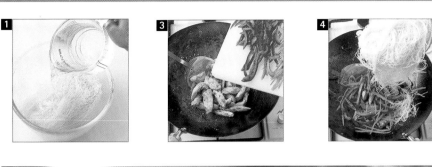

1 Soak the rice noodles for 4 minutes in warm water. Drain thoroughly and set aside until required.

2 Heat the peanut oil in a preheated wok or large heavy-based frying pan (skillet) and stir-fry the chicken slices for 2-3 minutes.

3 Add the garlic, ginger and Chinese curry powder and stir-fry for a further 30 seconds. Add the red (bell) pepper and

mangetout (snow peas) to the mixture in the wok and stir-fry for 2-3 minutes.

4 Add the noodles, soy sauce, Chinese rice wine and chicken stock to the wok and mix well, stirring occasionally, for 1 minute.

5 Sprinkle the sesame oil and chopped coriander (cilantro) over the noodles. Transfer to serving plates and serve.

VARIATION

You can use pork or duck in this recipe instead of the chicken, if you prefer.

Speedy Peanut Pan-Fry

Thread egg noodles are the ideal accompaniment to this quick dish because they can be cooked quickly and easily while the stir-fry sizzles.

NUTRITIONAL INFORMATION

Calories 563	Sugars 7g	
Protein 45g	Fat 33g	
Carbohydrate ...22g	Saturates 7g	

5 MINS   15 MINS

SERVES 4

INGREDIENTS

300 g/10½ oz/2 cups courgettes (zucchini)

250 g/9 oz/1⅓ cups baby corn (corn-on-the-cob)

250 g/9 oz thread egg noodles

2 tbsp corn oil

1 tbsp sesame oil

8 boneless chicken thighs or 4 breasts, sliced thinly

300 g/10½ oz/3¾ cups button mushrooms

350 g/12 oz/1½ cups bean sprouts

4 tbsp smooth peanut butter

2 tbsp soy sauce

2 tbsp lime or lemon juice

60 g/2 oz/½ cup roasted peanuts

salt and pepper

coriander (cilantro), to garnish

1 Using a sharp knife, trim and thinly slice the courgettes (zucchini) and baby corn (corn-on-the-cob). Set the vegetables aside until required.

2 Cook the noodles in lightly salted boiling water for 3–4 minutes.

3 Meanwhile, heat the corn oil and sesame oil in a large wok or frying pan (skillet) and fry the chicken over a fairly high heat for 1 minute.

4 Add the courgettes (zucchini), corn and mushrooms and stir-fry for 5 minutes.

5 Add the bean sprouts, peanut butter, soy sauce, lime or lemon juice and pepper, then cook for a further 2 minutes.

6 Drain the noodles thoroughly. Scatter with the roasted peanuts and serve with the courgette (zucchini) and mushroom mixture. Garnish and serve.

COOK'S TIP

Try serving this stir-fry with rice sticks. These are broad, pale, translucent ribbon noodles made from ground rice.

Yellow Bean Noodles

Cellophane or thread noodles are excellent re-heated, unlike other noodles which must be served as soon as they are ready.

NUTRITIONAL INFORMATION

Calories 212   Sugars 0.5g
Protein . . . . .28g   Fat 7g
Carbohydrate . . .10g   Saturates 2g

5 MINS   30 MINS

SERVES 4

I N G R E D I E N T S

175 g/6 oz cellophane noodles

1 tbsp peanut oil

1 leek, sliced

2 garlic cloves, crushed

450 g/1 lb minced (ground) chicken

425 ml/¾ pint/1 cup chicken stock

1 tsp chilli sauce

2 tbsp yellow bean sauce

4 tbsp light soy sauce

1 tsp sesame oil

chopped chives, to garnish

1 Place the cellophane noodles in a bowl, pour over boiling water and soak for 15 minutes.

2 Drain the noodles thoroughly and cut into short lengths with a pair of kitchen scissors.

3 Heat the oil in a wok or frying pan (skillet) and stir-fry the leek and garlic for 30 seconds.

4 Add the chicken to the wok and stir-fry for 4–5 minutes, until the chicken is completely cooked through.

5 Add the chicken stock, chilli sauce, yellow bean sauce and soy sauce to the wok and cook for 3–4 minutes.

6 Add the drained noodles and sesame oil to the wok and cook, tossing to mix well, for 4–5 minutes.

7 Spoon the mixture into warm serving bowls, sprinkle with chopped chives and serve immediately.

COOK'S TIP

Cellophane noodles are available from many supermarkets and all Chinese supermarkets.

Quick Chicken Noodles

Chicken and fresh vegetables are flavoured with ginger and Chinese five-spice powder in this speedy stir-fry.

NUTRITIONAL INFORMATION

Calories	266	Sugars	........4g
Protein	........25g	Fat	..........13g
Carbohydrate	...12g	Saturates	.......2g

10 MINS · 15 MINS

SERVES 4

INGREDIENTS

175 g/6 oz Chinese thread egg noodles

2 tbsp sesame or vegetable oil

25 g/1 oz/¼ cup peanuts

1 bunch spring onions (scallions), sliced

1 green (bell) pepper, deseeded and cut into thin strips

1 large carrot, cut into matchsticks

125 g/4½ oz cauliflower, broken into small florets

350 g/12 oz skinless, boneless chicken, cut into strips

250 g/9 oz mushrooms, sliced

1 tsp finely grated ginger root

1 tsp Chinese five-spice powder

1 tbsp chopped fresh coriander (cilantro)

1 tbsp light soy sauce

salt and pepper

fresh chives, to garnish

1 Put the noodles in a large bowl and cover with boiling water. Leave to soak for 6 minutes.

2 Heat the oil in a wok and stir-fry the peanuts for 1 minute until browned. Remove from the wok and leave to drain.

3 Add the spring onions (scallions), (bell) pepper, carrot, cauliflower and chicken to the pan. Stir-fry over a high heat for 4–5 minutes.

4 Drain the noodles thoroughly and add to the wok. Add the mushrooms and stir-fry for 2 minutes. Add the ginger, five-spice and coriander (cilantro); stir-fry for 1 minute.

5 Season with soy sauce and salt and pepper. Sprinkle with the peanuts, garnish and serve.

VARIATION

Instead of ginger root, ½ teaspoon ground ginger can be used.

Vary the vegetables according to what is in season. Make the most of bargains bought from your greengrocer or market.

Chicken on Crispy Noodles

Blanched noodles are fried in the wok until crisp and brown, and then topped with a shredded chicken sauce for a delightfully tasty dish.

NUTRITIONAL INFORMATION

Calories 376	Sugars 2g
Protein 15g	Fat 27g
Carbohydrate ...17g	Saturates 4g

🍤 🍤 🍤

35 MINS   🕐 25 MINS

SERVES 4

I N G R E D I E N T S

225 g/8 oz skinless, boneless chicken breasts, shredded

1 egg white

5 tsp cornflour (cornstarch)

225 g/8 oz thin egg noodles

300 ml/½ pint/1⅔ cups vegetable oil

600 ml/1 pint/2½ cups chicken stock

2 tbsp dry sherry

2 tbsp oyster sauce

1 tbsp light soy sauce

1 tbsp hoisin sauce

1 red (bell) pepper, seeded and very thinly sliced

2 tbsp water

3 spring onions (scallions), chopped

1 Mix together the chicken, egg white and 2 teaspoons of the cornflour (cornstarch) in a bowl. Leave to stand for at least 30 minutes.

2 Blanch the noodles in boiling water for 2 minutes, then drain thoroughly.

3 Heat the vegetable oil in a preheated wok. Add the noodles, spreading them to cover the base of the wok. Cook over a low heat for about 5 minutes, until the noodles are browned on the underside.

Flip the noodles over and brown on the other side. Remove from the wok when crisp and browned, place on a serving plate and keep warm. Drain the oil from the wok.

4 Add 300 ml/½ pint/1¼ cups of the chicken stock to the wok. Remove from the heat and add the chicken, stirring well so that it does not stick. Return to the heat and cook for 2 minutes. Drain, discarding the stock.

5 Wipe the wok with kitchen paper (paper towels) and return to the heat. Add the sherry, sauces, (bell) pepper and the remaining stock and bring to the boil. Blend the remaining cornflour (cornstarch) with the water and stir it into the mixture.

6 Return the chicken to the wok and cook over a low heat for 2 minutes. Place the chicken on top of the noodles and sprinkle with spring onions (scallions).

Sticky Chicken Drumsticks

These drumsticks are always popular – provide plenty of napkins for wiping sticky fingers or provide finger bowls with a slice of lemon.

NUTRITIONAL INFORMATION

Calories	213	Sugars	........14g
Protein	........27g	Fat	...........6g
Carbohydrate	...14g	Saturates	......2g

🝰 🝰

5 MINS   30 MINS

SERVES 4

I N G R E D I E N T S

10 chicken drumsticks

4 tbsp fine-cut orange marmalade

1 tbsp Worcestershire sauce

grated rind and juice of ½ orange

salt and pepper

T O   S E R V E

cherry tomatoes

salad leaves

1 Using a sharp knife, make 2–3 slashes in the flesh of each chicken drumstick.

2 Bring a large saucepan of water to the boil and add the chicken drumsticks. Cover the pan, return to the boil and cook for 5–10 minutes. Remove the chicken and drain thoroughly.

3 Meanwhile, make the baste. Place the orange marmalade, Worcestershire sauce, orange rind and juice and salt and pepper to taste in a small saucepan. Heat gently, stirring continuously, until the marmalade melts and all of the ingredients are well combined.

4 Brush the baste over the par-cooked chicken drumsticks and transfer them to the barbecue (grill) to complete cooking. Barbecue (grill) over hot coals for about 10 minutes, turning and basting frequently with the remaining baste.

5 Carefully thread 3 cherry tomatoes on to a skewer and transfer to the barbecue (grill) for 1–2 minutes.

6 Transfer the chicken drumsticks to serving plates. Serve with the cherry tomato skewers and a selection of fresh salad leaves.

COOK'S TIP

Par-cooking the chicken is an ideal way of making sure that it is cooked through without becoming overcooked and burned on the outside.

Chicken & Peanut Pizza

This pizza is topped with chicken which has been marinated in a delicious peanut sauce.

NUTRITIONAL INFORMATION

Calories . . . . .418 Sugars 7g
Protein . . . . .22g Fat 19g
Carbohydrate . . .43g Saturates 5g

2³/₄ HOURS   20 MINS

SERVES 4

INGREDIENTS

2 tbsp crunchy peanut butter

1 tbsp lime juice

1 tbsp soy sauce

3 tbsp milk

1 red chilli, deseeded and chopped

1 garlic clove, crushed

175 g/6 oz cooked chicken, diced

1 quantity Bread Dough Base

1 quantity Special Tomato Sauce (see page 142)

4 spring onions (scallions), trimmed and chopped

60 g/2 oz Mozzarella cheese, grated

olive oil, for drizzling

salt and pepper

1 Mix together the peanut butter, lime juice, soy sauce, milk, chilli and garlic in a bowl to form a sauce. Season well.

2 Add the chicken to the peanut sauce and stir until well coated. Cover and leave to marinate in a cool place for about 20 minutes.

3 Roll out or press the dough, using a rolling pin or your hands, into a 25 cm/ 10 inch circle on a lightly floured work surface. Place on a large greased baking tray (cookie sheet) or pizza pan (tin) and push up the edge a little. Cover and leave to rise slightly for 10 minutes in a warm place.

4 When the dough has risen, spread the tomato sauce over the base, almost to the edge.

5 Top with the spring onions (scallions) and chicken pieces, spooning over the peanut sauce.

6 Sprinkle over the cheese. Drizzle with a little olive oil and season well. Bake in a preheated oven, at 200°C/400°F/Gas Mark 6, for 18–20 minutes, or until the crust is golden. Serve.

Salads

Very often salads are nothing more than a few sad leaves of green lettuce with a slice of tomato. Make the most of the versatility of chicken and combine it with the delicious selection of fresh fruit and vegetables now available to create any number of hot and cold salads, which can be

eaten either as side dishes or as meals in themselves. In some of the following salad ideas, sweet and savoury flavours are mixed, while in others spices and

rich international flavours give an interesting twist to traditional ideas. If you are looking for low-fat recipes, remember that dressings often contain

fat, so use them sparingly.

Duckling & Radish Salad

Juicy duckling breasts are coated with sesame seeds, then cooked, thinly sliced and served with a crisp salad.

NUTRITIONAL INFORMATION

Calories	328	Sugars	.......0.2g
Protein	........22g	Fat	..........24g
Carbohydrate	....7g	Saturates	.......4g

5 MINS   10 MINS

SERVES 4

INGREDIENTS

350 g/12 oz boneless duckling breasts, skinned

2 tbsp plain (all-purpose) flour

1 egg

2 tbsp water

2 tbsp sesame seeds

3 tbsp sesame oil

½ head Chinese leaves (cabbage), shredded

3 celery sticks, sliced finely

8 radishes, trimmed and halved

salt and pepper

fresh basil leaves, to garnish

DRESSING

finely grated rind of 1 lime

2 tbsp lime juice

2 tbsp olive oil

1 tbsp light soy sauce

1 tbsp chopped fresh basil

1 Put each duckling breast between sheets of greaseproof paper (baking parchment) or cling film (plastic wrap). Use a meat mallet or rolling pin to beat them out and flatten them slightly.

2 Sprinkle the flour on to a large plate and season with salt and pepper.

3 Beat the egg and water together in a shallow bowl, then sprinkle the sesame seeds on to a separate plate.

4 Dip the duckling breasts first into the seasoned flour, then into the egg mixture and finally into the sesame seeds, to coat the duckling evenly.

5 Heat the sesame oil in a preheated wok or large frying pan (skillet).

6 Fry the duckling breasts over a medium heat for about 8 minutes, turning once. To test whether they are cooked, insert a sharp knife into the thickest part – the juices should run clear. Lift them out and drain on kitchen paper (paper towels).

7 To make the dressing for the salad, whisk together the lime rind and juice, olive oil, soy sauce and chopped basil. Season with a little salt and pepper.

8 Arrange the Chinese leaves (cabbage), celery and radish on a serving plate. Slice the duckling breasts thinly and place on top of the salad.

9 Drizzle with the dressing and garnish with fresh basil leaves. Serve at once.

Layered Chicken Salad

This layered main course salad has lively tastes and textures. For an interesting variation, substitute canned tuna for the chicken.

NUTRITIONAL INFORMATION

Calories	352	Sugars	.........9g
Protein	........29g	Fat	...........9g
Carbohydrate	...43g	Saturates	......2g

1 HOUR   40 MINS

SERVES 4

INGREDIENTS

750 g/1 lb 10 oz new potatoes, scrubbed

1 red (bell) pepper, halved, cored and deseeded

1 green (bell) pepper, halved, cored and deseeded

2 small courgettes (zucchini), sliced

1 small onion, thinly sliced

3 tomatoes, sliced

350 g/12 oz cooked chicken, sliced

snipped fresh chives, to garnish

YOGURT DRESSING

150 g/5½ oz/⅔ cup low-fat natural yogurt

3 tbsp low-fat mayonnaise

1 tbsp snipped fresh chives

salt and pepper

1 Put the potatoes into a large saucepan of cold water. Bring to the boil, then reduce the heat. Cover and simmer for 15–20 minutes until tender.

2 Meanwhile place the (bell) pepper halves, cut side down, under a preheated hot grill (broiler) and grill (broil) until the skins blacken and begin to char.

3 Remove the (bell) peppers and leave to cool, then peel off the skins and slice the flesh. Set aside.

4 Cook the courgettes (zucchini) in a small amount of lightly salted boiling water for 3 minutes.

5 Rinse the courgettes (zucchini) with cold water to cool quickly and set aside.

6 To make the dressing, mix the yogurt, mayonnaise and snipped chives together in a small bowl. Season well with salt and pepper.

7 Drain, cool and slice the potatoes. Add them to the dressing and mix well to coat evenly. Divide between 4 serving plates.

8 Top each plate with one quarter of the (bell) pepper slices and cooked courgettes (zucchini). Layer one quarter of the onion and tomato slices, then the sliced chicken, on top of each serving. Garnish with snipped chives and serve.

Chicken & Spinach Salad

Slices of lean chicken with fresh young spinach leaves and a few fresh raspberries are served with a refreshing yogurt and honey dressing.

NUTRITIONAL INFORMATION

Calories 235   Sugars 9g
Protein . . . . .37g   Fat 6g
Carbohydrate . . . .9g   Saturates 2g

3¹/₂ HOURS   25 MINS

SERVES 4

INGREDIENTS

4 boneless, skinless chicken breasts,
   150 g/5½ oz each

450 ml/16 fl oz/2 cups Fresh Chicken Stock
   (see page 14)

1 bay leaf

225 g/8 oz fresh young spinach leaves

1 small red onion, shredded

115 g/4 oz fresh raspberries

salt and freshly ground pink peppercorns

fresh toasted croûtons, to garnish

DRESSING

4 tbsp low-fat natural (unsweetened) yogurt

1 tbsp raspberry vinegar

2 tsp clear honey

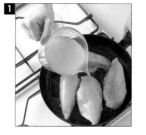

1 Place the chicken breasts in a frying pan (skillet). Pour over the stock and add the bay leaf. Bring to the boil, cover and simmer for 15–20 minutes, turning half-way through, until the chicken is cooked through. Leave to cool in the liquid.

2 Arrange the spinach on 4 serving plates and top with the onion. Cover and leave to chill.

3 Drain the cooked chicken and pat dry on absorbent kitchen paper (paper towels). Slice the chicken breasts thinly and arrange, fanned out, over the spinach and onion, on a large platter. Sprinkle the salad with the raspberries.

4 To make the dressing, mix all the ingredients together in a small bowl. Drizzle a spoonful of dressing over each chicken breast and season with salt and ground pink peppercorns to taste. Serve the salad with freshly toasted croûtons.

VARIATION

This recipe is delicious with smoked chicken, but it will be more expensive and richer, so use slightly less. It would make an impressive starter for a dinner party.

Chicken & Grape Salad

Tender chicken breast, sweet grapes and crisp celery coated in a mild curry mayonnaise make a wonderful al fresco lunch.

NUTRITIONAL INFORMATION

Calories 413   Sugars 20g
Protein . . . . .39g   Fat 20g
Carbohydrate . . .20g   Saturates 3g

🍲 25 MINS   🕐 0 MINS

SERVES 4

INGREDIENTS

500 g/1 lb 2 oz cooked skinless, boneless chicken breasts

2 celery sticks (stalks), sliced finely

250 g/9 oz/2 cups black grapes

60 g/2 oz/½ cup split almonds, toasted

pinch of paprika

sprigs of fresh coriander (cilantro) or flat-leafed parsley, to garnish

CURRY SAUCE

150 ml/¼ pint/½ cup lean mayonnaise

125 g/4½ oz/½ cup natural low-fat fromage frais

1 tbsp clear honey

1 tbsp curry paste

COOK'S TIP

To save time, use seedless grapes, now widely available in supermarkets, and add them whole to the salad.

1 Cut the chicken into fairly large pieces and transfer to a bowl with the sliced celery.

2 Halve the grapes, remove the seeds and add to the bowl.

3 To make the curry sauce, mix the mayonnaise, fromage frais, honey and curry paste together until blended.

4 Pour the curry sauce over the salad and mix together carefully until well coated.

5 Transfer to a shallow serving dish and sprinkle with the almonds and paprika.

6 Garnish the salad with the coriander (cilantro) or parsley.

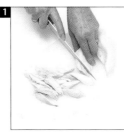

Chargrilled Chicken Salad

This is a quick starter to serve at a barbecue – if the bread is bent in half, put the chicken salad in the middle and eat it as finger food.

NUTRITIONAL INFORMATION

Calories	225	Sugars	.........5g
Protein	........16g	Fat	..........12g
Carbohydrate	...15g	Saturates	......2g

10 MINS   15 MINS

SERVES 4

INGREDIENTS

2 skinless, boneless chicken breasts

1 red onion

oil for brushing

1 avocado, peeled and pitted

1 tbsp lemon juice

125 ml/4 fl oz/½ cup low-fat mayonnaise

¼ tsp chilli powder

½ tsp pepper

¼ tsp salt

4 tomatoes, quartered

½ loaf sun-dried tomato-flavoured focaccia bread

green salad, to serve

1 Using a sharp knife, cut the chicken breasts into 1 cm/½ inch strips.

2 Cut the onion into eight pieces, held together at the root. Rinse under cold running water and then brush with oil.

3 Purée or mash the avocado and lemon juice together. Whisk in the mayonnaise. Add the chilli powder, pepper and salt.

4 Put the chicken and onion over a hot barbecue and grill for 3–4 minutes

on each side. Combine the chicken, onion, tomatoes and avocado mixture together.

5 Cut the bread in half twice, so that you have quarter-circle-shaped pieces, then in half horizontally. Toast on the hot barbecue (grill) for about 2 minutes on each side.

6 Spoon the chicken mixture on to the toasts and serve with a green salad.

VARIATION

Instead of focaccia, serve the salad in pitta bread which have been warmed through on the barbecue (grill).

Spicy Chicken Salad

This is an excellent recipe for leftover roast chicken. Add the dressing just before serving, so that the spinach retains its crispness.

NUTRITIONAL INFORMATION

Calories	225	Sugars	........4g
Protein	........25g	Fat	..........12g
Carbohydrate	....4g	Saturates	......2g

10 MINS ·   0 MINS

SERVES 4

INGREDIENTS

225 g/8 oz young spinach leaves

3 sticks (stalks) celery, sliced thinly

½ cucumber, sliced thinly

2 spring onions (scallions), sliced thinly

3 tbsp chopped fresh parsley

350g/12 oz boneless, lean roast chicken, sliced thinly

DRESSING

2.5 cm/1 inch piece fresh ginger root, grated finely

3 tbsp olive oil

1 tbsp white wine vinegar

1 tbsp clear honey

½ tsp ground cinnamon

salt and pepper

smoked almonds, to garnish (optional)

1 Thoroughly wash and dry the spinach leaves.

2 Toss the celery, cucumber and spring onions (scallions) with the spinach and parsley in a large bowl.

3 Transfer the salad ingredients to serving plates and arrange the chicken over the salad.

4 To make the dressing, combine the grated ginger, olive oil, wine vinegar, honey and cinnamon in a screw-topped jar and shake well to mix. Season with salt and pepper to taste.

5 Pour the dressing over the salad. Scatter a few smoked almonds over the salad to garnish (if using).

COOK'S TIP

For extra colour, add some cherry tomatoes and some thin strips of red and yellow (bell) peppers and garnish with a little grated carrot.

Waldorf Chicken Salad

This colourful and healthy dish is a variation of a classic salad. You can use a selection of mixed salad leaves, if preferred.

NUTRITIONAL INFORMATION

Calories	471	Sugars	........19g
Protein	........38g	Fat	..........27g
Carbohydrate	...20g	Saturates	......4g

30 MINS   0 MINS

SERVES 4

INGREDIENTS

500 g/1 lb 2 oz red apples, diced

3 tbsp fresh lemon juice

150 ml/¼ pint/⅔ cup low-fat mayonnaise

1 head of celery

4 shallots, sliced

1 garlic clove, crushed

90 g/3 oz/¾ cup walnuts, chopped

500 g/1 lb 2 oz lean cooked chicken, cubed

1 cos (romaine) lettuce

pepper

sliced apple and walnuts, to garnish

1 Place the apples in a bowl with the lemon juice and 1 tablespoon of mayonnaise. Leave for 40 minutes or until required.

2 Slice the celery very thinly. Add the celery with the shallots, garlic and walnuts to the apple, mix and then add the remaining mayonnaise and blend thoroughly.

3 Add the chicken and mix with the other ingredients.

4 Line a glass salad bowl or serving dish with the lettuce.

5 Pile the chicken salad into the centre, sprinkle with pepper and garnish with apple slices and walnuts.

VARIATION

Instead of the shallots, use spring onions (scallions) for a milder flavour. Trim the spring onions (scallions) and slice finely.

Coronation Salad

This dish is based on Coronation Chicken which was invented to celebrate Queen Victoria's coronation as a symbol of Anglo-Indian links.

NUTRITIONAL INFORMATION

Calories 236   Sugars 24g
Protein . . . . .7g   Fat 5g
Carbohydrate . . .43g   Saturates 1g

25 MINS   0 MINS

SERVES 4

I N G R E D I E N T S

1 red (bell) pepper

60 g/2 oz/⅓ cup sultanas (golden raisins)

1 celery stick, sliced

125 g/4½ oz/¾ cup sweetcorn

1 Granny Smith apple, diced

125 g/4½ oz/1 cup white seedless grapes, washed and halved

250 g/9 oz/1½ cups cooked basmati rice

60 g/2 oz/½ cup cooked, peeled prawns (shrimp) (optional)

1 cos (romaine) lettuce, washed and drained

1 tsp paprika to garnish

DRESSING

4 tbsp low-fat mayonnaise

2 tsp mild curry powder

1 tsp lemon juice

1 tsp paprika

pinch of salt

1 Deseed and chop the red (bell) pepper.

2 Combine the sultanas (golden raisins), red (bell) pepper, celery, sweetcorn, apple and grapes in a large bowl. Stir in the rice, and prawns (shrimp), if using.

3 For the dressing, put the mayonnaise, curry powder, lemon juice, paprika and salt into a small bowl and mix well.

4 Pour the dressing over the salad and gently mix until evenly coated.

5 Line the serving plate with cos (romaine) lettuce leaves and spoon on the salad. Sprinkle over the paprika and serve.

COOK'S TIP

Mayonnaise can be bought in varying thicknesses, from the type that you spoon out of the jar to the pouring variety. If you need to thin down mayonnaise for a dressing, simply add water little by little until the desired consistency is reached.

Chicken & Paw-Paw Salad

Try this recipe with a selection of different fruits for an equally tasty salad.

NUTRITIONAL INFORMATION

Calories	408	Sugars 8g
Protein	........30g	Fat 28g
Carbohydrate	...10g	Saturates 5g

5 MINS   15 MINS

SERVES 4

INGREDIENTS

4 skinless, boneless chicken breasts

1 red chilli, deseeded and chopped

30 ml/1 fl oz/1⅞ tbsp red wine vinegar

75 ml/3 fl oz/⅓ cup olive oil

1 paw-paw (papaya), peeled

1 avocado, peeled

125 g/4½ oz alfalfa sprouts

125 g/4½ oz bean sprouts

salt and pepper

TO GARNISH

diced red (bell) pepper

diced cucumber

1 Poach the chicken breasts in boiling water for about 15 minutes or until cooked through.

2 Remove the chicken with a slotted spoon and set aside to cool.

3 To make the dressing, combine the chilli, red wine vinegar and olive oil, season well with salt and pepper and set aside.

4 Place the chicken breasts on a chopping board. Using a very sharp knife, cut the chicken breasts across the grain into thin diagonal slices. Set aside.

5 Slice the paw-paw (papaya) and avocado to the same thickness as the chicken.

6 Arrange the slices of paw-paw (papaya) and avocado, together with the chicken, in an alternating pattern on four serving plates.

7 Arrange the alfalfa sprouts and bean sprouts on the serving plates and garnish with the diced red (bell) pepper and cucumber. Serve the salad with the dressing.

VARIATION

Try this recipe with peaches or nectarines instead of paw-paw (papaya).

Chicken & Noodle Salad

Strips of chicken are coated in a delicious spicy mixture, then stir-fried with noodles and served on a bed of salad.

NUTRITIONAL INFORMATION

Calories 217	Sugars 1g	
Protein 21g	Fat 11g	
Carbohydrate 9g	Saturates 2g	

🍲 10 MINS   🕐 10 MINS

SERVES 4

I N G R E D I E N T S

1 tsp finely grated fresh ginger root

½ tsp Chinese five-spice powder

1 tbsp plain (all-purpose) flour

½ tsp chilli powder

350 g/12 oz boned chicken breast, skinned and sliced thinly

60 g/2 oz rice noodles

125 g/4½ oz/1½ cups Chinese leaves (cabbage) or hard white cabbage, shredded finely

7 cm/3 inch piece of cucumber, sliced finely

1 large carrot, pared thinly

1 tbsp olive oil

2 tbsp lime or lemon juice

2 tbsp sesame oil

salt and pepper

TO GARNISH

lemon or lime slices

fresh coriander (cilantro) leaves

1 Mix together the ginger, five-spice powder, flour and chilli powder in a shallow mixing bowl. Season with salt and pepper. Add the strips of chicken and roll in the mixture until well coated.

2 Put the noodles into a large bowl and cover with warm water. Leave to soak for about 5 minutes, then drain them well.

3 Mix together the Chinese leaves (cabbage) or white cabbage, cucumber and carrot, and arrange in a salad bowl. Whisk together the olive oil and lime or lemon juice, season with a salt and pepper, and use to dress the salad.

4 Heat the sesame oil in a wok or frying pan (skillet) and add the chicken. Stir-fry for 5–6 minutes until well-browned and crispy on the outside. Remove from the wok or frying pan (skillet) with a perforated spoon and drain on absorbent kitchen paper (paper towels).

5 Add the noodles to the wok or frying pan (skillet) and stir-fry for 3–4 minutes until heated through. Remove from the wok, mix with the chicken and pile the mixture on top of the salad. Serve garnished with lime or lemon slices and coriander (cilantro) leaves.

Potato & Chicken Salad

The spicy peanut dressing served with this salad may be prepared in advance and left to chill a day before required.

NUTRITIONAL INFORMATION

Calories	802	Sugars	........15g
Protein	........35g	Fat	..........55g
Carbohydrate	...45g	Saturates	......10g

5 MINS   15 MINS

SERVES 4

INGREDIENTS

4 large waxy potatoes

300 g/10½ oz fresh pineapple, diced

2 carrots, grated

175 g/6 oz bean sprouts

1 bunch spring onions (scallions), sliced

1 large courgette (zucchini), cut into matchsticks

3 celery sticks, cut into matchsticks

175 g/6 oz unsalted peanuts

2 cooked chicken breast fillets, about 125 g/4½ oz each, sliced

DRESSING

6 tbsp crunchy peanut butter

6 tbsp olive oil

2 tbsp light soy sauce

1 red chilli, chopped

2 tsp sesame oil

4 tsp lime juice

COOK'S TIP

Unsweetened canned pineapple may be used in place of the fresh pineapple for convenience. If only sweetened canned pineapple is available, drain it and rinse under cold running water before using.

1 Using a sharp knife, cut the potatoes into small dice. Bring a saucepan of water to the boil.

2 Cook the diced potatoes in a saucepan of boiling water for 10 minutes or until tender. Drain and leave to cool until required.

3 Transfer the cooled potatoes to a salad bowl.

4 Add the pineapple, carrots, bean sprouts, spring onions (scallions), courgette (zucchini), celery, peanuts and sliced chicken to the potatoes. Toss well to mix all the salad ingredients together.

5 To make the dressing, put the peanut butter in a small mixing bowl and gradually whisk in the olive oil and light soy sauce.

6 Stir in the chopped red chilli, sesame oil and lime juice. Mix until well combined.

7 Pour the spicy dressing over the salad and toss lightly to coat all of the ingredients. Serve the potato and chicken salad immediately.

Oriental Chicken Salad

Mirin, soy sauce and sesame oil give an oriental flavour to this delicious salad.

NUTRITIONAL INFORMATION

Calories 361	Sugars 2g
Protein 34g	Fat 16g
Carbohydrate . . .17g	Saturates 3g

5 MINS   35 MINS

SERVES 4

I N G R E D I E N T S

4 skinless, boneless chicken breasts

75 ml/3 fl oz/⅓ cup mirin or sweet sherry

75 ml/3 fl oz/⅓ cup light soy sauce

1 tbsp sesame oil

3 tbsp olive oil

1 tbsp red wine vinegar

1 tbsp Dijon mustard

250 g/9 oz egg noodles

250 g/9 oz bean sprouts

250 g/9 oz Chinese leaves (cabbage), shredded

2 spring onions (scallions), sliced

125 g/4½ oz mushrooms, sliced

1 fresh red chilli, finely sliced, to garnish

1 Pound the chicken breasts out to an even thickness between two sheets of cling film (plastic wrap) with a rolling pin or cleaver.

2 Put the chicken breasts in a roasting tin (pan). Combine the mirin and soy sauce and brush over the chicken.

3 Place the chicken in a preheated oven, 200°C/ 400°F/Gas Mark 6, for 20–30 minutes, basting often.

4 Remove the chicken from the oven and allow to cool slightly.

5 Combine the sesame oil, olive oil and red wine vinegar with the mustard.

6 Cook the noodles according to the instructions on the packet. Rinse under cold running water, then drain.

7 Toss the noodles in the dressing until the noodles are completely coated.

8 Toss the bean sprouts, Chinese leaves (cabbage), spring onions (scallions) and mushrooms with the noodles.

9 Slice the cooked chicken very thinly and stir into the noodles. Garnish the salad with the chilli slices and serve.

Chinese Chicken Salad

This is a refreshing dish suitable for a summer meal or light lunch.

NUTRITIONAL INFORMATION

Calories	162	Sugars	.........3g
Protein	........15g	Fat	..........10g
Carbohydrate	....5g	Saturates	.......2g

25 MINS   10 MINS

SERVES 4

I N G R E D I E N T S

225 g/8 oz skinless, boneless chicken
  breasts

2 tsp light soy sauce

1 tsp sesame oil

1 tsp sesame seeds

2 tbsp vegetable oil

125 g/4½ oz bean sprouts

1 red (bell) pepper, seeded and thinly sliced

1 carrot, cut into matchsticks

3 baby corn cobs, sliced

snipped chives and carrot matchsticks,
  to garnish

S A U C E

2 tsp rice wine vinegar

1 tbsp light soy sauce

dash of chilli oil

1 Place the chicken breasts in a shallow
  glass dish.

2 Mix together the soy sauce and
  sesame oil and pour over the chicken.
Sprinkle with the sesame seeds and let
stand for 20 minutes, turning the chicken
over occasionally.

3 Remove the chicken from the
  marinade and cut the meat into
thin slices.

4 Heat the vegetable oil in a preheated
  wok or large frying pan (skillet). Add
the chicken and fry for 4-5 minutes, until
cooked through and golden brown on
both sides. Remove the chicken from the
wok with a slotted spoon, set aside and
leave to cool.

5 Add the bean sprouts, (bell) pepper,
  carrot and baby corn cobs to the wok
and stir-fry for 2–3 minutes. Remove from

the wok with a slotted spoon, set aside
and leave to cool.

6 To make the sauce, mix together the
  rice wine vinegar, light soy sauce and
chilli oil.

7 Arrange the chicken and vegetables
  together on a serving plate. Spoon
the sauce over the salad, garnish with
chives and carrot matchsticks and serve.

Hot and Sour Duck Salad

This is a lovely tangy salad, drizzled with a lime juice and fish sauce dressing. It makes a splendid starter or light main course dish.

NUTRITIONAL INFORMATION

Calories	236	Sugars	.........3g
Protein	........27g	Fat	..........10g
Carbohydrate	...10g	Saturates	.......3g

40 MINS   5 MINS

SERVES 4

INGREDIENTS

2 heads crisp salad lettuce, washed and separated into leaves

2 shallots, thinly sliced

4 spring onions (scallions), chopped

1 celery stick, finely sliced into julienne strips

5 cm/2 inch piece cucumber, cut into julienne strips

125 g/4½ oz bean sprouts

1 x 200 g/7 oz can water chestnuts, drained and sliced

4 duck breast fillets, roasted and sliced

orange slices, to serve

DRESSING

3 tbsp fish sauce

1½ tbsp lime juice

2 garlic cloves, crushed

1 red chilli pepper, seeded and very finely chopped

1 green chilli pepper, seeded and very finely chopped

1 tsp palm or demerara (brown crystal) sugar

1 Place the lettuce leaves into a large mixing bowl. Add the sliced shallots, chopped spring onions (scallions), celery strips, cucumber strips, bean sprouts and sliced water chestnuts. Toss well to mix. Place the mixture on a large serving platter.

2 Arrange the duck breast slices on top of the salad in an attractive overlapping pattern.

3 To make the dressing, put the fish sauce, lime juice, garlic, chillies and sugar into a small saucepan. Heat gently, stirring constantly. Taste and adjust the piquancy if liked by adding more lime juice, or add more fish sauce to reduce the sharpness.

4 Drizzle the warm salad dressing over the duck salad and serve immediately with orange slices.

Index

A

Aromatic and Crispy Duck 209

B

Baked Chicken and Chips 91
Bang-Bang Chicken 55
Barbecued Chicken 132
Barbecued Chicken 85
Barbecued Chicken Legs 165
Barbecued Duckling 206
Boned Chicken and Parmesan 129
Braised Chicken 166

C

Cajun Chicken Gumbo 220
Cashew Chicken 161
Celery and Cashew Chicken 163
Chargrilled Chicken Salad 244
Cheesy Baked Chicken 101
Chicken and Almond Rissoles 47
Chicken and Asparagus Soup 22
Chicken and Balsamic Vinegar 135
Chicken and Bean Soup 27
Chicken and Beans 217
Chicken and Cheese Jackets 48
Chicken and Chilli Bean Pot 221

Chicken and Corn Sauté 182
Chicken and Ginger Stir-Fry 75
Chicken and Grape Salad 243
Chicken and Leek Soup 23
Chicken and Lemon Skewers 100
Chicken and Lobster on Penne 137
Chicken and Noodle One-Pot 228
Chicken and Noodle Salad 249
Chicken and Pasta Broth 24
Chicken and Paw-Paw Salad 248
Chicken and Peanut Pizza 237
Chicken and Plum Casserole 94
Chicken and Potato Bake 83
Chicken and Rice Casserole 227
Chicken and Seafood Parcels 149
Chicken and Spinach Lasagne 153
Chicken and Spinach Salad 242
Chicken and Sweetcorn Soup 30
Chicken and Tomato Lasagne 151
Chicken and Vegetables 186
Chicken Cacciatora 130
Chicken Chop Suey 160
Chicken Chow Mein 230

Chicken Consommé 20
Chicken Fajitas 108
Chicken Fu-Yong 188
Chicken in Spciy Yogurt 73
Chicken Jalfrezi 115
Chicken Lasagne 131
Chicken Marengo 126
Chicken Noodle Soup 31
Chicken Noodles 231
Chicken on Crispy Noodles 235
Chicken or Beef Satay 57
Chicken Pasta Bake 150
Chicken Pepperonata 140
Chicken Risotto Milanese 223
Chicken Scallops 136
Chicken Soup with Almonds 37
Chicken Spring Rolls 51
Chicken Tikka 95
Chicken Tikka Kebabs 72
Chicken Tikka Masala 99
Chicken Tortellini 146
Chicken with a Yoghurt Crust 62
Chicken with Bean Sprouts 170
Chicken with Black Bean Sauce 172
Chicken with Bramble Sauce 114
Chicken with Chilli and Basil 195
Chicken with Green Olives 134
Chicken with Lime Stuffing 111

Chicken with Mushrooms 177
Chicken with Orange Sauce 139
Chicken with Peanut Sauce 194
Chicken with Peppers 183
Chicken with Rice and Peas 219
Chicken with Two Sauces 76
Chicken with Vegetables 148
Chicken with Vegetables 178
Chicken with Vermouth 98
Chicken with Whisky Sauce 88
Chicken Wonton Soup 32
Chicken Wontons 58
Chicken, Noodle and Corn Soup 33
Chilli Chicken 192
Chilli Chicken Meatballs 106
Chilli Coconut Chicken 171
Chinese Chicken Rice 226
Chinese Chicken Salad 252
Chinese Omelette 53
Citrus Duckling Skewers 109
Clear Chicken and Egg Soup 35
Cock-a-Leekie Soup 26
Coconut Chicken Curry 189
Coronation Salad 247
Cranberry Turkey Burgers 40
Crispy Chicken 190
Crispy Stuffed Chicken 87
Crostini all Fiorentina 49
Cumin-Spiced Chicken 179
Curried Chicken and Corn Soup 36

D
Dickensian Chicken Broth 25
Duck in Spicy Sauce 202
Duck with Berry Sauce 119
Duck with Broccoli and Peppers 199
Duck with Ginger and Lime 210
Duck with Leek and Cabbage 200
Duck with Lime and Kiwi Fruit 201
Duck with Mangoes 198
Duck with Pineapple 197
Duckling and Radish Salad 240

F
Festive Apple Chicken 86
Filipino Chicken 81
Fragrant Spiced Chicken 218
Fruity Duck Stir Fry 208

G
Garlic and Herb Chicken 154
Garlic and Lime Chicken 173
Garlic Chicken Cassoulet 215
Garlicky Chicken Cushions 124
Ginger Chicken and Corn 69
Golden Chicken Risotto 222
Golden Glazed Chicken 110
Green Chicken Stir-Fry 169
Grilled Chicken 133

H
Harlequin Chicken 71

Honey and Soy Chicken 184
Honeyed Chicken Wings 54
Honeyed Citrus Chicken 89
Honey-Glazed Duck 196
Hot and Sour Duck Salad 253
Hot and Sour Soup 21
Hot and Spicy Chicken 225

I
Indian Charred Chicken 207
Italian Chicken Parcels 143
Italian Chicken Spirals 125
Italian-Style Sunday Roast 155

J
Jamaican Hot Pot 116
Jerk Chicken 82

K
Karahi Chicken 79
Kung Po Chicken 168

L
Layered Chicken Salad 241
Lemon and Chicken Soup 29
Lemon and Sesame Chicken 193
Lemon Chicken 162
Lime Chicken Kebabs 80
Lime Fricassée of Chicken 92

M
Marinated Chicken Kebabs 113
Marmalade Chicken 104
Mediterranean Chicken 96
Mexican Chicken 84

Minty Lime Chicken 107
Mustard-Baked Chicken 127

N
Noodles in Soup 211

O
Oat-Crusted Chicken Pieces 44
Orange Chicken Stir-Fry 174
Orange Turkey with Rice 216
Oriental Chicken Salad 251

P
Pan-Cooked Chicken 128
Parma-Wrapped Chicken 145
Parsley, Chicken and Ham Pâté 42
Pasta and Chicken Medley 144
Pasta with Chicken Sauce 142
Peanut Sesame Chicken 187
Peking Duck 204
Peppered Chicken 181
Pesto-Baked Partridge 157
Pot Sticker Dumplings 52
Potato and Chicken Salad 250
Pot-Roast Orange Chicken 77
Poussin with Dried Fruits 70

Q
Quick Chicken Chow Mein 229
Quick Chicken Noodles 234

R
Red Chicken Curry 205
Red Chicken with Tomatoes 191
Rice with Five-Spice Chicken 224
Rich Chicken Casserole 147
Roast Baby Chickens 185
Roast Duck with Apple 121
Roman Chicken 141
Rustic Chicken and Orange Pot 112

S
Sage Chicken and Rice 214
Sesame Ginger Chicken 59
Skewered Chicken Spirals 138
Slices of Duckling with Pasta 156
Spanish Chicken Casserole 102
Speedy Peanut Pan-Fry 232
Spiced Apricot Chicken 67
Spicy Chicken Drumsticks 118
Spicy Chicken Noodle Soup 34
Spicy Chicken Salad 245
Spicy Chicken Tortillas 46
Spicy Peanut Chicken 180
Spicy Sesame Chicken 103
Spicy Tomato Chicken 93
Spring Rolls 50
Springtime Chicken Cobbler 105
Springtime Roast Chicken 90
Steamed Chicken Parcels 64
Steamed Duck Buns 56
Sticky Chicken Drumsticks 236
Sticky Chicken Drummers 45

Sticky Chicken Wings 63
Stir-Fried Ginger Chicken 164
Sweet and Sour Chicken 68
Sweet and Sour Drumsticks 43
Sweet Mango Chicken 175
Szechuan Chilli Chicken 176

T
Tagliatelle and Chicken Sauce 152
Tasmanian Duck 117
Teppanyaki 66
Thai Red Chicken 65
Thai-Style Chicken Skewers 74
Turkey and Vegetable Loaf 41
Turkey with Cranberry Glaze 203
Turkey with Redcurrant 120
Two-in-One-Chicken 78

V
Vegetable and Chickpea Soup 28

W
Waldorf Chicken Salad 246
Whisky Roast Chicken 97

Y
Yellow Bean Chicken 167
Yellow Bean Noodles 233